Arguments against Secular Culture

Robert Miller

Arguments against Secular Culture

SCM PRESS LTD

0 334 02604 0

First published 1995
by SCM Press Ltd
26–30 Tottenham Road, London N1 4BZ

Typeset at The Spartan Press Ltd,
Lymington, Hants
Printed and bound in Great Britain by
Mackays of Chatham PLC, Chatham, Kent

For Harold and Mary

Contents

PART II

Psychophysical Parallelism: In Defence of an Alternative Metaphysics

11 Organized Religion and its Relation to Metaphysics 135

11.1 Roles of religious organizations 135

11.2 Comment 137

12 Weakness of Psychophysical Parallelism: Confronting Neural Determinism 141

PART III

Reconstruction by Creation of Myths

13 The Creation and Uses of Myths 161

14 Myths for the Modern Mind: Determinism as the Central Myth of the Secular Society 170

14.1 Determinism as an assumed answer to an unanswerable question 170

14.2 The psychological functions of the belief in determinism 175

15 Myths for the Modern Mind: Subsidiary Myths of the Secular Society 179

15.1 'Classical science' versus the 'science of history' 179

15.2 Darwinism: the prime example of a 'science of history' 183

15.3 Critique of Freud and Marx as theories of history 195

15.4 Functions of modern historical myths, for the 'post-religious age' 197

15.5 A metaphysical alternative to determinism, to the assumptions of Darwinism, and to other modern myths 202

15.6 Can we ever deliberately adopt a myth? 207

16 What are the Necessary Myths? 216

Notes 221

Index 229

Acknowledgments

This essay has grown almost imperceptibly, from small beginnings a few years ago, and only gradually did it take the form of a book. Some inner, half-conscious motive, rather than a deliberate decision must have been the driving force. Perhaps it was passing my fiftieth year, which made me want to try to sum up my overall philosophical viewpoint. A book dealing with the relation between science and religion draws on all one's experiences of life, whether professional or more personal. For all these reasons, I am tempted to acknowledge the contribution of everyone I have ever met, some of whom have provoked me, others of whom have guided me to the point where I had to write this. However, this is not possible, so I will record my debt to only a few people, who are special for me. First of all I must thank my parents. This book expresses views which are in some ways different from their own. Nevertheless, without directing me in any obvious way, they kept alive in me an interest in the relation of science to religion, and also kept alive some of their own religious beliefs, albeit outside any church. My father in particular helped me with some of the detail, especially the references to the early history of physics, and some of the literary references were suggested by my mother. I would also like to give special thanks to Dugald Wilson and Janet Dunn. I have had many discussions with them in the years since arriving in New Zealand, and they gave me support and encouragement which played a part in my starting work on this book. I would like to thank Norman J. Barnes, who, many years ago, through music, showed me that there was a wider world than that contained by science. I thank three people who gave me much needed support during my years as a research student, George Gordon, Peter Usherwood, and the late Charles Phillips. I thank Valentino Braitenberg, who gave me important clues to how brain research can become holistic. I thank Almut Schuz for introducing me to the autobiography of Alexander Luria, and for some suggested improvements in the presentation of this book. I thank Olga Vinogradova, for a number of sparkling insights, which I have incorporated. I thank Dorothy Oorschot, who read an early version of this book, and has given me steady support. I thank Rick Beninger and Vern Quinsey. A very recent conversation with them (as we walked through the snow on the waterfront at Kingston, Ontario) persuaded me to make some modifications in the later part of this book. I also thank the two persons who have been head of the Anatomy Department in Otago, since I arrived there in 1977, Bill Trotter and Gareth Jones. They have guided me in different ways; but both provided an environment where there was sufficient freedom to work out ideas on a broad philosophical scale such as are presented here. Many other people (those who have provoked rather than guided me) I will not name; but many of them are actually trusted friends.

Robert Miller

Dunedin
February 1995

I

Introduction

It is impossible to avoid the historical roots of the culture one lives in. In a culture with Christian roots, it is impossible to avoid the influences of Christianity. Atheism in the culture of 'Western' industrialized countries is usually a particularly Christian form of atheism. Perhaps the most influential example of this close similarity of opposites is in the communist idealism which has dominated large parts of the globe for the major part of this century. It arose within a 'Western' Christian culture (albeit from one originally of Jewish rather than Christian faith);' and, though communism is explicitly atheistic, the communist vision of an ideal society on earth seems to have been an obvious transposition of the Christian notion of the kingdom of heaven. This close kinship of apparent opposites can also be seen on the smaller scale of individual beliefs about religion. In a recent letter in *Nature*,[1] the late Albert Einstein is quoted as referring to 'the crusading spirit of the professional atheist whose fervor is mostly due to a painful act of liberation from the fetters of religious indoctrination, received in youth'. Can we get beyond this attitude, to find an approach to religion which is not merely a reaction to (and reflection of) what we most despise in it?

This book is probably aimed more at people outside the established churches (of whom I am one), rather than those within them. It takes for granted the claims of Christianity and the counter-claims amongst the atheists (themselves reflections of Christianity). Amidst that uncompromising rivalry, the book attempts to define a position in no-man's land. At this position, there is undoubtedly a danger of being obliterated in the cross-fire. But if this can be avoided, the book may convince a few readers that some (but not all) aspects of conventional religious belief have a validity for contemporary times. It is argued that this validity derives from the actual position mankind occupies, and the fundamental dilemmas he faces. In some respects these dilemmas are very new, but in other important respects they are no different from those faced by pre-Christian societies, and by primitive peoples still found in the modern world. It is hoped that the attitude to religion developed in this book bears little direct relation to the centuries of tradition of organized religion (on the one hand) or to that variety of atheism which derives from a painful liberation from childhood Christian beliefs (on the other). However, both of these two stances, caricatured perhaps, will be taken as points of departure.

My own religious development and experience certainly did not escape the influence of the dominant religion, but (possibly fortunately) never led to my becoming committed in any serious emotional sense to a faith which I later had to abandon.

At the age of seven I suddenly refused to attend Sunday School. This was probably because I found the Sunday ritual intensely embarrassing. Probably the idea of dressing up in one's 'Sunday best' was the worst aspect of churchgoing for me at this stage. My parents, with a serious, though very liberal attitude to their religion, did not try to force the issue. So I reached the end of adolescence with one form of Christianity as important in my family, but nevertheless as an outsider to any institutionalized church.

At the end of my school years I thought it was time I formed a clear view of religion, and this coincided with my first exposure to evangelical Christianity. There was an evangelical group run by the neighbouring Anglican church, and I and some of my friends were attracted into it as a new form of social outlet. Then there was the Billy Graham crusade. I went there, with some foreknowledge, expecting to be bowled over by overwhelming emotion. In fact, while several of my friends were 'converted' (a short-lived episode for most of them), I was left quite unmoved.

At university I was again exposed to various versions of evangelical Christianity, which never led to any real commitment on my part; and I was generally disappointed by all my student encounters with organized religion. I could not, at this time, define the reason for this. In retrospect the reason is clearer. What I was really seeking, as most confused young adults seek, was an anchor of some sort. What these evangelists were offering was an anchor as part of a religious power structure. I also suspect, though it was never explicit, that some of the evangelical groups who tried to exert hold over me, were at the same time offering fellowship to people of homosexual orientation, at a time before any attempt at liberalization of attitudes on this issue had occurred in British society. My sense of disappointment probably arose from the fact that for me the only anchor worth considering was based on honest attempts to resolve age-old philosophical and metaphysical issues underlying religious belief, free from any institution, power hierarchy or hidden agenda.

My viewpoint on metaphysical matters was already forming at this stage, and owed nothing at all to my spasmodic contacts with institutional religion. My school education had been mainly in the sciences, towards the end focussing on the biological sciences. Specifically I was beginning to have some leaning towards neurobiology. But I was also very fortunate in having a very good musical education during my school years. The juxtaposition of these very different disciplines may have been a crucial influence in the philosophical stance I started to develop.

On the one hand, when I read philosophy written by neurobiologists, what was emphasized was that the brain, (including the human brain, and, implicitly, the mind it embodied) was a *mechanism*. In fundamental principle it was no different from other mechanisms, and could be studied in the same *objective* ways as any other mechanism. I came across this idea for the first time at the age of seventeen on reading *Doubt and Certainty in Science* by J. Z. Young, a book which left me thunderstruck.[2]

On the other hand, in my musical education there was a good deal of training of the ear, and development of one's aural imagination. These processes emphasized the reality of *subjective* experiences, and subjective qualities, rather than the objectivity of the brain mechanisms which made them possible. One specific influence which occurred during my musical education was introduction to the poems of Thomas Traherne (a seventeenth-century 'metaphysical' poet), whose poem 'Dies Natalis' was the text for one of the musical set works I studied. The tone of that poem struck an immediate resonance with me, and has stayed with me ever since, reinforced in later years, when I read other poems of Traherne.

Possibly it was the juxtaposition of the objectivity of biological science with the subjectivity of my musical education which was important in the development of my metaphysical views. Whatever the truth of this, by the age of twenty, by which time I had started more serious study of the central nervous system, my belief in some form of psychophysical parallelism had crystallized. These views have stayed with me since then, elaborated, and (especially in the last ten years) amended considerably, but the basic belief has not been eroded. They have always been linked in my mind with a basic theistic belief. In contrast to the theistic belief I was developing, I observed that many of my fellow students who became more deeply involved with the power structure of evangelical religion, usually became fervent atheists within a few years of leaving university. But my own developing beliefs can only have been indirectly influenced by the religious organizations I encountered, because my derivation of theistic belief from juxtaposition of subjective and objective views of the world was never remotely suggested in these organizations.

Added to these influences was an extended period when I faced the experiences of serious mental illness. At one stage in this chapter it seemed quite possible (to me at least) that I would end up living permanently in an institution; and, faced with this terrible thought, I could easily have taken my own life. This sort of protracted episode leaves indelible memories and scars, though I also derived something very positive from it, in that it later gave a clear direction and powerful motive to the neuroscience research I embarked upon. But the actual experience contributed strength and depth to the philosophical viewpoint I adhered to. Once again it forced upon me the reality of subjective experience, but now not only as an aesthetic exercise (as in my musical studies), but, because of the strong contrast between the pleasant and the terribly painful experiences of life, it brought into sharp relief the implications of subjective experiences for human values and value systems.

Somehow, in the aftermath of those terrible years I survived as a research student in the biological sciences, developing and deepening my interest in the nervous system. The scientific content was always enthralling. But during those years I felt again a growing sense of disappointment with the philosophical package that seemed implicitly to go along with the actual science I studied. Looking back on the twenty-five years (or more) that I have been studying the brain I have never lost the sense that I was basing my work on philosophical premises quite different from, and mainly opposed to those adopted by most of my colleagues. Indeed this sense has deepened, as I became aware that the scientific materialist view of life was now not only dominant amongst biological scientists, but was also coming to be the dominant ideology in the wider culture of the society I lived in.

In 1977 I came to live in New Zealand. This did nothing to erode my viewpoint on philosophical matters. In fact New Zealand, which is probably one of the most secular countries in the 'Western' world, has brought the contrast between my own views and the culture which surrounds me, into even clearer focus. It is not at all that I feel alienated by that culture. I am profoundly grateful for the new life which became possible after I emigrated. Alienated I *may* be in one sense, but no more so than in almost every other every social group or culture I have been part of. I am quite well accustomed to that situation, because I know no other. Rather it is that the 'orthodox' atheist/materialist world view which surrounds me is, I think, based on an almost incredibly narrow range of experience. Its proponents are blind as bats, in my view, protected from most of the important and influential aspects of human *moral* experience (taking human experience in a wide historical sense). So my alienation is of little real concern to me. Rather I should call it a disjunction between my own philosophical views and the dominant world view around me, a nearly-complete philosophical estrangement. My sense of estrangement from the society in which I live is perhaps the major impetus which has led me to write this book.

The other theme of this book, which emerges in its second part, has developed for me only in the last ten years. Gradually the awareness has been forced on me that the psychophysical parallelism which was adequate as a basis for my scientific endeavours until a few years ago is not enough as a basis for wider aspects of one's life. There are many puzzles which life presents to a questioning mind which cannot ever be answered by science, nor by any other means. These are questions recognized by the ancients, and by less 'advanced' peoples in the modern world. The force of these questions should actually be no less for modern educated people than for these supposedly 'backward' peoples. In fact, of course, these unfathomable questions may be often ignored by those who are so full of enthusiasm for the achievements of modern science and technology. Such people deny the force of the basic issues which have always perplexed mankind. Unfathomable these questions may be; but nevertheless insistent and provocative. We may not be able to find an assured 'answer' to these riddles, but we need some way of living with them.

In recent years it has become ever more clear to me that the only type of resolution we can find to these issues lies in what is generally referred to as mythology. The word 'myth' may arouse a certain disdain to the modern scientific mind, but I believe myths are just as important to the modern mind as they were to the ancients and to primitive peoples of the contemporary world. In fact I have come to think that some of the fundamental beliefs espoused by many scientists, and claimed by them to have a scientific basis, are not really scientifically validated beliefs at all (as their adherents would suppose) but in all important respects function as myths for the modern mind.

The book is divided into three parts, each with its subdivision into chapters. In Part I, I try to define what I think is the dominant philosophical viewpoint amongst educated people in the modern Western world. I explain the relationship of this viewpoint to the growth of scientific knowledge. In particular, I emphasize that the modern materialist viewpoint is in no way a continuation of the four centuries of scientific progress since the Renaissance, but is a gross distortion of the philosophical framework underlying that history of progress. I suggest that the trend which has become dominant in the last generation is destructive of many of the positive aspects of the pre-existing world view, though I certainly do not advocate a complete return to that view, because it too led to cruelties and injustices.

In Part II, I explain the psychophysical parallelism, which has been the guiding philosophy for me until about ten years ago. Overall, the merits of this philosophy (in my view) is that it preserves the reality of subjective experience, and with it preserves at least the possibility of a real scheme of values. At the same time it does not at all undermine the endeavours of scientists in areas such as the brain sciences, which are so heavy with philosophical implications. However, at the end of this section I confront a major shortcoming of this philosophy, that although it may provide a basis for aesthetic values, it fails completely to provide a basis for moral values, to give a way of dealing with the insistent and inescapable question, 'What do we live by?' On this issue the destructive power of the implicit philosophy of modern science wins against my earlier beliefs.

In Part III, I build another tier upon this philosophy, pleading for a humility in the face of insoluble religious questions, rather than a brash belief that they are soluble either within the framework of scientific materialism, or by authoritarian religious dogmatism. I introduce the concept of myths, not in pejorative terms, but as something whose real function we should try to understand, so that we can realize our own need for myths, just as much as primitive man needed them. Finally I offer my suggestions of what might be the most fundamental myths which we require. These are not very outlandish. In fact the surprise may come because they are so commonplace, and actually already an enduring and accepted part of the fabric of life for most of us. However, it is necessary to spell them out, explain how they are derived, and how they are compatible with all the empirical evidence we have (though, being myths, not actually proved by that evidence). Moreover it is required to designate them as [necessary myths] rather than factual statements, and point out what this implies for the way we handle these beliefs. Despite the obvious nature of the myths I describe, and our familiarity with them from ages of history, it is necessary to be quite explicit about them because, implicitly, some trends of modern thinking seem to be undermining them at a very fundamental level.

There is one other thing to say, by way of introducing this book: It is not meant to be a scholarly treatise. If it were, it would have had to be filled out with many more references, would have been substantially longer, and would have been aimed at a narrower readership. As it is, the book is intended more as my own personal statement, aimed widely at those with interest in the relation between science and religion, but without any special professional expertise. Since it is a personal statement, rather than a scholarly treatise, I hope the reader will forgive me when he or she notices that I am better read in scientific matters than in theological ones.

Part I

Philosophical Roots of the Modern Secular Society and their Destructiveness

2

Definition of Scientific Materialism

A generation ago, when I was an adolescent, it was possible to believe that the fundamental beliefs of most 'Western' style societies were still based on Christian (or Judaeo-Christian) religion. I believe that is no longer the case. I believe that the most influential belief system in the developed world is now scientific materialism. The change I refer to has actually been much more gradual than this. It started with the conflicts of science and religion in the Italian Renaissance, and was propelled further by the Newtonian revolution. It came to have a rather different slant, and a wider impact with theories such as those of Darwin which claimed to be both scientific and concerned with history. However, I believe it is only in the last generation that these post-Darwinian changes have had a wide enough impact to become the dominating philosophy of our culture. In this sense, in the battle between science and the Christian religion, science has won. It may not have won the argument; but it has won the allegiance of the broad mass of people.

What are the characteristics of this belief system? How has it come to be the dominant 'orthodox' view amongst educated people?

The first possible mistake to correct is that this materialism consists chiefly of the hankering after material possessions, in the wealthy countries of the world. This may sometimes be related to the underlying belief system, but if it is, it is one of the more superficial manifestations of the underlying fundamental philosophy.

The fundamental belief is that matter, the substance of the material world, is the only basic form of reality. In this statement, the word 'matter' should include 'energy', because of the realization by twentieth-century physics that matter and energy are interconvertible. Undoubtedly the matter and energy of the world can present themselves in limitless conformations and give rise to limitless natural phenomena. Some writers would suggest that there are complex *emergent* properties of matter which, while not going beyond what is contained in the basic principles of the behaviour of the material world, nevertheless cannot be

logically derived from those principles, because of the limits of
inference when dealing with complex systems.[1] Nevertheless all these
things, matter, energy, and all the complex properties of their combinations (whether or not they are classed as 'emergent') – in other
words the whole of 'nature' – are, in the materialist world view, aspects
of a single reality, the objective world. Always those conformations and
phenomena are to be grasped objectively. Implicitly the materialist
believes that, if there cannot be a description of those objects or events
which is objective (that is agreed publically) then one has to doubt that
they really exist. With this materialist belief there is no sense of the
fundamental reality of the world of subjective experience.

Don Cupitt contrasts the modern view with the tradition started by
Descartes more than three hundred years ago. He writes:

> The Cartesian tradition began with the subject and then tried to
> construct the public realm as a system of private points of view . . .
> The recognition of the logical primacy of the public, entering social
> science through Durkheim, and linguistic philosophy through Witt-
> genstein, has been crucial for twentieth century thought.[2]

One of the most striking statements of this creed of objectivity comes
from the distinguished French molecular biologist, the Nobel Laureate
Jacques Monod. In his book *Chance and Necessity* he writes: 'The
cornerstone of the scientific method is the postulate that nature is
objective.'[3]

Monod's book will be referred to a number of times in this work.
For the present, it is merely necessary to mention that this statement of
Monod is not actually an unqualified acceptance of the materialist
position, and a denial of the world of subjectivity. The above quotation
continues by saying that this postulate of objectivity is 'in other words
the *systematic* denial that "true" knowledge can be reached by inter-
preting phenomena in terms of final causes – that is to say, of purpose'.
Here he is contrasting the word 'objective' not with the word
'subjective', but with the word 'projective'.[4] This should give us pause
before categorizing Monod as a naive materialist. After reading the last
chapter of his book one gets the impression that this statement of one
of the most basic tenets of the scientific enterprise is, for Monod,
almost an Aunt Sally, a clear target for us to aim our own arguments
against.

In fact, in the present book, the logical primacy of the public view of reality is not accepted; but neither is the subjective view of reality given primacy either. The two are regarded as entirely interdependent.

3

Materialism and Definitions of Mind

If one espouses the pure-blooded materialist philosophy, it obviously has profound implications for one's concept of mind and consciousness. With this philosophy, is it actually possible to believe in the existence of mind and consciousness? If so, what would be the implications for the relationship between mind or consciousness and the material world (e.g. our brain)? The answer to these questions hinges absolutely on how the words 'mind' and 'consciousness' are defined.

To many philosophers, and most psychologists and neuroscientists, the words 'mind' and 'consciousness' are defined in terms of certain 'strategies of information processing'. There are a number of equivalent phrases and concepts in use. In the discipline of computer science we are used to machines carrying out a series of operations (the 'programme' or part of it) which, taken together, have a certain function or goal. The word 'algorithm' would be used in this discipline instead of the phrase 'strategy of information processing'. Similarly amongst mathematicians who consider the mind, the debate is whether the mind (or its components) are 'computable'.[1]

From Freudian psychology we inherit the concept of the unconscious mind. This is a strategy of behaviour which is not admitted by the subject who performs it, but which can be revealed by studying the behaviour or speech utterances he or she emits, and which is directed to achieving a certain (unconscious) goal.

Amongst contemporary psychologists the 'psyche' they study is defined entirely as patterns or strategies of behaviour emitted in certain circumstances, often achieving a specific goal. For instance the whole of learning theory can be seen as a set of concepts defining possible or probable strategies of information processing during learning. The experimental side of this discipline has invented a wide variety of methods for demonstrating, as clearly as possible, just what strategy of information processing may be used in different circumstances of learning. Likewise, the processes which occur during visual perception may be 'dissected' to lay bare the basic features and combinations of features of the visual world which, when assembled together, underlie the way we analyse the varied information coming to us through our eyes. These two examples equate different aspects of mind ('learning' and 'seeing') with the corresponding algorithms for information processing.

This way of defining the psyche was not always characteristic of psychology. Last century, introspection was held to be the major window on the mind. It is an enduring legacy of the behaviourist school of psychology, and one which is essential to any hope of a science of the brain and its integrated functions, that the psyche is defined in this way, at least in part.

Amongst philosophers, the word used for this approach to the mind is 'functionalism', implying that the essence of the mind or its components is to achieve a certain function, or to carry out certain logical steps. Churchland for instance writes: 'The core of functionalism is the thesis that mental states are defined in terms of their abstract causal roles within the wider information-processing system'.[2]

Moving closer to the core of the philosophical argument, the word 'consciousness' may also be redefined as 'self-consciousness' and then dissected conceptually as the strategy of information processing which allows a machine to be informed about at least a part of its own operations. For instance Edelman[3] envisages that conscious states result from signals from one part of the brain re-entering that part, so that it can be informed of its own state, just as it can be informed about the external environment. In principle, experimental methods might also be devised to demonstrate just such a form of information processing in animals. For example a commonly used way of investigating drug effects on the brains of animals is to show that the experimental animal, typically a rat, can 'distinguish' one injected drug from another. This is achieved by training the animal to perform one response when injected with one drug, and another when a different drug is injected. There is no sense organ such as the eye or the ear by which the experimental animal can recognize which drugs it has been injected with. One must presume that some aspects of the global inner state of the animal's brain can control behaviour, just as external sensory stimuli control behaviour in conventional learning tasks.

These definitions of mind, from computer science, psychology or philosophy, reflect the dominant ideology of our times. However, such definitions of mind (as 'strategies of information processing') are not the only possible ones. Many people (perhaps especially those in the creative arts) might define mind as a *collection of subjective qualities and impressions, indefineable in public terms*. Although it is impossible to be certain, these subjective qualities and impressions may be rather different from person to person, some of them being possibly of rather rare occurrence, as experiences, in the population as a whole. Such rare experiences may nevertheless be tremendously vivid to the person who experiences them, and central to their artistic activities.

How do these differences of definition influence one's views on the existence and status of mind or consciousness?

Some materialists abolish mind altogether as an 'internal variable' for which there is no evidence. They do not admit to the existence of subjective qualities; nor do they believe in the reality of internalized strategies of information processing, because these would have to be inferred rather than directly observed. When it comes to the psychology of living things, including humans, they are concerned only with establishing lawful relations between things which in a very strict sense are observable. This approach is adopted by some in the 'behaviorist' school of psychology, which flourished in North America in the earlier years of this century. For them, outward behavior was the only reality worth considering. We will consider them in more detail later.

Another type of materialist viewpoint, while acknowledging an entity corresponding to what is called mind or consciousness, would argue that all the phenomena of mind and consciousness are complex derivatives of the material constituents of the world as 'emergent properties'. When one enquires further into this contention, one invariably finds that the words 'mind' and 'consciousness' are defined in terms of strategies of information processing rather than as subjective qualities. It is, of course, very difficult to analyse and demonstrate the complex patterns of psychological information processing in anything like complete detail. Nevertheless in so far as one can identify such strategies, they are explicit and open to public scrutiny, and therefore objective. One can thus apparently achieve an objective description, in part or in its entirety, of mind or consciousness.

Such objective definitions of the information processing demonstrable in objective behaviour can, of course, in principle be related to brain mechanisms, just as the behaviour of a computer can be related to the physical hardware, and the software (or 'programme'). Thus, if mind is defined in terms of a strategy of information processing it certainly is derivable in principle from the physical matter of which the brain is composed. Thus, given its definition, mind *must* be one of the high-level properties of the machine we call our brain.

At this point, views diverge amongst materialists about the nature of mind. Some would reason that any mental faculty which we think we have, but which cannot be rendered as an explicit algorithm or strategy of information processing, cannot be accommodated by their view of mind. Such a philosopher, on meeting an acquaintance whom he thinks he recognizes, should be troubled that he cannot say explicitly what is the combination of facial features by which he recognizes the acquaintance.

Other materialist philosophers would be more accommodating: Since 'mind' and 'consciousness' are also viewed as emergent properties, it is also allowed that these formulations are merely provisional attempts to define something which may always escape full definition. They should therefore accept the products of the information processing in the mind, even if not explicitly analysed, without too much question.

What about the philosopher who defines mind in terms of a collection of subjective impressions and qualities? Materialism does not admit the reality of such subjective things. Thus, it is unlikely that this philosopher be a materialist. It is not impossible, however. He might admit the existence of subjective phenomena in so far as he regards them as *epiphenomena* arising from the function of the brain.

Otherwise this philosopher might be classed in one of two broad positions: He might be an idealist (for whom the subjective world of mind is the *only* reality). Alternatively, he may be a dualist of one sort or another, allowing the existence of two fundamentally different forms of reality ('mind' or 'spirit', and matter). Whichever of these positions he adopts about the nature of reality, if he defines mind in terms of subjective qualities, there is no natural expectation that these subjective qualities can, by any logical feat, be derived from the material properties of the brain. Admittedly the world of subjective qualities may *correlate* with physical processes in the brain, but that correlation does not mean that the subjective qualities can be *logical* derivatives of objective facts about the brain. Subjective qualities cannot be derived from objective facts. However such a philosopher will be able to give some status to mental faculties which he feels he has within him, without being able to explain how those faculties work. Such a philosopher will accept with ease the possibility that he recognizes a familiar face, even though he cannot say how this remarkable feat is done. Polanyi[4] develops this idea most fully. He recognizes that in most of our day-to-day skills, we 'know more than we can say'. Many of us may be able to swim or to ride a bicycle; but few of us know explicitly how this is done. The same is also true for all our skills of knowing and understanding at a more intellectual level.

Thus the question of the existence of mind or consciousness and whether they are or are not part of the material universe hinges emphatically upon a purely semantic question. Are 'mind' or 'consciousness' to be defined with regard to publicly demonstrable strategies of information processing? If this answer is given, many materialists (the 'emergent' materialists) will readily admit the existence of mind. Alternatively mind and consciousness may be defined with reference to the fact that they contain some 'subjective qualities' (which are quite elusive, because they are private to the individual subject). If this answer is given, mind exists for the dualist and for the idealist, but not usually for the materialist, who denies the existence of the subjective world. Once the question of definition of mind has been answered, the answer to the question about the relation between mind/consciousness and the matter of the brain follows automatically, and in a rather trivial manner. Generally the answer will accord with the prior assumptions (about whether or not matter is the single fundamental reality).

In my own view these two concepts of mind, (the 'strategies of information processing', and the 'collection of subjective qualities') are categorically totally different. In my experience many people will deny one or other of the concepts. Nevertheless, they *are* very closely related. It is thus easy to understand that definition of mind or consciousness becomes unclear because of confusion of these categories. The very word 'psychology' is quite ambiguous in this respect. The materialist I caricature here would not believe that there can be any reality to the notion of 'subjective qualities', and would define mind and consciousness in terms of algorithms of information processing. Other people would quite naturally try to define mind in terms of those elusive subjective qualities which they feel the mind contains, and thus provide a definition of mind which is essentially subjective.

The point I have just made about the different definitions which may be offered for mind and consciousness is quite central to the argument of the first two parts of this book. In Part II this source of confusion is referred to a number of times. While writers about the problematic mind/brain relationship attribute the problem to various conceptual confusions, I believe they have almost all missed the crucial point. It is this. Intuitively most of us are in fact aware of the dualism between our subjective inner world and the public, objective outer world. This is a very fundamental belief, but one for which we nevertheless now have a rather limited language at our disposal, especially in a world where the objective 'wonders of science' are so dominant. Thus for many of us, that fundamental belief becomes hidden or repressed, because it is difficult to express it explicitly. However, we have a much richer vocabulary for the world of mind when it is given an objective definition. Therefore, just because of the language at our disposal, mind and consciousness are defined in familiar objective terms. In the process the issue of the status of mind, and its relationship to brain, body, and matter generally are entirely prejudged.

Our fundamental intuition about the subjective nature of mind is lost in these descriptions. Although we may be puzzled and unconvinced that the objective analyses of mind really capture the essence of the problem, the power of the language which is readily at our disposal is so great that we cannot escape from its grasp. Subjectivity, and our initial intuition, are thus denied. This is of considerable practical importance in psychiatry. The reason why mental illness is a source of such fear and denial can be attributed in part to the fact that we (who are all liable to be afflicted by psychiatric illness) have a very limited vocabulary for such essentially subjective realities.

In comment I should also suggest that the actual vividness and experiential impact of those supposed 'subjective qualities' varies considerably amongst persons; so that what is blindingly obvious to one person is easily denied by another. It is well recognized by psychologists that the strength of 'mental imagery' varies considerably from person to person.[5] Moreover, one of the themes of the following sections is that, in recent history, a change has occurred in the way we are allowed to make our judgments. Hitherto we have been used to recognizing complex qualities or concepts (and some have developed great skill in this) in one step, just as we recognize a familiar face, or a colour. By allowing such judgments to be made, a tacit belief was accepted that there really were such 'subjective qualities', activated when each complex concept is recognized. Nowadays such qualitative judgments are suspect, as being 'too subjective', and are increasingly replaced by operationalized schemes, which segment the judgment into a number of criteria, with explicit rules as to how each is to be scored, and how the scores are to be combined to make the final assessment. This change in approach also probably has its basis in personality characteristics, with underlying differences in brain dynamics. The difference between the style of the earlier qualitative judgments and the modern operationalized ones corresponds almost exactly to what is said to be the difference between the right ('non-dominant') hemisphere function and the left ('dominant') hemisphere function. It is often said that modern culture relies too much on left hemisphere functions, and not enough on those of the right hemisphere.

Perhaps these deep (and largely unrecognized) differences in the psychological makeup of each protagonist is an element which contributes to the intransigence with which this debate is usually conducted. But there is a cultural bias as well as an individual psychological one. And in present times I maintain that the dominant view is that mind is to be defined in objective rather than subjective terms. In the sections below I give a variety of examples of this tendency.

4

The Scientific Obsession with Exclusive Objectivity

Individual human judgments and intuitions, unaided by any discipline, are remarkably fickle. Different persons see and hear different things in the world when regarding the same sights and sounds. The emphasis they place on the things they see and hear vary greatly from person to person. One of the ultimate goals of science, and indeed of any type of knowledge, is to provide a description of the world which is objective, that is, free as far as possible from the biases of individual observers. The scientific goal of achieving a publicly agreed description of nature is the origin of the materialist philosophy, which emphasizes, to the status of a dogma, the unreliability of every individual subjective judgment. However, in the sections which follow, I hope to show that the derivation of the materialist philosophy from this goal of science is invalid, because an essential part of the development of science has always involved the acknowledgment (and refinement) of human skills in acquiring subjective impressions and intuitions.

In this chapter, I will deal with some of the methods of science used to ensure objectivity, and will provide some well-known examples from the history of science, and others from the areas of modern science with which I am most familiar. In chapter 5, I will give examples of how these methods and habits of thought have invaded the thinking of our whole culture, not only in strictly scientific topics, but also in inumerable other everyday matters, especially in matters of human value.

4.1 Objectivization by quantitative descriptions in the physical sciences

Descriptions may be qualitative or quantitative. The former may contain a wealth of detail, but usually do not present the actual evidence for each conclusion in a manner where it can be critically evaluated, or can form a basis for attempts at precise replication. Such descriptions may thus be rather authoritarian. A fundamental characteristic of most scientific methods, once they establish themselves, is therefore to insist on quantitative methods against qualitative descriptions. Usually quantitative descriptions use our familiar decimal system of numbers. In some cases qualitative descriptive data may be in 'categorical' form (that is recording whether a quality is 'present' or 'absent'). Data coded in this precise way can also be regarded as being quantitative, except that a 'binary' numerical system is used rather than a decimal one (see section 4.5 on statistical methods).

Economic Quantitation has been carried to its finest precision in the physical sciences, especially in physics. It has been a major aspect in the process of obtaining an objective view of the world. It is certainly true that the success of modern science depends heavily on its use of quantitative methods. The invention of reliable yardsticks to give a quantitative measure for any variable of interest greatly enhances the precision of any scientific argument. This is because there are precise mathematical methods for demonstrating the relationship between quantitative measures, and for manipulating information expressed quantitatively. Such precise argument is not available for qualitative descriptions. Thus, in many examples, quantitation is a powerful and perfectly valid part of scientific reasoning. However, it is not necessarily so. In some other examples it is invalid, even absurd.

If one goes back to a time in the history of science before quantitation was the accepted method for most description, and puts oneself in the shoes of thinkers of those times, it would be hard to present an *a priori* argument why quantitative description should be preferred to other forms of description. The scientist who first pioneered the idea of quantitation and simple elegant mathematical relationships was Galileo, though of course Newton later adopted the method far more extensively. Looking at the whole body of Galileo's work, it is difficult to conclude that his development of this method was based on a logical derivation from more fundamental principles. There were too many mistakes in his reasoning (for instance his theory of the tides), and too many assertions with clear empirical implications that were not in fact put to the test. Instead we must conclude that Galileo had some sort of *faith* in this method. The role of quantitation and simple mathematical relationships in physics became the accepted hallmark of scientific method as a result of experience, which showed it to be the most fruitful method in practice. Possibly Galileo's faith was based in part on some such experience. His father, a professional musician, was interested enough in the physics of sound to conduct a series of experiments on the simple whole number ratios of lengths of vibrating strings which produced the simple and most agreeable harmonic intervals of music. Galileo must have been aware of these experiments, and may have developed his method as a result. The quantitative method could not have been known in advance by any *a priori* reasoning.

The process of quantitation has been applied to all basic variables, both the fundamental ones of mass, length and time, and a host of other more complex and subtle variables derived from them. How has the step of quantitation been made?

Consider first the fundamental variables, mass, length and time. The quantitation of mass and length must have had very early historical origins. A basic prerequisite would be that a civilization had a system of numbers well enough developed to do simple arithmetic. Any civilization that traded in precious metals (for instance) would have needed to weigh the metals, and it would soon have become clear that quantitative measures of weight could be combined according to the rules of arithmetic. Here we have the earliest examples of those simple mathematical relationships which so impressed Galileo. (At that stage of course the distinction between mass and weight could not be made. Weight depends on both mass and the force of gravity, and in early times the force of gravity was not recognized, let alone the fact that it varied in different parts of the universe.) For both weight and length the step towards quantitation must have depended on the direct subjective impact of the objects to be weighed or measured on the basic senses – the visual impression of length, or the weight of an object one can feel when one holds it in one's hand. Indeed, in the twentieth century the developmental psychologist Jean Piaget[1] has investigated the age at which a child comes to regard such basic qualities as being capable of quantitative evaluation. These studies do not of course answer whether the appreciation of length, weight, volume (etc.) as quantities is an innate development, as opposed to one strongly influenced by our culture. However, this is not the basic point. It is this: Whether one is talking about historical development, or the cognitive development of an individual human, objective quantitation of mass and length originated from subjective appreciation of different degrees of a quality, dependent on the subjective impression received from basic senses.

The quantitation of the time variable, so fundamental to post-Renaissance science, is a more interesting case, because important steps in the process occurred more recently, and are therefore matters of recorded history. In the science of the ancient Greeks there were no accurate time-pieces for measuring intervals of time as short as minutes or seconds. There were therefore severe limitations on the use of time as a quantitative variable, for instance in laboratory experiments. Greek science therefore tended to be static rather than dynamic, and could not give any substance to, or accurate prediction from the idea of natural laws of causation. In the times of the ancient Greeks and Romans the number of 'hours' in day-time and night-time was often decreed to be the same (i.e. 12), regardless of the time of the year.[2] In the early Renaissance, Johannes Kepler noted some interesting numerical coincidences in the orbit times and distances from the sun of the planets. Some of these were later given a rational basis, while others never were, and are nowadays dismissed as 'mystical numerology'.

The explicit realization that time could be quantified quite accurately is probably to be attributed to Galileo more than to any other scientist. His studies of motion, and the 'natural' characteristics of acceleration in falling bodies made explicit assumptions about time as a precise quantitative variable. In his analysis of swinging pendulums, time was also used as a precise quantitative variable. In so doing he paved the way for explicit formula for simple harmonic motion. His work also led to the first accurate clocks, which were built in Galileo's lifetime, the yardstick by which such precise quantitative time could thenceforth be measured. Accurate experiments in the new science of mechanics by Galileo and other pioneers were thus made possible. Moreover a truly rational science of planetary motion could be built on this framework by Newton.

But what did Galileo's bold step rest upon? It must have rested on his very own subjective assessment of the qualitative feeling of time passing. The story of Galileo timing the frequency of the candelabra swinging in an Italian church, using his own pulse as the measure of time, is familiar. While there is little proof that this actually happened, it is quite plausible that it did. In Galileo's experiments with inclined planes, the acceleration of bodies must have been timed somehow; but there were no chronometers in existence more accurate than the human pulse.[3] Let us assume that in those earliest experiments the human pulse actually was used for timing. We then ask the question: How did Galileo know that his own pulse was regular, and could be used for approximate measurement of time? Undoubtedly, he guessed (or assumed) that this was so because of his own subjective sense of rhythm. It is perhaps no accident that Galileo's father was a professional musician. Galileo must have been very familiar with the idea that the temporal measures of a rhythmic piece of music could be laid out as measures of length, written along the staves of a musical manuscript.

The realization that time in the intervals of seconds or minutes could be measured quantitatively in a public, objective way was an enormous conceptual step forwards; but nevertheless one cannot avoid the conclusion that it relied initially on a subjective, qualitative hunch, in the mind of a single person. Here we have a very important instance where the subjective and the objective depend on each other; where quantitative and qualitative assessments of the world are not in antithesis to each other, but are complementary.

In the years since the scientific Renaissance, many other physical variables came to be treated quantitatively. In many cases this involved extension of the quantitation of mass, length and time. Sometimes new concepts were given precise definition by mathematical combinations of other fundamental variables. For instance, velocity, momentum, energy, force, torque and a variety of other variables can be defined as combinations of measurements of mass, length and time, made in various situations. Sometimes extensions were made from the everyday scale to the scale of very large or very small events, in which case much more specialized measuring devices were needed. For instance it became possible to measure the velocity and wavelength of light and sound; to measure 'atomic weight'; or to measure the distance separating us from identified stars, using the time taken for light to travel from them to us – expressed as 'light years' – as a measure of distance. Nevertheless the original methods of weighing and measuring mass, length and time would be involved indirectly, for calibration of the specialized measures, or in the experimental procedures involved in deriving the micro- or macro- measurements.

All these advances were logical extensions of the original concepts of mass, length and time, and were not derived from subjective appreciation of any new qualities. But since mass, length and time originated in such subjective impressions, the extensions of these quantitative concepts to areas where direct sensory experience is impossible also ultimately depended on such subjective sensory experiences, as well as on the logical processes by which the extension was made.

However, some other quantitative variables arose independently from the fundamental variables of mass, length and time, and only later were integrated into that conceptual scheme. In such cases, the impetus to quantitate the new variable may have come from other kinds of subjective appreciation of the different degrees of a particular quality. The obvious example is temperature. We are all subjectively familiar with different degrees of 'hotness'; but only when it was realized that most substances (whether solids, liquids or gases) expand when they are heated was it possible to invent a scale for temperature – that is, to produce the first thermometer. Later, of course, when it was realized that the temperature of an object was a property derived from the degree of motion of its individual atoms or molecules, it became possible to derive temperature from the laws of motion, and thus to integrate the concept of temperature fully into the basic scientific scheme of mass, length and time. Once again, however, we have a case where the subjective (qualitative) and the objective (quantitative) assessments of a variable are complementary, the former being an essential precursor to the latter.

In the birth of the science of chemistry accurate measurement of the weights of solids and liquids, and of the volumes of gases, played an important part. It was found that when chemical combination occurred, different elementary substances combined in characteristic ratios of weight or volume. Alternatively, where an elementary substance could combine in several ways with another substance, the amount of the elementary substance in the different compounds would always be as simple whole number ratios to each other. These characteristic and simple whole number ratios of the masses of combining substances played an important part in defining the concepts of atoms and molecules. Another major conceptual advance came when the realization was made by Van't Hoff that the component atoms which combine to make a molecule are arranged in the same three-dimensional space with which we are familiar in everyday life, but on a vastly smaller scale. In both cases, the advances in chemistry are elaborations and extensions of the descriptive schemes of physics in which mass, length and time are central.

The sciences associated with the discovery of electricity brought in a whole new range of concepts of, and ways of integrating the physical view of the world. Other sorts of forces (magnetic and electrostatic) became explicable. A new window on chemical structure was opened up, by the realization that chemical combinations and dissociations could be achieved electrolytically. In due course this discipline of electrochemistry provided new insights into the structure of atoms. The modern view of the nature of light and other electromagnetic radiation would have been impossible without the nineteenth century study of these aspects of electricity. But all these advances in physics and chemistry did not go beyond the quantitative descriptive language using mass, length and time, which had its real birth at the Renaissance.

Towards the end of the nineteenth century, this view of the physical universe seemed almost complete. A completely objective view of the physical world seemed close at hand, and subjectivity could be regarded as a primitive approach. In the twentieth century there have been two profound revolutions in physics – Einstein's theory of relativity, and the quantum theory, which have changed all that. Far from abolishing the subject who makes the observations, these revolutions have brought the subject and object (observer and observed) into inseparable interaction. With Einstein's Theory of Relativity modern physics shows that what is observed on axes of space and time depends on the relative movement between the observer and what is observed. Thus the endeavours of the experimental physicist depend on (and tell us about) the properties of the observer as much as about what is observed.

With Heisenberg's Uncertainty Principle (central to the quantum theory) physics deals with fundamental limits on accuracy of measurement, at least for fundamental particles. The velocity and position of such a particle cannot be measured without it interacting with another particle, fired on the initiative of the experimentalist. The observer cannot find anything out about such a particle without altering its 'unobserved state'. In this circumstance the more accurately one measures velocity the less accurately one can ever measure position, and *vice versa*.

There is a line of philosophical reasoning which makes further use of these developments, concluding that they have profound implications for the nature of mind. The argument goes as follows: In relativity theory, the measurements made by an observer depend on the attributes of the observer (his velocity). In quantum theory the observation that is made can be said not to reflect what is actually present at that time: It is one of many possible states, being the one at which, by chance, reality is forced to 'crystallize out' in response to the act of observation. Thus, reality is very different in the observed and the unobserved state. For both relativity and quantum theory, it is impossible to define an objective reality, independent of the observer. Both physicists[4] and some psychiatrists[5] have drawn from these experiments implications for the philosophical issue of mind/brain relationships. If this claim is correct, it cannot be ignored; and if incorrect, the flaw in the reasoning needs to be clarified. I believe there is a flaw in the reasoning. Specifically, I believe that the experiments and theory of neither relativity nor quantum theories has a bearing on what I believe to be the central aspect of the mind/body issue. The question is however confused by the alternative definitions of mind (mentioned in chapter 3), and which tend to prejudge the issue in a tautologous manner. What I believe to be the central enigma here, the metaphysical relationship of subjective to objective reality, is not addressed by either of these physical revolutions, despite their very great practical and theoretical implications. The detailed analysis of this line of reasoning, in my view confused and incorrect, appears in section 9.6 of Part II.

4.2 *Objectivization in the biological sciences*

In biology many of the methods of the physical sciences are adopted with little modification. Mass, length and time are measures applicable as much in biology as in other sciences. Admittedly, many of the chemical constituents are different in living organisms from those found in inorganic chemistry. It was a major landmark when it was shown that a simple molecule – urea – which could be synthesized by inorganic means, was identical with the compound found in living things. This was the start of a long process of analysing the constituents of living things in the same materialist terms adopted for inanimate matter, which has culminated, in our own time, with the elucidation of the chemical structure of the genetic material of all living things.

However, a distinguishing feature of biology is the considerable amount of available detail of anatomical structure. A large part of early research consisted of qualitative descriptions of the bodily form of organisms, either as their external form (which later became particularly useful for attempts at classification) or using dissection to reveal internal structure. Such descriptions were obtained either by observation with the naked eye, as in many dissections of living things, or by the use of microscopes of various sorts. Those who presented the first descriptions of a new set of structures were scientists with skills of observation way beyond those of ordinary people. The contribution made by these scientists was subjectively-based in two different ways. In the first instance the early descriptions of these pioneers relied on subjective visual impressions which the object of study made on the individual investigator. Only later did such descriptions receive validation by replication of these subjective visual impressions by other observers. In addition, however, the description of any complex structure is subjective in a quite different way: Rendering the complexity of what strikes the eye into a meaningful written description for others to read involves always a *selection* of detail. *A priori* there are no rules for such selection. They are the free and subjective choices of the investigator. We see in anatomy textbooks the things that have 'struck the eyes' of anatomists through the centuries, but this choice is really rather arbitrary. Why for instance is it that points of attachment of muscles to bone are emphasized, but not the length of the lever arms by which those muscles act?

This free selection of a descriptive language, such as is adopted for anatomical structure, is rather different from what obtains in the physical sciences. In the latter, a variable is only accepted as valid for descriptive purposes if it can be measured, and the quantitative measures so obtained obey the basic rules of arithmetic. In the qualitative descriptions of much of biology, there is no such obvious criterion, yet it is nevertheless important that the description be made. In many instances the traditional descriptive forms survive without much question, even over the centuries, with no more secure foundation than the authority of the person who first proposed them. In some cases however, a form of validation does occur for the selective process underlying a descriptive scheme. The validation is much slower, and by more complex means than the actual visual images recorded by the observer. How is it achieved?

The choice of descriptive language (such as a classification scheme) can become validated *by the use to which it can subsequently be put*. Succinctly, if there is no *a priori* criterion for choice of descriptive language, we must say 'if it works, use it'. In science the most important function of description is to provide a basis, later, for explanation, the demonstration of *why* things are as they are. Therefore, as far as descriptive science goes, we can say in general that a principle for the selection of which data are relevent is validated when the data included by the selection can be used as part of an explanatory framework. Sometimes this is easy. The distinction made by the early microscopists between epithelium, endothelium and mesoderm followed easily from a natural distinction: The inner and out lining layers of the body serve the functions required at an interface with the external world, or the internal contents of an organ such as the stomach (respectively), whereas the tissue lying between these two layers can be expected to have quite different functions, and correspondingly different architecture. Therefore this division of tissue types is useful in explaining very basic functions of tissues, whereas others (for instance the colour of the cells when stained in certain ways) is not useful in this basic way. For the joints between bones, the *shape* of the articulating surfaces is an obvious point to be emphasized in descriptions and classifications, because it is this which determines and explains which varieties of movement are possible. An engineer makes rather similar distinctions, for instance between hinge and ball-and-socket joints.

In other cases the principles to be emphasized in description and classification give rise to far more trouble. A pioneer in the description and classification of plants, Linnaeus, emphasized that the reproductive parts of plants were those which gave the surest guide to the natural order by which plants could be classified. At the time, and for a long time afterwards, there was no sure validation for this dictum of Linnaeus. It could however be argued that the validation of Linneaus' classification scheme came with Darwin's theory of evolution by natural selection. If reproductive fitness was the sole determinant of evolutionary change, the reproductive parts would arguably be those which change least in the course of evolution.

Another example comes from the pioneer genetic studies of Gregor Mendel. He emphasized that the ratios between the numbers of offspring (from a particular match of parents) having different discrete characteristics was of vital importance to understanding genetics. It should be explained that the science of statistics had not yet been born at the time Mendel was working, and that his own results had so much variance that they would probably not have withstood scrutiny by modern statistical tests. The results were ignored for the next fifty years, and could have been discarded as 'mystical numerology' such as that used by Kepler. But with the discovery of chromosomes, and their behaviour during production of the gametes involved in sexual reproduction, it became clear that the simple whole number ratios which Mendel had believed to apply to his studies of garden peas was a straightforward inference to be made if chromosomes were the vehicle for inheritance.

In such cases, it is usual, along the way, before such proper validation occurs, that there be many disagreements about how one selects what is relevant. In addition, in the time before the selective principles of a descriptive scheme have been properly validated, the choice of one, rather than another scheme of description often has to rely on no more solid foundation than the authority and prestige of the original investigator.

From a methodological point of view, the thing to be noted in these cases is that the selection of what is relevant in a description is not evident *a priori* but can be discerned only when the consequences of a particular choice become clear. This may disatisfy some logicians. But it is absurd to base all reasoning and all science on self-evident *a priori* principles. There must be some way of establishing premises to start from. Moreover in some traditional forms of reasoning (e.g *reductio ad absurdum*) the validity of premises is determined only at the end of the process, when one finds whether the conclusions are sense or nonsense. No doubt there are sometimes initial constraints which allow one to choose the premises to start from; but where there are no such constraints, as when a completely new field for descriptive science is opened up, a slower process, *a posteriori*, has to be used. Indeed, even with the choice of precise quantitative forms for description, the validity of that form is not self evident, but arises from its proven usefulness. Likewise, Galileo's method for quantifying time, by reference to pendular motion was not correct *a priori*, but was validated by the uses to which such a manner of description could subsequently be put.

Careful notice should be taken of this *a posteriori* principle ('if it works, use it'): It arises several times in later parts of this work, applied then not only in scientific descriptions, but also in metaphysical descriptions, and ultimately in formulating credible myths about our place in the universe. In all cases, its use is restricted to situations where there are no other prior constraints, and one has a free choice, provided only that no contradictions arise from one's choice of descriptive form.

As for quantitative approaches to objectifying visually-based descriptions, this has lagged behind the qualitative descriptions, with their inevitable subjectivity, by generations, sometimes centuries. In fact, in a modern subject called stereology, we are only in the last decade inventing methods of getting unbiased quantitative information about three dimensional structure from cross-sectional pictures, for instance as seen in the microscope. This is sometimes done with the breezy energy of those who think that for the first time they are being truly scientific about biological structure, and with some scorn for the qualitative descriptions of the past. This attitude does not give the credit due to the early pioneers. This scornful attitude is probably motivated in part by the belief that subjectivity has no part in science. The reality of course is quite different. Subjective assessment, in the first instance by a single individual, is an essential precursors to objectivization and quantitation. H.-J. Gundersen, a modern pioneer in the science of stereology writes as follows:

> Humans have five senses like most living creatures: smell, sight, touch, taste and hearing ... As opposed to most lower species, stereologists have at least four extra senses or probes which are sensitive and very specific for four geometric modalities of 3-dimensional objects; volume, surface, length and number.[6]

EIGHT (P.A. ROSS)

Apart from the considerable arrogance of this statement, one may note that the stereologists' statistical tools are equated with the human primary senses; whereas in reality they are *mathematical extensions* of information gained by the primary sense of sight, just as described for many physical variables in the previous chapter.

4.3 Objectivization in psychological sciences

As mentioned above, quantitation of the temperature variable started from subjective awareness of the quality, and degrees of 'hotness', and only later was integrated into the theoretical framework of the rest of physics, defined by its fundamental variables. In the science of psychology attempts have been made to define a large number of variables, in a manner similar to that used for the original definition of the temperature variable, but with varying degrees of success. In a few cases these variables have been properly validated, by integrating them into the theoretical framework of the rest of science. In these few cases, it has been achieved by showing that these variables correspond well to physico-chemical processes in the brain, or in sensory or motor organs. Many other variables hang in limbo, so to speak, useful within the subject of psychology, but not yet properly validated and incorporated into the physico-chemically defined functions of the nervous system. A few examples of these variously-successful attempts at quantification are appropriate.

Perhaps the closest analogy to the quantification of temperature is in sensory psychophysics. Subjectively we are aware that the sensations we receive from each of our sensory systems can vary in 'intensity', though it is not obvious how to quantitate this intensity. Last century, Weber and Fechner[7] found a way of solving this problem by evaluating the 'just-noticeable-differences'. Weber conducted experimental tests of discrimination of differences of intensity, using, for instance, weights of graded size, tones and lengths. He found that the 'just-noticeable-difference' (jnd) bore a regular quantitative relation to the objective measure of the weights being discriminated. The size of the just-noticeable-difference was roughly proportional to the size of the weights themselves. For instance in lifting weights, two different weights had to differ by at least the ratio 39/40 for the difference to be noticeable. This ratio held true regardless of the actual size of the weights. Similar results have been obtained using a variety of sensory stimuli. More recently there have been many qualifications and criticisms of this type of finding. Nevertheless, the basic relation is still a well-known starting point for the discipline of psychophysics, and is now known as the Weber-Fechner law. From this it was possible to provide an objective scale for the subjectively-appreciated intensity of each stimulus. By defining all just-noticeable-differences for a particular sensory modality as equal, one has a yardstick to measure the total (subjective) intensity of any stimulus. In principle this intensity would be expressed as 'so many jnds'.

Thus far, the psychological scale for intensity of a perceived stimulus, defined as the increments known as jnds corresponds to the physical scale for temperature defined by increments of expansion of the fluid in a thermometer. The integration of this psychophysical scale into the fabric of mechanistic neuroscience is in the realm of sensory physiology rather than psychophysics. Specifically it lies in the relation between the objective stimulus magnitude and the quantitative aspects of the response of the corresponding sense organs. Generally speaking, the objective magnitude of a stimulus bears a logarithmic relation to the magnitude of the increase in impulse firing rate produced in the nervous system by the stimulus. Simply put, when the intensity of a sensory stimulus is increased by regular *multiples*, the corresponding increase in impulse frequency is also regular, but consists of regular *additions* rather than regular multiples. Examples of this fact are cited by Granit.[8] If one takes the subjective capacity to discriminate as reflecting a small constant difference in impulse frequency, this logarithmic relationship observed physiologically would necessarily generate relations similar to the Weber-Fechner law as seen psychophysically. But the revelation of this objective logarithmic relation does not detract from the original law, which was itself derived from the universal appreciation of degrees of subjective intensity for the various types of stimulus which continually bombard us.

Another pair of concepts which have been important in the history of psychology are those of reward and reinforcement. The first controlled investigations of these concepts were initiated by Thorndike, at the end of the last century. He showed that animals such as cats, presented with the problem of finding food hidden in a complex apparatus, would repeat the response or response sequence which on previous occasions had obtained for them the food. Objectively the concept which came out of such experiments was that of reinforcement: Behaviour which fulfills certain basic 'motives' for an animal tends subsequently to be produced more easily, that is, it is reinforced. However, it is difficult to believe that this objective formulation was the whole story. Somewhere in Thorndike's thinking, which led to his puzzle box experiments, must have been the idea that when humans perform acts which fulfill their motives or intentions, it also made them experience a transitory subjectively pleasant feeling, a short-lived euphoria. Thorndike's actual phrasing for his celebrated Law of Effect was as follows:

> Of several responses made to the same situation, those which are accompanied by or closely followed by satisfaction to the animal will, other things being equal, be more firmly connected with the situation, so that when it recurs, they will be more likely to occur . . .[9]

Use of the term 'satisfaction' seems to refer to a subjective experience. This could perhaps be described as the origin of the reward concept.

However, the history of psychology in the first half of the twentieth century, especially in North America, was dominated by the attempt to abolish any reference to subjective qualities such as rewarding experiences, from the vocabulary of students of animal behaviour and learning. For myself I am not convinced that they succeeded in abolishing the concepts of subjective qualities from their own thinking (see below).

Amongst the large research literature produced by the early psychologists were some studies of the relative reinforcing effects of motivationally favourable stimuli of various sizes (e.g. food 'rewards' of different sizes). In fact these never led to any generally accepted quantitative measure of reward magnitude, in the manner of the Weber-Fechner law, because there were too many additional influences which determined the reinforcing effect of a standard rewarding stimulus. Nevertheless, as psychological concepts, reward and reinforcement became very important ways of describing the results of experiments on animal learning.

Despite its psychological complexity, the reward-reinforcement concepts are amongst the few where the concept has been validated and fully integrated into the mechanistic neuroscience. This process of validation started in the mid-1950s when Olds and Milner showed that there were regions of the brain which, if stimulated electrically, could produce objective changes in an animal's behaviour similar to the reinforcing effects of a food reward. For instance, an animal would tend to return to the place where it had previously received such brain stimulation, or it would perform behavioural acts which had previously been followed by the brain stimulation. In the years since then, a vast amount of research has given us an increasingly clear account of the regions in the brain and the chemical messenger substances which mediate this internal reward. We are now reaching the stage where the biophysics of the process are being investigated, and the nerve networks which can lead to such reward-mediated changes of behaviour are becoming the subject of simulation on computers. Thus the process is far advanced of integrating a concept, which was originally confined to the discipline of psychology, into the chemistry, physics, anatomy and cybernetics of the brain.

Now let us move to some examples where the process of objectification and quantification have been attempted, have indeed become very influential, but are nevertheless far less convincing and satisfactory, when judged by the criteria used in the rest of science.

The subject of reward and reinforcement introduces the fashion in early twentieth-century North American psychology called 'behaviorism'. The founder of this movement was J. B. Watson. He states explicitly his view that until behaviorism appeared, psychology was non-scientific. In particular, referring to earlier psychology he states 'its subject matter is not objective', and that 'introspection [is] a serious bar to progress'.[10] The new science had to concentrate solely upon the objective observables of behaviour. Thus there could be no clues to objective facts gained from examining one's own subjective experience, and no suggestion of internal, non-observable variables in explanation of behaviour.[11]

Predictably perhaps, much of Watson's book, entitled *Psychology from the Standpoint of a Behaviorist*, is concerned with the anatomy and physiology of the nervous system and sense organs, such as was known at the time Watson was writing. But, apart from this, Watson could not really maintain his credo in a consistent fashion. He gives himself away when trying to define thought. For him, thought is synonymous with 'implicit language habits'. By this he means most specifically 'subvocal speech'. Undoubtedly there are some people in whom subvocal speech can actually be observed when they are reading to themselves, or thinking. But Watson goes well beyond what can actually be observed. He writes:

> A man may sit motionless at his desk with pen in hand and paper before him. In popular parlance we may say he is idle or 'thinking', but our *assumption* is that his muscles are really as active and possibly more active than if he were playing tennis.[12]

He assumes that what he has not actually observed does in fact occur, to fit his objectivist view of thought. It is hard to believe that Watson was really relying on direct observation to form his view, rather than on his own subjective experience of thought-words 'going through his head'. He even tries to defend himself against this obvious objection:

> The introspectionist claims that the behaviorist first uses the method of introspection to find thinking, and having once found it, shuts his eyes and turns his back upon the original method, and begins to externalize the process . . . The behaviorists' answer is that he can at present arrive at this conclusion only by making a logical inference.[13]

In view of Watson's earlier admission that he assumes subvocal speech though he cannot observe it, the claim of a purely logical inference from observation is incredible.

Another behaviourist, Clark Hull, had a more accomodating view of introspection. He writes:

> At all events, verbal reports [i.e. of internal states] in some manner are frequently useful; e.g. in clinical situations where a precise and objectively metricized history of the ailing subject is lacking and where time or energy would not be available to make exact calculations concerning relevant habit structures . . . Consequently, introspective reports concerning internal conditions are useful for rough qualitative purposes; nevertheless they become inadequate wherever primary quantitative laws are in the process of systematic formulation or precise validation.[14]

This position differs little from that advocated by me, except in matters of emphasis.

Amongst the behaviourist school, the scientist who was most thorough and consistent in his rejection of mentalist language was B. F. Skinner. He does not reject conceptual terms for the description of behaviour, but insists that they be not used to refer to mental states, but rather to aspects of information processing directly derivable from empirical observations. Thus he is somewhat critical of both the mentalist and the materialist:

> The materialist, reacting from a mentalist system, is likely to miss behavior as a subject matter, because he wishes to have his concepts refer to something substantial. He is likely to regard conceptual terms referring to behavior as verbal and fictitious and in his desire for an earthy explanation to overlook their position in a descriptive science.[15]

Against the mentalist he writes:

> The traditional description and organization of behavior represented by the concepts of 'will', 'cognition', 'intellect' and so on cannot be accepted so long as it pretends to be dealing with a mental world, but the behavior to which these terms apply is naturally part of the subject matter of the science of behaviour.[16]

> The important objection to the vernacular in the description of behavior is that many of its terms imply conceptual schemes. I do not mean that a science of behavior is to dispense with a conceptual scheme, but that it must not take over without careful consideration the schemes which underlie popular speech. The vernacular is clumsy and obese; its terms overlap with each other, draw unnecessary or unreal distinctions, and are far from the most convenient in dealing with the data.[17]

His plea might well have been made by an advocate for Newtonian physics, for whom the words force, mass, weight, momentum etc suddenly had come to have precise mathematical definitions, in contrast to the use of some of these terms in loose ways before the Newtonian scientific revolution took place.

Skinner believed that 'the mind' or 'consciousness' is a metaphor or a construct. He writes:

> Self-knowledge, consciousness, or awareness became possible only when the species acquired verbal behavior . . .
>
> Many mentalistic or cognitive terms refer not only to contingencies but to the behavior they generate. Terms like 'mind', 'will' and 'thoughts' are often simply synonyms of 'behavior'.[18]

For him the central realities are the observables of behaviour, and anything mentalistic is an epiphenomenon, or an unnecessary projection from behaviour.

It is interesting to quote his views on our sense of time.

> A writer has pointed out that 'the conductor of an orchestra maintains a certain even beat according to an internal rhythm, and he can divide that beat in half again and again with an accuracy rivalling any mechanical instrument'. But is there an *internal* rhythm? Beating time is behavior. Parts of the body often serve as pendulums useful in determining speed, as when the amateur musician beats time with a foot or the rock player with the whole body . . . The conductor beats time steadily because he has learned to do so under rather exacting contingencies of reinforcement. The behavior may be reduced in scale until it is no longer visible to others. It is still sensed by the conductor, but it is a sense of behavior, not of time. The history of 'man's development of a sense of time' over the centuries is not a matter of cognitive growth but of the invention of clocks, calendars and ways of keeping records, in other words of an environment that keeps time.[19]

This behaviourist view of the human sense of rhythm contrasts curiously with what must have been Galileo's approach to quantifying time (discussed in section 4.1). For Galileo an assumption must have been made that an internal sense of rhythm was a clue to an accurate temporal measure. Skinner assumes the relation to be exactly reversed. If the sense of rhythm in a conductor is really a 'sense of behavior', it is implied that some agent (perhaps even a 'subject') must be aware of that behaviour. How is that agent informed of the regularity of the rhythm in the conductor's beat, if there is no internal sense of rhythm? Like Watson, Skinner tends to assume covert behaviour when it cannot be observed. For one who holds that the sense of time is given by behaviour rather than by an internal sense, consider the powerful impact that can occur in jazz music of a 'syncopated rest'. Here, a powerful beat of the music may occur in total silence, with no associated behaviour by the musicians. Yet its musical impact can be very strong, perhaps more strong just because the beat occurs in total silence.

Psychology has come a long way since Watson, and there are now very few adherents to the behaviourist creed in anything remotely resembling its original form. Nevertheless, the above illustrations are apt, because the tendency to exclusive objectivity which Watson's behaviourism represented occurs in a wide variety of other ways in quite contemporary science. Within psychology, behaviourism as such may be superseded, but has had a profound impact which still endures. The original idea that one should shun all internal variables, and concentrate only on the observable behaviour is not now widely held. There *is* now a consensus, that for scientific study of psychological processes, one should try to define the internal strategies of information processing. The impact of behaviourism is that these strategies cannot be convincingly discovered from introspection, but must be inferred from objective evidence of behaviour, although they are not directly observable. They are therefore still, in a sense, objective. This is a considerable advance in methodology and philosophy. Mentalism in in the form of Cartesian dualism has been mainly abandoned.[20] Less categorical forms of mentalism are advocated by many writers.[21] But mentalism in so far as it implies a belief that there actually *exists* an internal subjective world, is generally scorned.[22] A major thrust of the present book is that this modern emphasis is a mistake. For the time being it is sufficient merely to point out that the rejection of this form of mentalism is the *assumption* of the modern science of behaviour, rather than its conclusion.

4.4 Objectivization in the social sciences

It is hard to draw a dividing line between psychology and sociology. However, there is a methodology, found in both, but more typical in sociology, which is different from the examples given above. A large number of variables exist in the disciplines of psychology and sociology for which operational methods have been devised to allow quantitation. These methods purport to measure such things as 'intelligence', personality variables such as 'extroversion/introversion', descriptions of interpersonal interactions such as 'expressed emotion', or sociological parameters, such as 'social class'. On the surface these abstract nouns seem to denote variables as substantial as mass, length, time or 'hotness'. It could be suggested that they arise from similar subjective intuitions as these physical variables; and if they do, they should be objectively quantifiable in a similar way. However, the methods that *are* used to quantify these abstract psychological and social qualities are rather different from those used to quantify basic physical variables, or even the psychological intensity of a stimulus as implicit in the Weber-Fechner law.

Usually a 'rating scale' is used to quantify these variables. This may consist of a series of tests to be performed (e.g. items in an intelligence test); or it may consist of a series of questions to be asked of the subject; or it may consist of other sorts of items of information to be obtained about the person or psychological situation under study. The exact performance of the test, the exact phrasing of the questions, or the definition of the type of information to be obtained, is of greatest importance. These details may be elaborated at great length to ensure that the investigator knows exactly how to score the responses given by his subjects. Special training of a team of investigators may be required to ensure that they all operate in the same way. Often the precise wording of an item or question is critical; and where a rating scale needs to be used in several languages, the reliability of a translation when back-translated into the original language must be established. These complex and varied procedures are adopted to ensure that different investigators provide similar ratings when presented by the same experimental subject. Overall the method is designed to ensure the 'objectivity' of the use of the rating scale, that is, its freedom from noise or subjective bias. Success in this is generally checked explicitly by testing the 'inter-rater reliability' of the rating scale used.

In addition there may be explicit statements of the rules by which information from the different components of a rating scale are to be combined to give a final score. These rules may involve merely adding up the answers to all the questions in the test (e.g. giving one mark per question), but often much more complex rules are developed, even to the extent of writing computer programmes to derive the end score from the raw data. Again, since the data processing is explicit and carried out by precisely specified rules, it is free from observer bias, and therefore 'objective'.

Of course, measures using rating scales are never as accurate and reliable as measurements of physical variables. The important thing is that different investigators, or the same investigators at different times, use the rating scale in exactly the same way. Given this, and in so far as one is concerned with collecting descriptive data about sociological or psychological matters, independent of the personal biases of those collecting the data, these methods have considerable use. The usefulness of such methods for purposes of prediction is obvious in many aspects of modern life, for instance in predicting the results of forthcoming General Elections, or for demonstrating shifts in public opinion over the years. Nevertheless, as in descriptive anatomy, the principles of selection of the items in any rating scale are, in the end, the subjective choice of the person(s) who developed each rating scale, and the method of scoring.

Moreover, it may easily be asked whether an abstract noun like 'intelligence' denotes any quality which exists in the same substantial way as 'mass' or 'temperature'. Such questions go beyond mere description because they appear to raise theoretical questions about the reality and validity of the underlying variables. When such questions arise, an extension of the above methods is sometimes used to demonstrate the 'validity' of the underlying concept which the rating scale is supposed to measure. Multivariate statistical methods are used in this, and there are a variety of detailed methods for this. Basically these methods calculate the degree to which the different measures of the variable assessed by a rating scale correlate over the population of subjects used in the assessment. For instance, if 'blue eyes' and 'fair hair' always occur together, and there are no cases of 'blue eyes' and some other hair colour, or of 'fair hair' and some other eye colour, one can say that the measures of eye colour and hair colour are highly correlated. This procedure is carried out for all possible pairs of measures of the variable with which the rating scale is concerned. Then, those groups of variables which show acceptable levels of mutual correlation are taken as representing a valid concept. Thus, for instance, it would be possible to calculate which items in an intelligence test are 'the better ones' in that they correlate with a greater number of other item scores, or with the overall total score. In this way, so it is claimed, psychological and sociological constructs can be 'validated', implying perhaps that when they are so validated, they become variables as substantial as those in the physical sciences. Cronbach and Meehl,[23] for instance, make an explicit analogy between the processes involved in establishing a scale of temperature, with that involved in scaling intelligence. Their analogy has several serious flaws, however. The

Binet intelligence test, to which they refer (the forerunner of later intelligence tests), is not a single measure (like the mecury thermometer) but a series of measures, each influenced by several variables, with the total score supposed to 'average out' the extraneous variables. Correlations between the results obtained with various types of thermometer are far more precise than those between different types of intelligence test. Above all there is no *theory* (linking performance on intelligence tests to a well defined concept of intelligence) which can rival the kinetic theory (relating the well validated concepts of molecular motion and kinetic energy to temperature). Not surprisingly, intelligence testing has been criticized because it reflects things other than the supposed concept of 'intelligence'.

When such methods are used, it is common, after a while, for mistakes to be recognized, and revisions to be made. For instance the personality variable 'psychoticism' was measured in the personality inventory of Eysenck, this word seeming to imply that persons scoring high on this variable would be more prone to psychotic illnesses such as schizophrenia and mania. The modern view, however, holds that this scale really measures something approximating to what is nowadays called 'psychopathy', a personality type which has little relation to psychotic illnesses. A generation ago it was claimed that a characteristic psychological trait of someone with schizophrenia was 'overinclusiveness', a tendency, so it was believed, to include a much wider range of instances in the definition of any concept than was the case in 'normal' individuals. A variety of tests were devised to 'measure' the degrees of this quality. However, this concept rather fell out of favour when it was realized that *general* over-responsiveness to the test items could account for many of the differences between normals and those with schizophrenia, as registered by these tests. Likewise, intelligence tests have often been criticized because they are influenced by a great many factors other than some 'innate' quality of intelligence. These include such things as the extent of training in the particular test, the similarity of the test material to situations common in the prevailing culture, as well as how the subject is feeling on the day of the test. If there is so much argument about the results of tests of this nature, it makes one suspect that the method itself has a basic fallacy of some sort built into it. What could this be?

It is the mutual correlation of different measures of a variable on which the validity of that variable is mainly postulated. This is the questionable part of the process. It is often said that correlation does not prove causation, because correlation between A and B can arise for reasons other than that 'A causes B'. (For instance B might be the cause of A, or there might be a common cause of both.) Likewise, mutual correlation of two measures of a supposed sociological 'variable' might occur for many reasons other than that the variable is a solid and totally coherent construct. In the case of intelligence tests, a high degree of correlation between the different measures of 'intelligence' may arise because the subjects as a group have cultural experiences which differ in systematic ways, rather than because intelligence is a coherent quality which can be measured as readily as temperature. The role of calculations of correlation in this sort of psychological research is really similar to that in analysis of causal hypotheses: In the latter case, calculations of the degree of correlation can falsify a causal hypothesis, but strictly cannot verify it. In psychological and sociological research, the correlations analysed by multivariate statistics can falsify a claim that the different measures of a 'variable' are coherent, but cannot verify such a claim. This method of validation of a concept is therefore itself invalid.

What would be more impressive would be to derive, in as precise a way as possible, the *logical* relations between the concept to be measured (and the various measures of it) and other more fundamental variables, ultimately linked with the basic measures of mass, length and time. This is how the temperature variable became incorporated into the rest of physics, how the Weber-Fechner law was integrated into physiology, and how those few fully-validated psychological variables such as reward/reinforcement were integrated into physiological psychology. However, most psychological variables, and all sociological ones, fall short with regard to this type of validation. They are thus not integrated into the structure of scientific knowledge as a whole.

The reader should not misunderstand the drift of the above paragraphs. Rating scales contribute a great deal to descriptive accounts in psychology, psychiatry and sociology, regardless of whether the variables measured are validated or not. But to use those variables as if they were validated in the strong way that is possible in physics and chemistry leads to problems. In particular, when measures of such variables are introduced into other deductive arguments (such as in formulating theories or for developing explanatory arguments), their use tends to become circular. This is because the unstated assumptions buried within the original rating scale or its scoring system come to influence the conclusion, without it being clear that they really are prior assumptions rather than products of the argument.

The use of data from complex rating scales is particularly dangerous when applied in practical decision making. There was a time in Britain when important decisions about which child went to which secondary school hung on each child's performance in an intelligence test such as mentioned above. This practice has long been abandoned for reasons already outlined. But the same methodological flaws are being repeated at present in other areas of practical decisions making.

Two examples come quickly to mind. The first is the use of complex sociological rating scales to decide which psychiatric patients deserve various psychiatric diagnoses. Of course, in social terms it is clearly a very important decision to designate someone as 'schizophrenic', and it is thought of cardinal importance to do this precisely and consistently (though one hears sometimes of psychiatrists who change a diagnosis, because it is likely to have a less severe effect on a patient's employment prospects.) But when such a definition of schizophrenia also becomes the concept which brain scientists are trying to explain, the definition is an impediment to research. The second example, which will be expanded below, is the use of rating scales purporting to assess the 'quality of life' of a medical patient to help make difficult decisions about priorities for health spending. In such examples, insistence on the validity of the construct embodied in a particular rating scale when it has actually no such validity usually amounts to the originator of the rating scale claiming a superior authority. This has of course occurred many times before, using simpler descriptive systems.

One may ask, Why were the subjective intuitions which led to concepts such as mass, length, time and temperature so successful whereas those which underlie concepts such as 'intelligence' are much less so. The answer is probably that for the physical variables mentioned, a scientific concept is derived directly from a single type of subjective percept, which can then be objectified by measures along a single axis. To some extent the same is true for concepts such as 'reward/reinforcement'. Concepts such as intelligence, however, are not rooted in a single category of perception. In origin they are conceptualizations derived from many fundamental categories of information. There is then no unambiguous way in which those types of information should be integrated to form a scientific concept.

Finally in this section let me mention a few instances where quantitative description is totally invalid, but is pursued quite dogmatically, for its own sake, with no regard for the fact that objective assessment as quantities must always derive from subjectively-appreciated qualities. One example of this absurdity appears sometimes in review articles within the biological or psychological sciences. Faced with mountains of relevant experimental literature some researchers think they can cut corners on the vast task of scholarship required, and appraise the literature 'quantitatively'. Such writers will produce tables of all the research papers *for* and all those *against* a particular thesis, the thesis supported by the longer list being deemed the winner. There is in these writings no detailed critique of the individual merits and demerits of the papers on each side of the argument, for instance by comparing only those papers whose experimental approaches are very similar. Just the basic findings, as reported in the abstract, suffice for this tabulation, as though all studies providing information relevant to a particular issue can be compared on an equal basis. The alternative approach is for each result to be judged, case by case, on its own merits, to see whether the quality of the evidence *for* or *against* a particular viewpoint is stronger, regardless of its quantity. If quantity of scientific papers reaching a certain conclusion is to be reckoned as our measure, regardless of their quality, why not count the number of words written for or against a particular viewpoint, or simply weigh the papers for and against a particular proposition? We reach the absurdity of the University of Lagado, so beautifully described by Jonathan Swift in one of Gulliver's travels.

4.5 *Statistical analysis in science*

The above sections concentrated on the actual recording of data especially with quantitative measurements using variables validated with varying degrees of success. Quite apart from the recording of data there is *data analysis*. This is not entirely separate from the recording of data. For example, in the above section, calculations of correlation were, in some instances, necessary to validate chosen variables (in the social sciences). Generally speaking, however, the methods of data analysis make up the separate discipline called statistics. Much of this is concerned with detecting reliable differences or correlations amongst data sets where the actual measurements are only estimates of the underlying quantities. This involves a wide variety of methods of calculation applied to the recorded data. However, the aim of these calculations in all cases is to reduce the data to a single measure, a single yardstick. This yardstick is *probability*. The various statistical methods in use are usually designed to assess the probability that the observed values could have arisen by chance. If this is calculated to be unlikely, the 'null hypothesis' is rejected. For instance, one might have two lists of numbers representing the body weights of two populations of persons. The 'null hypothesis' would be that there is no significant difference between the two populations, that is, all the weights are from the same cross section of people. If, however, the 'null hypothesis' is rejected, one is led to the conclusion that the two populations are likely to be different 'to a certain degree of probability'. The calculations involved are often quite complex but, thanks to modern computer technology, this is far less tedious than it was a generation ago. Statistical methods can handle any quantitative variable. 'Categorical variables' (i.e. statements that a certain quantity is 'present' or absent') can be handled by other statistical routines. As mentioned above (section 4.1) categorical variables are also quantititive but use a binary numerical scheme rather than a more traditional one.

Overtly, all statistical methods are explicit, quantitative and objective. However, when we look more closely we find that, as with quantitative methods of measuring physical variables, the quantitative methodology of statistics relies on an interplay between objective and subjective, the latter making the former possible.

Take for instance the basic yardstick of statistics – probability. Quantitative it certainly is, but now in a more abstract sense than the physical variables discussed above. Basic concepts of probability have a mathematical derivation. But they would not have arisen if most of us did not also have a subjective feel for probability, that is, for the likelihood of certain events occurring in certain circumstances. Quantitative statements of probability presumably developed from these subjective feelings in a manner rather akin to the development of a temperature scale from our subjective feelings of different degrees of hotness, although the basic insight when statistics is formalized is mathematical rather than empirical.

Over the years a consensus has been reached that events that are less likely than 1 in 20 are to be taken as serious indications that the 'null hypothesis' may be rejected. But such a cut off point has no logical foundation whatsoever. There is no real reason why one should set the cut off point at $p<0.05$ rather than at $p<0.1$ or at $p<0.0001$. The value of 1 in 20 is perhaps the most agreeable figure for most scientists, a pragmatic compromise. Actually, within the discipline of psychology, experiments have been done to assess how likely an event has to be objectively before it becomes subjectively convincing to an experimental subject. The result is that different persons, and different personality types, have systematically different subjective statistical criteria for assessing whether an event is a significant departure from randomness. Indeed, from the discipline of learning theory, it can be shown that different ways of presenting favourable and unfavourable outcomes induce different subjective assessments of the likelihood of a forthcoming event having a favourable outcome. 'Partial reinforcement', that is, presentation of a reward on only a fraction of the instances when the to-be-rewarded behaviour is emitted, is in some ways a more powerful means of reward than reward on every occasion, because animals so manipulated cling more tenaciously to the acquired habit when there is no reward following it at all. They seem to have been influenced to believe in a stronger likelihood of the occurrence of reward than animals trained in with reward on every trial. Similar principles appear to apply to humans as to experimental animals. Much of the gambling industry exploits the factors determining subjective estimation of probability.

The interplay between subjective and objective assessments is raised in another way by the discipline of statistics, this time in a far more fundamental and philosophical way. It will be noted that statistical tests are designed to disprove the 'null hypothesis' of randomness in a data set. Thus, statistical tests never prove anything, either that two populations of values are different, or that they are the same. They disprove the hypothesis of randomness, to the stated degree of probability. At a time after statistics as a discipline had been developed, a philosophy was being developed by Karl Popper, which was remarkably similar in form. Popper[24] suggested that science never verifies any statement, but rather is always attempting to falsify hypotheses. A scientific statement is then one which is, in principle, falsifiable. Truth may be earnestly sought, but is nevertheless quite elusive. But then comes the paradox: All the descriptive data (from which any of the competing hypotheses arise) are collected on the assumption that in some sense they are true. After all, in the process of description, the primary sense data which permit the description are taken at face value, unless there are strong reasons to doubt them. Nevertheless, objectively all we can apparently do is prove a hypothesis to be false. The existence of 'truth' seems to be in the subjective world, and therefore perhaps suspect.

4.6 Neglected methods and approaches in contemporary science

Summarizing the argument so far, we see that the sciences have always had a tendency to emphasize the quantitative and objective. We have also seen that in modern times this emphasis has led to some rather dubious attempts at quantitation, and some downright absurdities. At the same time, there are some aspects of the traditional method of science which are severely neglected at present, and this also arises from a general neglect of the base of subjective impressions from which science develops.

Several very direct examples of this are found in psychiatric research. Many psychiatric patients write autobiographical accounts of their experiences; and some psychiatrists find it valuable to collect and read them. Some academic journals (e.g. *Schizophrenia Bulletin*) regularly publish short autobiographical accounts. Nevertheless, in academic psychiatry as a whole there is a severe neglect of such idiographic accounts of psychiatric illness as a serious object of scientific study. It is exceedingly rare to see any autobiographical work cited in the reference lists of scientific papers in psychiatry. For purposes of scientific study it is preferable to present a breakdown of the symptom profiles, averaged across large numbers of patients, by established rating scales with acceptable inter-rater reliability, rather than to present a small number of detailed idiographic accounts. It is difficult to avoid the conclusion that anything as subjective as a first person account of experience is suspect. Such primary sources are only useful when rendered tractable by having been filtered through the web of rating scales and statistics. The flaw in this attitude is obvious: There could be no data at all for the raters and statisticians were it not for the existence of the subjective phenomena in the first place. Well-written detailed autobiographical accounts are an important insight into that essentially private subjective experience. Sure, there is an advantage to be gained from the rigour of the social science method. But there is also something to be gained from the detailed idiographic account, quite different from what is emphasized by the social science method. A single careful account can show something that no amount of rigorous use of rating scales can show: the precise sequence of occurrence of symptoms in an individual patient (sometimes even on a second-by-second basis). This can be an important constraint on one's hypotheses about the possible logical or causal relation of one symptom to another, in terms of strategies of information processing in the mind/brain. Such very detailed longitudinal information can sometimes be far more useful in deriving scientific theories than any amount of cross-sectional information derived from rating scales.

Amongst the various trends in twentieth-century psychiatry, the one which corresponds most closely to the approach I have just advocated, was that developed by Karl Jaspers, while still a young man, and before he became a professional philosopher. He suggested that there was important knowledge to be obtained about the formal aspects of subjective experience in psychiatric patients. That knowledge was not to be obtained by observation, and its acquisition did not depend on 'explanation' in its usual scientific form. He distinguished two forms of comprehension, *Erklären*, and *Verstehen*, which may be roughly translated as 'explanation' and 'understanding'. The latter, comprising a rather intuitive grasp of another person's experience, and the way in which one pattern of experience may be related to others, was to be used in the description of the subjective experience of psychiatric patients. Jaspers' work was not translated into English until the 1970s.[25] It has in fact had a major influence on the British instruments for describing abnormal psychological states, but this nevertheless has been a rather indirect influence, without due credit having been given to Jaspers. The empirical and pragmatic approach typical of British scientific traditions does not square easily with the more metaphysical assumptions underlying Jasper's attempts to capture the details of a subjective reality.

The same comment can be made about the style of descriptive prose by clinical researchers. Looking back to papers written forty years ago one sometimes comes across careful, eloquent and informative descriptions. In even earlier days such accounts were the main vehicle of communication in medical research. Nowadays such accounts might not be acceptable to research journals. Comparisons would have to be double-blind and reliable rating scales would have to be used. But it is impossible to conduct a double-blind trial, or consider using a validated rating scale unless earlier studies using more subjective methods have already given the impression that there is some relation worth testing objectively. However, nowadays, those impressions and hunches are rarely reported in the scientific literature. The researcher would be prevented from publically expressing his or her immediate impressions of the matter he or she studies. They remain part of the private wisdom of each investigator, private perhaps because, in the competitive world of modern science, it is giving away too much to publish one's hunches too freely.

Nevertheless, today's scientists rely extensively on hunches reported in earlier years. Just one example will suffice. In the early years of treatment of psychotic illnesses with drugs of the chlorpromazine type, a German psychiatrist, H.-J. Haase came to the conclusion that the dose of such drugs which conferred the optimum benefit to patients was that which produced slight impairment of the patient's control of his or her movements, as detected in a handwriting test.[26] This conclusion has been largely ignored because it is was presented mainly as clinical description, rather than fully controlled scientific studies. In the years since then, much larger doses of these drugs have been routinely used on very large numbers of patients, often with serious side effects, which are sometimes irreversible changes. Yet in the last few years fully controlled studies are giving some indication that Haase's concept was correct, or at least, not very far from correct.

Exactly the same point can be made from a totally different source. The distinguished Soviet psychologist and neurologist, Alexander Luria, in an autobiographical account of his scientific career, ends with a chapter entitled 'Romantic science', referring to two of his own detailed studies of the psychology of single subjects. He writes:

In the previous century, when auxiliary laboratory methods were rare, the art of clinical observation and description reached its height. One is unable to read the classical descriptions of the great physicians J. Lourdat, A. Trousseau, P. Marie, J. Charcot, Wernicke, S. Korsakoff, Head and A. Meyer without seeing the beauty of the art of science. Now the art of observation and description is nearly lost . . . The physicians of our time having a battery of auxiliary laboratory aids and tests, frequently overlook clinical reality. Observation of patients and evaluation of syndromes have begun to give way to dozens of laboratory analyses which are then combined by mathematical techniques as a means of diagnosis, and as a plan of treatment.[27]

A much broader and more general area of neglect, at least in the biological sciences, is in the development of concepts and ideas. Mountains of experimental evidence accumulate in the medical libraries. A miniscule part of the biological and medical journals are concerned with integrating that information to derive unifying concepts. The intellectual skills required for such work are found very rarely amongst biomedical scientists. They are certainly not encouraged by the editorial policies of most journals, by academic departments or by the organizers of conferences. The granting bodies which give financial support for research almost never take such a variety of research seriously. This bias is again related to the emphasis on the objective at the expense of the subjective. A new scientific concept is incapable of quick, public replication, because it initially exists in the mind of a single imaginative person, cannot be photographed, or weighed or measured, that is, it lacks initially any public validation. Anyone familiar with the history of science will realize how misguided it is to ignore the subjective insights which give rise to new concepts; though familiarity with the history of science will also show that such misguided devaluation of new ideas is by no means confined to the present time.

Jacques Monod was quoted early in this work, as giving a clear statement of the postulate of objectivity inherent in the scientific enterprise. But when we see him writing about the psychology of scientific thinking, it becomes clear that he is not one of the radical empiricists with uncritical adherence to this postulate. He writes:

> I am sure every scientist must have noticed how his mental reflection at the deeper level is not verbal: it is an *imagined experience*, simulated with the aid of forms, or forces, or interactions which together barely compose an 'image' in the visual sense of the terms. I have even found myself, after lengthy concentration on the imagined experience to the exclusion of everything else, identifying with a molecule of protein.[28]

Penrose, an eminent mathematician, writes in similar vein.

> I simply do not trust my unconscious algorithmic actions when they are inadequately paid attention to by my awareness . . . For a simple example, one will have learnt the algorithmic rules for multipying two numbers together, and also for dividing one number by another . . . but how does one know whether, for the problem in hand, one should have multipied or divided the numbers? For that one needs to *think* and make a *conscious* judgement.[29]

Later he writes:

> Almost all my mathematical thinking is done visually and in terms of non-verbal concepts, although the thoughts are often accompanied by innane and almost useless verbal commentary.[30]

For myself, the process of scientific thinking is much more verbal than this, with lengthy inner verbal discourses occurring both before the moments of insight, and afterwards in checking those insights. But I also have had the experience of 'seeing' theories of brain function in visual form, of imaging patterns of myriad pulsating flashes of light against a dark background, these signifying the cascades of action potentials in vast constellations of nerve cells in action.

Monod even suggests that 'the right hemisphere is responsible for an important part, perhaps the more profound part of [this] subjective simulation'. But, in my experience, such insights into the thought processes of scientists is rare, and despite what Monod says is the experience of 'every scientist', the theoretical and conceptual approach which Monod exemplifies are also rare.

This neglect of conceptual development applies in many areas of biological research (and probably elsewhere in science). However, one example of it with which I am very familiar is in classification of psychiatric disorders. A generation ago it was realized that diagnostic labels were used in quite different fashions in different parts of the world, and also might be used inconsistently by different practitioners within one country. As a result of this a variety of schemes have been devised, in several countries, which operationalize the process of psychiatric diagnosis, so that all psychiatrists using a particular scheme will make broadly similar diagnoses when confronted by the same patients. This process gives some degree of objectivity to the process of psychiatric diagnosis, and undoubtedly aids communication about different types of mental illness. However, the operationalized criteria for diagnosis are only conventions. Thus many of the distinctions made between different mental illnesses may have no more fundamental a basis than a convention such as that used to distinguish a horse from a pony. A rather close analogy to the conventional distinction between horse and pony is found in the definition of schizophrenia by the American Psychiatric Association's prestigious DSM-III scheme. Having defined the necessary symptoms, a further criterion is stated that the symptom pattern must have existed for at least six months before the diagnosis of schizophrenia can be given. If the condition has lasted for five months and three weeks, the illness is called 'schizo-phreniform disorder'. It does not take much intelligence to realize that, if there is such a thing as schizophrenic illness it cannot exist for six months without at some time having existed for less than six months.[31]

In another scheme – the Present State Examination (or PSE) –

adopted by the British Psychiatric Association, the principle stated purpose is descriptive. In order to achieve a description of a patient's mental state which is, as far as possible, consistent between psychiatrists, the form of the interview is specified in great detail, as are the questions to be asked, and the way the answers are to be scored. Thus, different psychiatrists mean exactly the same thing when they report that a particular symptom or syndrome is present. This is a worthy purpose. The PSE is also linked with a computer programme (called CATEGO) by which these raw data can be combined to give syndromes, and ultimately, to give provisional diagnoses. Reading the small print of the PSE manual makes it clear that these latter objectives are regarded by the authors as less important, and not properly validated. Nevertheless the existence of the computer programme, and its wide publicization, have turned the PSE into an authoritative definition of schizophrenia and a variety of other mental disorders. For a generation of British psychiatrists, the PSE and CATEGO programme are *the* definition of schizophrenia, for use in all research studies, and there can be little further enquiry as to the validity of the concepts embodied therein.

What is missing in the DSM-III and other similar schemes is concern for actual concepts of mental illness, and the coordinated reasoning which gives rise to disease theories. These prestigious schemes give the glamour of an objective scientific decision to diagnosis, but hide the fact that there are very few, if any, validated disease theories in psychiatry. The net effect is that the definition of a particular psychiatric condition is in fact given by the fiat of a powerful professional organization, rather than on the basis of clear scientific understanding of psychiatric illness. The very prestige of these schemes may in fact be an impediment to thinking creatively about disease theories in psychiatry, since researchers may be constrained to think only in terms of the combinations of symptoms which correspond to the designated syndromes and diagnoses, rather than taking the combinations of symptoms which actually occur in patients in an open minded fashion and relating them to possible underlying brain mechanisms. Admittedly there are some scientific advantages of replicable diagnostic schemes. However, one suspects that the real driving force behind psychiatrists' obsession with replicable diagnosis is not strictly scientific at all, but derives from the powerful social roles that psychiatrists have to play. The prestige of the formalized diagnostic schemes gives them the air of a scientific advance, and masks their real function. Once again the obsession with objectivity tends to cut the investigator off from the subjective base from which true understanding takes its origin.

4.7 *Examples of the tyranny of the objective over the subjective*

The worship of objectivity is now a feature of our whole culture, not confined to an aspect of scientific study. In modern parlance the word 'subjective' has undeniable connotations of denigration. A common phrase in debate is, 'That's only a subjective opinion.' But why should it not be accepted that subjective statements are actually honest statements of a personal viewpoint, to be reckoned along with all others? To the objection 'that's only a subjective opinion' the retort could easily be made, 'so are all opinions'. Such denigration of the subjective in everyday parlance derives ultimately from science; that is it derives from the scientists' continual endeavour to establish objective, publically-agreed accounts of the things they study. But this denigration is also based on a false notion of science, which, as argued above, has its roots in subjectivity. What is specialist scientific use of language in one generation becomes everyday parlance amongst non-scientists a generation later, though often without full understanding of the scientific considerations of the original debate. The vicarious appeal to scientific authority can be found in many detailed examples. What I refer to here, however, is the appeal to what is thought to be the overall method and philosophy of science to support what are becoming widespread and prevalent social attitudes throughout our culture. The preceding section on the history of scientific method showed that subjective judgments were always essential to scientific progress, despite the endless quest for objectivity. Yet this sort of easy criticism of subjectivity generally succeeds in silencing all but the strongest-willed.

Let me give a few examples where the superficial gloss of scientific method has invaded life outside science, without the real substance of science as found in the historical core of scientific progress.

Take for instance the modern insistence on quantitative methods, encroaching into secondary schools, in subjects where it previously did not exist. This occurs in geography, zoology, social studies, politics. Something is gained in this, though it may not be appropriate to introduce such methods until students get closer to the research frontier. But also something very important is lost. Students mistake the form of science for its intellectual substance. They may lose confidence and belief in the importance of their own subjective hunches. They may lose the creative, imaginative side of their mental life, not least in scientific thinking. And they may quite misunderstand the historical processes from which our scientific culture has grown.

Another example of the attraction of the gloss of science, without its substance, is the modern trend to turn science into entertainment. We have dramatic public exhibits of various scientific phenomena, ranging from conservation of angular momentum, acoustic lenses, to lasers. These are overtly justified in educational terms, but generally fail to provide any insight into the conceptual basis of these phenomena. We have popular science programmes on the broadcast media with titles like 'The facts of the matter', as though science was only about facts. One is left with a sense of raw physicalism, as though what can be demonstrated publically and dramatically is the heart of science. Where is the communication of the subjective and conceptual insights which underlie these elegant demonstrations?

In modern 'literature' science fiction, and fantasy based on pseudo-science, seem to have largely replaced the deep insights into human nature found in the fiction of the nineteenth century. Where are the modern-day Tolstoys or George Eliots who, within the framework of a novel, could tell us so much both about practical human psychology, and about the complex interactions within human societies? From what source can we now gain such a wide overall vision of the nature of our personal and social existence as was available to the readers of these authors? There appears to be none. Instead, we have the international marketing of extravaganzas such as *Teenage Mutant Ninja Turtles* and *Jurassic Park* – perversions of science, but becoming a dominant cultural force. And rather than the wide vision of the best of nineteenth-century fiction, we have a myriad of specialist subcultures, each with its own inward-looking specialist ways of thinking, and each defending itself from other subcultures, rather than seeking to recognize each other's common humanity. Perhaps this is the price of modern science-based society, where each person's ultraspecialized expertise is thought to be a bigger contribution to society than any vision or idealism which can have wider currency.

Even modern trends in orchestral music playing betray the modern *Zeitgeist*. In the middle years of the century, orchestral performances were lavish, and emotional expression was florid, even extravagant. Nowadays the emphasis is on 'authentic' production, using period instruments, with brisk business-like rhythms and tempi replacing the strong emotions of a generation ago. The technicalities of the performance may be 'authentic', but apparently no one can believe in the authenticity of the intense emotional expression of earlier times.

I also point out a trend which has become widespread amongst people who are growing up today: to have no truck with religion in any form. I must again emphasize here that I myself have no links with any organized religious body; but I do not reject every aspect of religious thinking. Yet this is what appears to be the norm at present. Forget the power structures of the established churches by all means. But it seems possible to grow up now without having the remotest notion of the intellectual roots of religious belief in philosophy and metaphysics. Much of this 'new age' attitude no doubt results from the emptiness of the evangelical movements which flourished in the 1960s and 1970s. Those movements have surely reaped their predictable consequences. The role of religious movements will be considered later. However, the point here is that the widespread rejection of any and every aspect of religion is usually justified by reference to what is perceived as a 'scientific' attitude. Again I stress that it is false to equate science with anti-religious attitudes. Historically, scientists have had a wide variety of attitudes to religion, some being explicit atheists, other having a wide range of metaphysical and theological convictions. But undoubtedly those emminent scientists of the past had deeper and better thought-out views on these matters than those who now so easily reject religion outright in the name of 'modern science'.

5

Exclusive Objectivity in Matters of Value

5.1 Objectivization and operationalization of value-laden decisions

We have seen that in apparently factual matters of science one cannot escape from the subjective base for all descriptions, measurements and theories, though the culmination of each of these activities emphasizes their objective nature, and even carefully hides any hint of subjectivity. This is because individual human judgments and intuitions, unaided by any discipline, are remarkably fickle. This is more emphatically true for value judgments than for those of value-neutral sensory impressions which are the raw material from which science develops. It is demonstrably the case that unanimity in matters of value is more difficult to reach than in matters of scientific truth. Therefore, in moving from matters of fact to matters of value, one would have thought that judgments of a subjective nature would then more easily assert themselves. But once again there is a tendency at present to hide the subjective side of value judgments, reducing decisions on matters of value to operationalized procedures, without ever explicitly presenting the actual values which underlie the operational scheme. Often this produces a way of making clear decisions, in areas of inherent uncertainty. These procedures suffer merely from the weakness that they are in the end rather arbitrary. Operationalization and objectivization of value-laden decisions *may* be more dangerous than the hiding of the subjective side of 'neutral' scientific knowledge. This is because by concealing the subjective basis of our values it may become possible to exert considerable power, without accountability or proper control of that power. By claiming objectivity and scientific authority for a decision, it is more difficult to identify and attribute personal responsibility for the way decisions turn out.

Again a few examples are in order. In the section above on scientific method in the social sciences, I mentioned quantitative methods of assessing persons, as for instance in intelligence tests. To use such methods in academic research studies of mental ability is one thing. It is another to use them for practical assessment and decision-making about individual persons. In mass education such methods have been used as examination methods,[1] although the nation-wide use of such tests has long been abandoned in Britain. But what about when such psychological testing is used to assess job applicants? Quantitative assessments of people's performance are common in academic life (e.g. the number of publications, or the number of times they have been cited). I imagine there are similar practices in many other professions. Do these 'objective' tests really assess all the individual valuable qualities of a person, as can often be assessed subjectively by a wise and experienced person without the aid of the tests? Do they give a fair decision concerning those with hidden disabilities? Do they miss something qualitative or conceptual about a person (e.g. his/her originality, communication skills, ability to work with others and develop the potentiality of others)? Are they perhaps just a convenient way of making difficult decisions in a manner that leaves little room for argument? From my observation of procedures for admission to medical school (that highly sought-after holy grail, for many young people), based on academic ability alone, this is a reasonable interpretation.

Another example of the increasing objectivization of value-laden decisions is the increasing insistence on financial accounting in decision-making. This is of course fair enough in some degree. In the former Soviet Union, I am told, the price of bread was artificially kept so much below the cost of production that farmers would feed bread to their farm animals, rather than use the grain from which the bread was made for this same purpose. This is clearly an absurdity which would have never survived had there been proper financial accounting. But take another example. In the British city of Sheffield (my home town), the public transport system was for many years run with the help of massive subsidies from ratepayers, so that fares were kept artificially low. The aim appeared to have been, in the end, to have a completely free public transport system. Here it is not so clear that the policy was absurd. There are vast (but hidden) costs to a city arising from excess use of private motor transport, which are saved if public transport is free. But in fact in the accounting equations it is hardly ever possible to express in quantitative money terms all the advantages and disadvantages of a particular policy. So, when decisions are made on the basis of such 'full cost accounting' one may be given the glamour of a careful 'objective' decision, which is really at best somewhat arbitrary, and at worst a deliberate distortion or selection of the costs and benefits to achieve a certain end. The hollowness of the accountant's approach can be seen in Sheffield today. The policy of cheap public transport has been abandoned, the city is overwhelmed by private motor cars, and transport about the city is generally slower than ten years ago.

The role of money was originally as a useful measure for exchange of those goods and services which people value. In modern times we are reaching the stage where all matters of value must be expressed in monetary terms. Money becomes a quasi-objective measure of everything that is valuable. Implicitly, anything that cannot be measured with this yardstick, including good personal relationships with all those about one, are of no account on this scale, and become valueless.

Another very clear example of the operationalization of value judgments is in the field of health economics. Faced with the undeniable fact that medical technology is now capable of delivering more and better treatment that can possibly be paid for when provided on a mass scale by even the wealthiest countries, attempts have been made to apportion scarce resources according to a rational scheme. One much-discussed scheme starts from the practice, especially used in evaluating treatments for cancer, of comparing years of survival associated with the different treatments. The recent development of this, for more general use, takes not just the bald figures of years of survival to evaluate a particular treatment, but adjusts the sum of years survived for the 'quality' of life during those years. 'Quality' would be taken as 100% if there were no disabilities and no day-to-day suffering, but is reduced 'proportionately' (so to speak) if there is either disability or on-going suffering. Rating scales have been developed for assessing both of these reductions of quality of life. The resulting measure for the value of a particular treatment is expressed as 'quality-adjusted life-years' (or 'QALYs'). When the cost of a particular set of treatments is known, it is possible to calculate which way of dividing the available resources between different treatments achieves the greatest increase in QALYs.

This procedure has the merit of formalizing very difficult decisions where subjective biases, very variable between persons, would otherwise abound. However, it also brings in a great many difficulties. The use of rating scales to assess quality of life is perhaps the most obvious, following the discussion of rating scales in section 4.4 above. For descriptive purposes such rating scales may be useful. But their use for making value judgments of the respective merits of different medical treatments implies that they are fully validated measures of life quality.

As the previous discussion has shown, it is never possible to give the concepts defined by such rating scales a very secure validation, which can compare with the concepts of the physical sciences. Apart from that, the computation of QALYs assumes that one year at 100% quality is equivalent to 2 years at 50% quality, as calculated by these rating scales. That of course begs one of the questions which led to the initial dilemma. Above all, no amount of operationalizing of complex decisions can avoid the need to make moral and political decisions on these issues. Although one should try to reduce the subjective biases of an individual doctor in these processes, the moral and political dimension in these decisions must have its roots in subjective intuitions, hopefully turned into the best possible consensus by a political process. Reliance on QALY calculations does not necessarily achieve this consensus. As mentioned in a commentary in *The Lancet*[2] the use of QALYs would tend to make one think that these decisions are technical matters, when at root they are moral and political.

It is interesting to compare these procedures for policy decisions in health care with those adopted for the decisions made by individual doctors for (and in collaboration with) individual patients. 'Medical decision analysis' uses a quite different paradigm, where empirical data from analysis of past application of particular treatments in particular circumstances is used to give statistical predictions of the likely outcome of a certain course of action. Unlike the calculation of QALYs, this empirical basis is value-neutral, and can be taken as factual information upon which clinician and patient can jointly exercise their subjective and personal value schemes, to reach a decision. In modern times, when clearly the cost of a treatment may also be relevant to determine whether a particular treatment is a realistic option, the cost consideration could also appear at this stage. In any case, the value-neutral and the value-laden parts of the decision are kept separate, and the form of the decision is thereby clearer and (I believe) more legitimate.

In the days before medical care was subject to the scrutiny of accountants, there were certainly very great inconsistencies in the funding available for different sorts of treatment, and in different areas of medicine. Mental health services of course were always the poor relation. Will proper accounting change that? Possibly so. But if that happens, it will be because the true cost of mental illness becomes widely known and can then be part of the moral and political debate about priorities in health care. I see no evidence that the practice of using QALYs *per se* will contribute to this debate. After all, QALYs are used for comparing existing treatments. To mount a really effective mental health care system would mean doing something radically new, with few precedents from which to derive alternative costs. A decision to mount such a new mental health care system, if it is taken, must inevitably be taken on the basis of incomplete data.

In the end, of course, as politicians and others must be well aware, *most* of the really important decisions have to be taken on the basis of incomplete knowledge of advantages and disadvantages of a particular policy. Factual analyses such as estimates of various costs of a policy, estimated in various ways, and with various rating scales, can help reduce the uncertainty, but rarely do so completely. But after all that, subjective judgments have to play an essential part in guiding the decision-maker through his decisions. Most of all, subjective value judgments have to be *assumed*, because they are incapable of objective proof.

Where, in all the passion for objective accounting, has gone the concept of a 'wise' subjective decision in the face of uncertainty. Wisdom is an outmoded quality, because it cannot be defined objectively. Of course, it is easy to justify such an approach by asking, 'how does one recognize wisdom?' The fact that that question can be asked shows how far we have gone along the road of objectivization. Polanyi in defending the notion of 'personal knowledge' would have no doubt that the intellectual skills comprised by the term 'wisdom' actually exist, despite the fact that they cannot be operationalized.[3] He would also accept that in principle they can be recognized, just as we recognize a familiar face, although we cannot say how either feat is actually done.

It is pertinent to refer back to the comment made earlier about the dichotomy of psychological functions in the human mind/brain. Operationalization of complex decisions reflects an emphasis on the analytic, part-by-part functions (thought to be performed by the left hemisphere), and a neglect of the synthetic, holistic functions (attributed to the right hemisphere). Of course the two should work together and achieve a consensus. But, as with the psychiatrists' rating scales, it appears that one side of the decision-making process has been allowed to atrophy. A legalistic approach seems to be achieved rather than a scientific one, and there is the possibility (as with some legal decisions) that the decision is in the end an arbitrary compromise of many competing factors, rather than one impelled by a consistent strategy.

5.2 *Scientific materialism and value systems*

In practice, of course, despite these modern trends in objectifying value-laden decisions, it is impossible to live without expressing subjective opinions, and these opinions very often are about value judgments, what is good or bad aesthetically, or what is right or wrong morally. Everyone has to make such judgments, continually and every day. The typical materialist scientist I have caricatured in the previous chapter does this most effectively. When he or she is questioned about where those values come from it is unlikely that their subjective origin will be acknowledged. Instead the argument will probably go in one of two ways: (1) He or she may attempt to justify his or her scale of values by reference to supposedly objective facts about the biology of the human nature, and the evolutionary pressures which are supposed to have created the human species, and human nature with its particular psychological characteristics. (2) He or she may assert that the value scale their behaviour exemplifies consists only of relative values, with no relation to an absolute value scheme. These two attitudes to human values are rather different in many ways, but have one thing in common. The approach to matters of value (whether it is to justify a particular scale of values, or to suggest that no value scale can be justified in fundamental terms) is seen as secondary to so-called objective scientific facts. Let us consider both of these forms of argument in detail.

1. *The 'naturalistic fallacy'*

One of the older ways of turning value judgments from their inherently subjective character to apparently objective facts is to argue from what is (or what is supposed to be) a natural characteristic of human beings, to what ought to be the norm for human behaviour. It is assumed therefore that what is natural for the human species, for instance according to some evolutionary argument, ought to be done. It has been suggested some time ago by G. E. Moore[4] that such a style of reasoning, from what is the case, to what ought to be the case, is fallacious. The appeal to human *nature* in this style of argument is therefore called 'the naturalistic fallacy'. That this is a fallacy is based on the suggestion that matters of fact are quite independent of matters of aesthetic or moral value. These two are, so to speak, to be measured on axes orthogonal to each other. Reasoning about facts is to be based on factual premises; and reasoning about matters of value is to be based on premises of value. One cannot mix the two in a chain of reasoning.

But is the appeal to nature actually a fallacy? On first appearance it seems logical to say that it is. But consider some of the practices that have come about by the attempts to go against what is natural by those who think that the appeal to nature is a fallacy.

The worst example of this that comes to mind is the traditional Christian approach to sexuality. It is deeply ingrained in Christian culture of the past centuries to regard sexual activity in humans as less than ideal, and as impure. Admittedly a wide variety of Christian groups over the centuries have had views about sexuality more in tune with the biological motives which actually drive us. But nevertheless it cannot be doubted that from the earliest times when Christianity recognized itself as a church, there was a strong tendency to deny the validity of the sexual side of our being. The potent symbol of this is that Mary the mother of God was supposed to be a virgin and, as such, was a symbol of purity.[5] Even amongst modern 'mainstream' Christian opinion, which is more accepting of sexuality as such, there is still much unease about homosexuality; and attempts to show that it is morally wrong are often based on the assertion that it is 'unnatural'. The monumental distortion of human relations that has occurred over the centuries from such attitudes to sexuality, sanctioned by church doctrine, and still continuing, is in my view one of the strongest arguments against Christianity, with fundamental implications both in theory and in practice.

But, one may ask, to say this, is it also accepting that the 'naturalistic fallacy' is not a fallacy after all? To accept this argument against Christianity, does one also have to accept that anything that is natural is therefore morally acceptable. I think not.

When we have decisions to take which have a moral dimension to them, in sexual or any other matters, we cannot ignore the natural tendencies of ourselves and others involved. Apart from our actual desires and motivations it is natural for many humans to think in terms of principles. Principles of behaviour clearly can conflict with desires and motivations. Naturally (so to speak) serious dilemmas result. But nevertheless there *is* a choice in such situations, not only about the actual details of the decision, but also about underlying principles. The fact that the dilemmas are natural products of our cognitive and motivational make-up does not help us at all in resolving them. If we base our decisions just on what is supposed to be natural, and on our supposed evolutionary heritage, we ignore one important fact about nature and about evolution – that it is a process of change. That change might occur by natural selection (a topic discussed later) but, for humans, that evolutionary change is certainly mainly cultural change. And there is a certain sense in which, at the time we make critical decisions about our actions and the principles which should govern them, we are, in a small way, at the cutting edge of that change. If this is so, we cannot dodge making a decision, by relying on the authority of 'nature'. To be of any real significance, we must work out this decision from fundamental principles (possibly quite subjective at root), if any there be, rather than by reference to a supposedly static human nature, or what *has been* our evolutionary or cultural heritage.

2. *Relativity of values*

Another objection which might be raised by the materialist against serious attempts at moral thinking is to claim that all values are, in origin, relative rather than absolute. In support of this assertion he or she will point to the obvious fact that values vary widely from one culture to another, and from time to time in the course of history; and he or she may develop evolutionary or other arguments explaining why circumstances in one time or place have led to the emergence of each variety of value system. To such people, values are a product of all-pervasive but changeable social influences, and do not derive from any fundamental or absolute value scale. In contrast to those who appeal to an unchangeable human nature to justify unchangeable values (the naturalistic fallacy of the previous paragraphs), these protagonists believe that human nature is maleable in the face of environmental change, and that the value systems adopted by human societies are an equally-maleable response to such environmental change. Whereas the naturalistic fallacy argues from what is to what ought to be the case, the relativist argues from scientific (e.g. anthropological) facts to reach the conclusion that no value schemes can command strong allegiance.

Examples of this are abundant within the new discipline of sociobiology. Habits of societies which practice polygamy, monogamy or polyandry are 'explained' in terms of the best reproductive strategy when the ratio between numbers of males and females varies. Cannibalism may be explained as a society's response to living in an environment in which there is little other source of animal protein (such as in pre-European New Zealand).

But when one observes the behaviour of such moral relativists one cannot but be struck by a singular incongruity. Such assertions of the relativity of human values as ideas seem not to have any influence at all on the day-to-day excercise of those same persons' values. One example with which I am familiar is in the matter of ethical limitations on animal experimentation. Biological scientists appear to be more aware than a generation ago of the necessity for such limitations to their work. They will assent without demur to the ethicists who evaluate their grant applications and who assert that animals are sentient beings like humans. But in other circumstances they (often the same people) will argue against the existence of mind in animals, or of subjective facts (in man or animals) which must form the starting point in ethical matters. Suffering in animals, as a subjective experience, is no more real than it would be in a computer simulation of avoidance learning.

It is likewise very strange to find that those who argue strongly for such an ephemoral basis of values are also capable of very strong daily decisions on matters of value. How is it that my colleagues who espouse such a relativistic basis for their values nevertheless fight like tigers for what they believe are the best decisions in university administration and politics. It is strange that science, which sets such a great store by statements capable of the widest generalization over space and time, should be used to justify relative values only, without any generalization from the here-and-now to the universal case. The contradictions between the overt beliefs and the actual behaviour of the moral relativist usually stand out like a polar bear in Africa.

The incongruity between stated principle and observed behaviour of the moral relativist gives a clue as to what the flaw in their position may be. In practice it is difficult to avoid viewing our moral decisions as relative. But to admit the relativity of value decisions in practice does not prevent us from believing in absolute values in principle. What is the difference between absolute judgments in practice and in principle? If we believe in an ultimate value as an ideal, we are likely to make serious efforts to get as close to that ideal as possible, even if we accept that the ideal is unattainable, and that our efforts to approach the ideal involves the fallibility of subjective judgments. We are thus likely to believe that our moral decisions actually are *serious* ones, although, having taken them, we have no assurance that they are correct. If, on the other hand, we believe that moral decisions are 'only' relative ones, without an underpinning of any absolute (though actually unknowable) values, it follows that no decision on matters of value is really important. We would have lost the belief in the 'moral seriousness' of life. Thus the moral relativist may be correct in pointing out the adaptability of values in the face of changing circumstances in practice. But it is not valid to go from there to state, as a matter of principle, that there can be no universal human values. Probably it is that underlying and semi-conscious belief which is the basis of their strong stance on matters of value when they come up day-by-day.

Another aspect of the thinking of the moral relativist which is worth pointing out is this. The moral relativist seems assured of the accuracy of the factual or scientific assessments upon which he or she bases his case. For instance, the sociobiologist seems quite confident in ascribing a causal relation to the link between evolutionary pressures on a society and the sort of value system it comes to espouse. He seems ready therefore to accept the absolute basis of decisions about truth and falsehood, even when detailed questions about the mechanism of evolutionary change are demonstrably contentious. Yet decisions about truth and falsehood are in practice often almost as relative and fallible as are decisions on matters of value. Sociobiological hypotheses are far from universally accepted. As a more general illustration of this we may note that statistical tests do not prove the truth of anything. For instance they do not prove that two estimates of a numerical value are of the same quantity. Rather they establish (to a stated degree of probability) that the two estimates are *un*likely to be estimates of the same quantity. The philosopher Karl Popper has argued that our judgments of truth strictly speaking serve to falsify rather than to verify hypotheses.[6] However much we may seek it, objective truth itself is quite elusive.

Could it be that the mistake of the moral relativist is not so much that he believes in the relativity of all values, but that he believes too easily in the absoluteness of truth? He certainly *appears* to believe more firmly in the absoluteness of truth/falsehood distinctions than that of value judgments. If we first accept that truth is always relative, we may find it more palatable that we cannot get at an absolute value scale either, in practice. John MacMurray wrote:

> . . . so, Science is condemned to chase reality, as it were, round an endless rope, and cannot find anything on which to rest. As a result no scientific statement can ever be final. Its 'truths' exist provisionally and its whole business is to revise then continually.[7]

In the same way Popper asserts that though his aim is always to falsify hypotheses, this does not mean he is more interested in falsehood than in truth. Falsification is the only way he recognizes of approaching truth. As an eloquent analogy, Popper writes:

> The status of truth in the objective sense, as correspondance to the facts ... may be compared to that of a mountain peak usually wrapped in clouds. A climber may not merely have difficulties in getting there – he may not know when he gets there, because he may be unable to distinguish, in the clouds, between the main summit and a subsidiary peak. Yet this does not affect the objective existence of the summit.
>
> Though it may be impossible for the climber ever to make sure he has reached the summit, it will often be easy for him to realise that he has not reached it; for example when he is turned back by an overhanging wall.[8]

In Penrose's book *The Emperor's New Mind*, the author argues strongly against the claim of the artificial intelligence experts, that all the operations of consciousness are computable; and he therefore argues against the view that consciousness of sorts can actually be realized by man-made computing machines. The book is full of many interesting arguments, about both mathematics and physics. However, I suspect that there may be a false antithesis arising between consciousness and computability, closely linked to the issue of truth as an unattainable ideal. Computing machines, representing rigidly defined systems of axioms, may or may not succeed in reaching their conclusion, or deriving a mathematical proof. But if they do, the conclusions or the proof are an absolute derivation from the axioms. Not so the insights of human consciousness, whether they be the foresights of a master chess player, or the intuitions of a scientist or mathematician. These are approximations to an ideal, and require endless, obsessive checking, both empirically and theoretically.

The same attitude can be adopted about matters of value. We may never establish an absolute value scale in practice, but we can for ever be approaching it and approximating to it. And when we have at last achieved the humility of accepting that both truth and value are relative we start to confront the basic dilemmas of human existence, that we actually do still have real choices to make, which can help or hurt ourselves and others. We have to make decisions on these matters. When we face these decisions, the background belief that for matters of both truth and value unattainable ideals actually exist in some sense can nevertheless continue to have its attraction for us puzzled mortals. We have already noted, when considering statistics and Popperian philosophy, that objective truth does not exist. Perhaps we should say, therefore, that the ideals for both truth and value are in the subjective realm, the realm of ideas.

If we accept the idea that values are fundamentally more than just relative and have a real existence, even as unattainable ideals, it influences our views on other issues about morality. For instance, we may ask whether morality is at all subject to the constraints of systematic reasoning. In fact, systematic reasoning about morality is probably a feature characteristic mainly of the traditions of European thought, and the cultures derived from Europe. Professors of Philosophy in universities in the Far East teach mainly Western philosophy. According to Bertrand Russell,[9] this profound cultural difference between East and West has existed since the time of Pythagoras. What are the merits and disadvantages of a reasoned approach to morality?

If values are only relative, it is merely a matter of expediency that we choose one alternative strategy of action rather than another. Morality reduces to no more than 'custom' or 'habit'. If, on the other hand, morality is to be constrained by rational considerations, our decisions about morality may seem to have a more solid, timeless quality, even if the basic value premises are admitted to be inaccessible ideals, and therefore not to be known clearly in practice.

Moral reasoning appears to be a development of the more mundane mental processes which determine the purpose of day-to-day activities. In these cases we seek to coordinate our actions towards a predetermined goal, so that we do not undertake activities which undo other actions we have just done. If one has no predetermined purpose in mind, one is likely to be doing things at one time which undo those done at another. To put it crudely, we may be digging a hole with great energy one day, and the next day, quite arbitrarily, deciding to fill in the hole again. If one considers that moral reasoning is an extension of this purposeful coordination of actions, a principled and reasoned approach to morality appears to be needed.

To say this is not to argue for a rigid set of principles which apply invariably without regard to the situation. There may be fundamental principles which are not adaptable, and on which there can be no compromise. However, most specific decisions need not bring these principles into question. Underneath these immutable principles are a larger number of principles lower in the hierarchy. These may sometimes conflict with one another, and the conflicts are to be resolved by reference to the more fundamental principles, bearing in mind the actual situation to which they apply in practice. But even for the most fundamental principles, we must acknowledge, with humility, the uncertainty inherent in assuming the absolute truth of any proposition whether of fact or of value. Thus even in the most complex scheme of moral reasoning one should temper the rigidity (for instance of a black-and-white version of moral sin) with a knowledge of one's own subjectivity.

The issue is also raised of whether moral reasoning involves only case-by-case comparisons, or reasoning based on an initial hierarchy or network of underlying principles. Undoubtedly, most people, presented with a vignette of the 'situation ethics' type can make their judgments of the correct course of action. However, this may be totally unprincipled and unreasonable unless one actually has some underlying principles as a basis for the comparison. Perhaps then the real value of such single case studies is to use the situation to discover which, if any, are the underlying moral principles.

However, this still leaves open many questions. Where do the premises for such moral reasoning derive from? Two possible sources of those premises could be suggested. They may be accepted *a priori*, by adoption of some external authority, such as a religious text, or an authoritative religious organization. Alternatively, those initial premises for moral systems may be derived entirely from internal subjective intuitions, a source which may also be described as *a priori*. If so, it should be born in mind that the subjective intuitions from which moral systems derive differ from person to person.

In either case, however, it would be prudent to allow empirical considerations to influence moral descisions. When a moral dilemma presents itself to us, it involves the balancing of many factors. The particular way in which each such factor presents itself is of quite rare occurrence, perhaps unique. We therefore cannot anticipate in advance all the factors belonging to a particular dilemma, as a pre-ordained logical system. Therefore, there must be a certain empirical element in most moral decision-making. We learn how to balance the many factors by experience, and experience teaches us to make better decisions. On the other hand, the basis of morality cannot be wholly empirical either. In so far as it *is* empirical, there must also be some initial value scale against which we judge the results of our moral 'experiments'.

Yet another major question is, how wide and how general can be the principles by which we take moral decisions? We may not, of course, even be able to enunciate general principles, because we may never have been confronted by the particular test cases when, for instance, such principles are in serious conflict with self-interest. But, given the limited understanding we have, there are still difficulties of not admitting, even in principle, the possible claims of an ultimate goal. Different persons undoubtedly take differing degrees of foresight, and therefore coordinate their actions over different scales of time. If we consider only short-term goals, we are still likely to be revealed as undoing with one coordinated set of actions the achievment previously achieved by another such set of actions. Some people claim they find this acceptable, and regard life as cosmic drama, a comedy for some, a tragedy for others. I am not convinced by their actual behaviour that they really do believe this. They all do take long-term foresight for their decisions, though they may not have an explicit cosmic purpose in mind behind their actions; and when minor inconsistencies are pointed out between the objective of actions performed at different times, they are as easily shamed as everybody else. Thus, I argue, when one is really explicit about it, if one engages in purposeful activity at all, even on the smallest scale (and it is inconceivable that we behave in a completely purposeless fashion), one should at least try to extend the scale of that purpose, eventually to be guided by an ultimate purpose. But what can be that purpose?

It is not intended to suggest any firm answers to these questions here. In Part II, however, as part of the discussion of psychophysical parallelism, it will become clear that value systems, including moral value systems, need not be entirely relative, but can derive from more or less universal subjective intuitions coming from value-laden experiences. Given such fundamental backing to ones value systems, a reasoned approach to morality is not out of the question, using a hierarchy of principles, and moulded by experience. This, it is hoped, can be an antidote to the relativistic view of morality, in which the only matters of importance are expediency and acceptable customary behaviour.

6

Destruction by Objectivization

Historically, throughout the development of science, subjective and objective descriptions of the world have always been complementary, the aim being to start with a subjective insight and show then that it is also objectively true. However, in modern times this mutual relationship has largely been forgotten. Objective measurement is done with a scorn for the subjective insight from which the to-be-measured things emerged. Operationalized rules for assessing complex variables are pursued without regard for the conceptual insights which make such complex variables valid and worth assessing. Statistical methodology, in which statements can only be falsified and never verified, has led us to a view that truth itself is a mirage. Quantitation is sometimes pursued dogmatically for its own sake without anyone asking whether the figures one obtains at the end mean anything. The private and subjective aspects of scientific enquiry needed to build new theoretical schemes are largely ignored. Likewise, skills in observation are being lost because they are too subjective. The subjective base from which we derive our scales and systems of values are suppressed in deference to so-called objective ways of arriving at decisions in matters of human value. The passion for exclusive objectivity has become an ultimate goal. The distortion of science called 'objectivity' has become a replacement for God.

It is said that science pervades all aspects of modern life. The preceding sections have shown how the quest for objectivity and quantitative measurement has triumphed over subjectivity and qualitative judgments. It has triumphed in all sorts of ways, not least in the basis we attempt to provide for our value systems. It is widely thought that this trend is what is meant by being scientific. But is this really so? From our analysis of the historical development of science it is clear that it is not so. Subjectivity always occurred as an essential precursor and therefore as a complement to scientific objectivity. But nowadays the two are seen as antithetical to each other. The scientific quest for objectivity has become so single-minded that it has lost sight of its own origins. The result is destructive at a most profound level: destructive of our real understanding of science, destructive of our confidence in our own judgments, destructive of our skills in imaginative thinking, and in careful observation, and destructive of our ability to construct useful value systems.

Most surprising of all, the objectivist stance is also found amongst leading religious thinkers. Don Cupitt writes:

> Perhaps one reason for the very existence of society is that it, its public constructed world, and its god, are required to check the *I think*, and to inhibit its tendency to solipsism, inflation, self-deification, and madness . . . God and the public sphere, now they are established, must subordinate the self and subjectivity and secure their allegiance. This is done by demonstration of the logical priority and superior reality of God, society and the public realm, designed to convince us that the subjective realm is derived and quite properly subordinate. Kept in his place, the human subject will not lose his head: but by whatever means, that mad rush to solipsism must be checked.[1]

In a very similar vein, John Polkinghorne writes:

> A homicidal maniac hears the voice of God telling him to go out and kill prostitutes. That is why religion is not what one does with one's solitariness, why it can only be pursued within a community and following a tradition, with the correctives they apply to private judgements.[2]

Several points here deserve comment. First, the Roman Catholic church of the 1600s could easily have made such an authoritative statement to rebut the heresy of the supreme individualist, Galileo; and yet the scientific revolution he started now appears to have become the 'objective', 'public', 'authorized version' of reality. (Note that Cupitt does base his rejection of anything metaphysical on the 'established' corpus of scientific knowledge.) Second, it is arguable that it is the public 'objective' view of reality which is more dangerous than the solipsistic, subjective one. In the post-cold-war world, we see, in the Balkans and the frontiers of the former Soviet Union, alarming resurgences of nationalism and ethnic conflict. Seen from a distance, the intense tribal loyalties which motivate the various groups involved in these struggles are difficult identify with, or to take seriously. To the participants themselves, they represent the so-called objective view of truth, to which Cupitt refers. The world might just be a safer place if there were more solipsists who know what they as individuals stand for, rather than following the psychological pressures which grow within the groups they belong to, with the biological determinism of a pack of wolves. As for Polkinghorne's reference to the delusions of homicidal maniacs, he seems to be inferring that florid psychotic delusions can be kept in check by the authority of religious communities. But the psychiatric profession, as well as many of their patients, know better. Even when those delusions have the religious content to which Polkinghorne refers, the most fundamental treatment is drug therapy. Only when that has been initiated and started to become effective do psychological therapies and the social therapies which might be found in a religious community become meaningful. This difficult fact is discussed in greater depth in chapter 12. Apart from that, the striking thing about both these quotations is how British they both seem, so different from the sentiment which would be found in a small remote country of only three million people, many of whom are recent immigrants, seeking a new life, and where individuality still counts for something.

7

Origin of Scientific Materialism

The previous chapters have shown how, in modern times, a tyranny has developed in which objectivity, and the various methods for achieving it, have come to totally dominate earlier habits and skills which are denigrated as subjective, and therefore quite unreliable. The argument was constructed in such a way as to emphasize the emptiness of the modern style; for objectivity and its trappings, if pursued in defiance of subjective assessments, cuts us off from the primary source of information, and from the roots out of which objective science assuredly grew. This emptiness implicit in the modern approach seems very obvious to me. However, it is perhaps necessary to try to explain the historical trends out of which this situation, in some ways quite absurd in my view, has arisen.

1. A major factor in leading to the contemporary *Zeitgeist* is a shift in the areas where the most exciting scientific advances are perceived as taking place. In the first half of this century physics was at the forefront of scientific and intellectual progress. Nowadays the focus is on the biological sciences. How does this make a difference? I believe it is because there is a sense in which the advances in physics in the first half of the twentieth century were very fundamental advances not only for what is strictly scientific, but for our apprehension of reality in any form. They really did shape our fundamental perceptions of reality, how we come to know reality, and the limits on what we can know. The advances in biology in the second half of this century, while having enormous impact on practical aspects of our daily lives, are not fundamental in the same sense; or at least their potential impact at such a fundamental level has hardly been realized as yet.

As I explained earlier, the heart of classical physics was to reveal the basic variables by which the universe is to be described; initially mass, length and time, with a host of derivative variables following in the wake of the formulation of this language for description. This is fundamental enough. But the advances of twentieth-century physics are even more fundamental, in challenging the traditional clear separation between the subject and the object of study, between the observers and what is observed. These are obviously far more subtle notions than those of today, where objectivity is taken as a very simple-minded creed for the materialist.

But I believe that the modern materialist creed has not come from early twentieth-century physics, but from late twentieth-century biology. The nuts and bolts of biological research (including most of neuroscience) are not fundamental in the sense of modern physics. They apply the descriptive languages already derived in the pre-twentieth-century physical sciences to another realm of matter, that from which living organisms are formed. The description of living things is then inevitably as a complex mechanism described, like a motor car, as something objective and quite separate from the observer. The real interest at present lies, for the most part, in the details of this mechanism, taking for granted the language of classical physics and chemistry in which the analysis is couched.

What is now largely forgotten is where the basic language for description came from, and how it arose from essentially subjective impressions and conceptualizations. Even further from the reckoning is the fundamental inseparability of observer and observed which comes with twentieth-century physics.

Of course, not all modern biology is like this. Some of it is heavy with philosophical implications for how humankind should view itself. Evolutionary theory, for instance, attempts to be something more than this. It attempts to provide an underlying framework for the whole of biology. Its claim to explain the origin of the human species obviously makes the observer become part of the subject under observation. However, despite the great influence of these ideas, there is a body of opinion which holds that evolutionary theory is not a scientific theory in the traditional sense. A critique of the claims of evolutionary theory, along these lines, appears later in this work (chapter 15).

Another area where modern biology has the potential to be really fundamental in the way that advances in physics were fundamental, in the earlier years of this century, is the behavioural and neural sciences. Here, in principle at least, the observer confronts the fact that he is also the object being studied. The human faculties for knowing reality become the object of intense scientific study. Subjective and objective views become inextricably linked, as they became in twentieth-century physics.

One prime example of this is in the study of differences between the two cerebral hemispheres, especially as revealed in some epileptic patients in whom it has been necessary to sever the connections between the two hemispheres. This topic has been extensively researched by specialists. The apparent difference between the analytic, linguistic and deductive functions of the dominant hemisphere, and the holistic and inductive functions of the non-dominant hemisphere, has had considerable impact on modern culture. But, as a whole, it does not rival the overall influence of the vast amount of 'nuts and bolts' biology which is easier to comprehend, has a wider impact and promotes the naive objectivist position. In fact, that 'nuts and bolts' neuroscience is coming to overwhelm the style of brain science guided by and contributing to philosophical speculations. In the last two decades, we have seen a decline in the emphasis on understanding the information processing systems of the brain, let alone the integration of such systems to give a holistic account of human mentality. Instead the neurosciences are now dominated by neurochemical and molecular approaches, far removed indeed from the philosophical quest which motivated many scientists a generation ago (myself included) to enter this field.

The implicit inseparability of observer and observed was also realized by Karl Jaspers, the pioneer of phenomenological description in psychiatry. In defining the empathetic understanding which is possible for mentally ill patients he refers to three types of phenomena seen in those patients:

> The first group consists of phenomena known to us all from our own experience . . . Next there are phenomena which are to be understood as exaggerations, diminutions or combinations of phenomena we ourselves experience . . . How far such 'understanding' can go in such cases, when we cannot base it on any conscious experiences of a similar kind, is a question that cannot be conclusively answered . . . The third group of pathological phenomena are distinguished from the two previous groups by their complete inaccessibility to any empathic understanding. We can only get closer by analogy and metaphor. We perceive them individually, not through any positive understanding of them but through the shock which the course of our comprehension receives in the face of the incomprehensible.[1]

The point to be made from these quotations is that in all three groups mentioned by Jaspers, the assessment of the patient's experience is made by comparison with elements which are shared with (or alternatively are foreign to) the physician's own experience. The 'observations' are thus as much about the observer as about the observed.

In psychiatry there is also a relationship between observer and observed reminiscent of Heisenberg's uncertainty principle. In the interchange between a psychiatrist and his patient, it is impossible for the former to learn some aspects of the latter's condition without asking the patient searching, even provocative, questions. The process of such questioning can deeply influence the patient. Thus, the information the psychiatrist obtains is not a true reflection of the state of the patient before the consultation started.

Pertinent as these illustrations are, they are mainly from a previous generation of psychiatrists. Modern psychiatry has now become closely allied to neuroscience, and the potential for really fundamental insights into the basic nature of reality, which the two disciplines together certainly have, has scarcely been realized yet. As just mentioned, in most of contemporary neurosciences at present the strategy is quite similar to that in the rest of biology – to apply the languages already created by physics and chemistry to the matter of the brain. It is possible to do this without any reference to the idea that a human brain embodies a mind or a person, or that the object of study may also be the subject which does the studying. Implicitly many neuroscientists are abolishing the idea of a mind or a person from their world view. That this trend of contemporary biology is actually in opposition to habits of thought now well established amongst physicists has been noted by Paul Davies. He writes:

> It is ironical that physics which has led the way for all other sciences, is now moving towards a more accomodating view of mind, while the life sciences, following the path of last century's physics, are trying to abolish mind altogether.[2]

It is just because biology, rather than physics, is the dominant science of the late twentieth century, that the objectivism implicit in most of modern biology has the greater impact on the totality of modern culture.

2. Apart from this shift in emphasis from physical to biological science, another tremendous influence of science as a whole is the wide variety of technological conveniences it has made possible. To make this point, one need only mention the electronics industry and its impact on forms of entertainment, the discovery of means of contraception which are mainly safe, and the ease of modern transport over large distances.

The effectiveness and power of these technologies certainly must be respected, even if we fear the environmental impact of modern technology. Paul Davies makes the point that although science has 'invaded our lives', 'it has not done so at the intellectual level. The vast majority of people do not understand scientific principles, nor are they interested.'[3]

I take issue with this statement. True, popular understanding of science may be quite shallow, but nevertheless the success of modern technology has deeply affected the way people think. Within the last generation technology has for the first time really had an impact on the mass of the population in Western countries. Popular and sometimes simple-minded religious belief has given way to a belief in science and technology, which is also often of a simple-minded form. I have already referred extensively to the attitude of exclusive objectivity which pervades modern culture. This is the simple-minded distortion of scientific thinking which the technological revolution has produced. Make no mistake: The success of science in everyday living has changed popular modes of thinking most profoundly.

3. Another of the emphases of modern science, which has grown with, and contributed to the modern dominance of exclusive objectivity, is concern for information processing strategies and information coding. This appears in a major way in several branches of biology, such as psychology and molecular biology, and of course is reinforced by the powerful information-processing machines which the computer revolution has spawned. This emphasis on information processing and information technology is something new, not found to a great extent in older physics. However, it carries with it another buttress for the modern trend to objectivism, and rejection of anything subjective. How does this come about?

To provide a description of the world in quantitative terms, ultimately as numbers, is to translate the reality of the world into a coded form. This is an explicit operationalized procedure, and as such, as we have seen, is entirely objective. In fact, when it is done properly, it is the most important form of objectivization which science has devised. The links with subjective appreciation of the variables being quantified, though quite basic, can actually be forgotten once the quantification is under way.

The same is true of any other code. Thus, the encoding of genetic information, or the coding of a calculation routine in computer programming language are entirely objective. The physical machinery which implements the programme, or decodes the genetic information, is essential, objective, and taken for granted. The history of science which led to the understanding of the physical principles governing that machinery, which at some time must have involved quite subjective steps, is again totally forgotten. The result is that information science, and information economies, have apparently escaped from the realm of the subjective into a brave new world where subjectivism is as outdated as the dinosaur. What is not realized is that this brave new world has no 'visible means of support' in the philosophical sense.

4. The modern obsession with exclusive objectivity is related in another way to the computer revolution. Whereas previously, complex qualities could only be judged subjectively, and sometimes idiosyncratically, such judgments are now replaced by computer algorithms. Computers can deliver their verdict, according to the chosen algorithm, with great speed, and it is easily possible to obtain a 'verdict' by several different algorithms, also with lightning speed. This process appears to remove the need for an observer from the process of description, and replaces his or her subjectivity by an operationalized objective approach. As I have argued above, all objective assessments of qualities have their origin in subjective impressions. In modern times the widespread use of computers is one amongst a number of forces which tend to divorce objective assessments from the subjective judgments in which they take their origin. The remarks of Erwin Schrödinger, made earlier this century, redress the balance, and are still quite up-to-date:

> The observer is never entirely replaced by instruments; for if he were he could obviously obtain no knowledge whatsoever . . . Many helpful devices can facilitate this work, for instance photometric recording . . . on which the position of the lines can be easily read. But they must be read! The observer's senses have to step in eventually. The most careful record, when not inspected, tells us nothing.[4]

5. Another major feature in the second half of the twentieth century is the dominance of the mass media, especially television, for providing the public with information. Everyone receives the same information by these means. Not surprisingly, this insidiously sets up as the criterion for truth that which is agreed publicly. Moreover, these media give us totally public presentations of images of reality in such a vivid fashion that nothing is left to the imagination of the viewer. Gone are the days of

the British radio comedy when half the fun depended on what one could *not* see but each could imagine in a different way on the basis of a few suggestive sounds. The total reality of the modern visual media makes us think that what we see on the television screen *is* reality. We thus lose our capacity for imaginative recreation, each of our own reality.

Likewise the recorded music industry brings into everyone's home breathtakingly perfect musical performances. Many of us think they are real performances, and to an extent they are; but they are highly selected and edited, to avoid the least imperfection. Some eminent musicians realize that the more satisfying musical experiences occur in live performances, just because of the idiosyncracies, the occasional blemish, and the way in which the persons who are performing touch, and are touched by, the audience. In jazz music the role of chance is yet more clearly recognized. The occasional mistake in fingering producing a wrong note is employed as a spur, by the talented performer, for further improvisation, which will resolve the tension between the solo line and the underlying harmony. One jazz virtuoso has even declared that the 'wrong note is the right note'. The chance element in such performances is lost in recorded versions. Again we see the contrast between the authorized version of public objective reality, and the more personalized version where subjective interpretations by performer or audience play a part.

6. A further reason why the bland objectivism of modern times has easily taken root is because of a point I have already made; that the majority of us live a relatively comfortable existence, made possible by modern technology. We are thus protected from the more unpleasant and intense experiences that have been naturally accepted throughout history until recent times. Few of us (in 'Western' countries) now know from personal experience of the darker side of human existence – illness, suffering, madness, isolation and death – as commonplace and everyday realities. In former times these were recognized as ever-present facts of life. Aldous Huxley expressed this well:

> The patience of common humanity is the most important and almost the most surprising thing in history. Most men and women are prepared to tolerate the intolerable.[5]

I am not implying that suffering inevitably makes people concentrate more on subjective experiences; and certainly not that suffering is a necessary part of one's education. But knowledge of the darker side of experience does make at least some people attempt to integrate their emotionally intense subjective experiences with the intellectual side of their minds with which they grasp objective reality. It is perhaps no coincidence that the culture in the second half of the twentieth century which has best integrated objective and subjective is that which has experienced the most profound suffering. I think of the former Soviet Union, a culture which was explicitly atheistic and dominated by philosophical materialism, but one in which the humanity of Solzhenitsyn, the vitality and compassion of Shostakovich, or the warmth of the psychologist Alexander Luria, managed to emerge.

7. Ideology also plays a part in the obsession with exclusive objectivity. A primary example of this is the influence of the Darwinian 'theory' of evolution. Darwinian evolution claims to be scientific. A critique of this widespread belief is presented later in this book. But whether it is or not, Darwinian thinking also has ideological implications, in that it encourages people to think in terms of vast populations of living things and eons of time, sometimes at the expense of the here and now, the small scale, the personal and the subjective. The evolutionary 'struggle for existence' is supposed to be an objective fact. The subjective experience of those who struggle is conveniently ignored in the sanitized neo-Darwinian version of world history. The same emphasis comes from many other trends of recent decades, for instance our continual exposure to arguments about large-scale social processes, macro-economic reasoning and the like (to say nothing of astrophysics, cosmology and the Law of Increasing Entropy, said to be the most fundamental of physical laws).

This emphasis on the macro at the expense of the small scale and personal is encouraged further by the power of modern communications and newsmedia. We know, if we read, that about twenty million Russian people died violent deaths in the Second World War. We see on our own TV screen (if we have one) that several million people are facing death by starvation in Ethiopia. We see hundreds of thousands of lives threatened in the voyeurist pictures of the war in the Persian Gulf. Few of us can actually comprehend what these facts mean as personal experiences. It would make a much bigger impact on most of us if we heard a single survivor of such events recalling how *all* his or her friends were exterminated in such events.[6]

Thinking in global terms is also an inescapable feature of modern concern with the environment. The industries which have allowed use of aerosol propellants and refridgerator coolants in our kitchens contribute to the global warming which may soon threaten low lying Pacific Islands. Undoubtedly it is necessary for some of us to think as accurately as possible in global terms, and for our consciousness to include the global environmental issues. But some way has also to be found of doing this without disregarding the implications at a personal, humanly comprehensible level.

The environmentalist movement has the slogan: 'Think globally, act locally'. Actually this could lead to some strange actions. For instance, I might consider that, since the weeds in my garden absorb carbon dioxide, and that carbon dioxide contributes to global warming, I would be helping to prevent global warming by letting my own little garden grow long and go to seed!

However, the serious point is this: that if we think only on a global scale, we cut ourselves off from the subjective focus which can be the only ultimate guide for our value judgments and decisions. For the large scale events we tend to deny the subjective personal aspect of the events, and think 'objectively' in terms of 'mass forces', governed by 'scientific principles'. We cannot put together in our consciousnesses the large scale and the personal, the here-and-now with the process of history, the finite and the infinite. The Christian religion actually has devised a way of doing this very well. The Christian story (or, as I will explain later, the Christian myth) is centred on an intensely personal event, the birth of a child, but at the same time makes the event of infinite significance, because it is the God-child. In contemporary culture most of us have lost the connection between the secular and the infinite. Somehow we must reinvent a way of connecting personal experience with the possibility of universal values. We must start our thinking about systems of values from the small scale and personal, deriving from our own subjective experience, but also go from there and extend to the global, universal case.

Mathematicians have actually derived a formal solution to this sort of conundrum. The only consistent way of handling infinity as a mathematical concept is by assuming that when any infinite quantity is subdivided, any of the resultant portions is also infinite. Translating this to the above argument would mean that it *is* valid to consider the suffering of a single human being, just one portion of infinite humanity, as also of infinite significance.

8. Amongst the features of modern culture which have predisposed many of us to accept the trend to universal objectivity, are some which are most pronounced in New Zealand. One of these is the influence of

the principle industry of New Zealand, the production of large numbers of livestock for slaughter. Success in this industry is necessarily expressed in economic terms. In the severe winter weather in 1992 over half a million livestock died before reaching the freezing works. While this was undoubtedly a tragedy, the farming practices which led to so many livestock being so vulnerable was defended on economic grounds. When this single industry is such a dominant part of the livelihood of a country it has inevitable consequences for the attitude of mind amongst many of the inhabitants. Life and death of animals are solely objective facts, expressed in economic terms. It is easy to translate this attitude to human life and death. A harsh value scheme sometimes appears, in which the agony and ecstasy of human or animal life is of no account.

9. The institutions of religion, as it has been expressed in recent times, have some responsibility for the trend to objectivism and materialism. The dominant expression of religion in the last thirty years has been fundamentalist in various ways. It has used the high pressure methods of the advertizing industry and the simplest, least subtle type of concept as its stock in trade. While this style of religion wins its adherents in the short term, it is hardly likely to win long term adherence amongst the more perceptive people. It is just these people whose thinking will in due course have most influence. It is hardly surprising that a stridently materialist culture should have grown as the deeply hostile antithesis to such a shallow variety of religion. Possibly the extremely secular culture of New Zealand arises in part because, in the earlier generations, when religious observance was more widespread, it was not based on strong philosophical or metaphysical roots. In this respect it may be contrasted with the European cultural tradition, where most of the best philosophers were of religious persuasion. In New Zealand, when religion is challenged by the growth of scientific attitudes, it is no longer possible to defend the traditional religious belief at any fundamental level. Sooner or later a clear gap is likely to appear between the traditional beliefs of the parents, and the 'modern' materialist views of their children. The alternative way things may go is of course the revitalizing of the most simplistic fundamentalisms. We are back where we started. The extremists on both sides call the tune, and any attempt to define one of the more subtle positions in 'no-man's land' is in danger of being shot to pieces from both sides.

10. Despite these comments about New Zealand, there is one feature of life in New Zealand which I perceive as a great advantage, as it must be for any small country. It is a powerful antidote to the implicit message

of modern materialist orthodoxy. This antidote is the pervasive environment in which the personal small scale aspects of life are much more important, relative to the events of world scale which so few of us can really grasp in the same vision as the small scale and personal. Politicians are not unapproachable isolated figures, but people who many of us actually know, for better or worse (and we can easily form our own judgments). Newspapers concentrate on the small scale. They may often be quite parochial, but avoid the tendency to ignore the human scale from which values derive. In a country with only three million people the pressure to division of labour into many minute fragments is less, and so is the pressure on each individual to specialize. It is therefore easier for people to acquire an integrated perspective of their life rather than the viewpoint seen from a narrow speciality, as tends to happen in bigger countries. Many New Zealanders, realizing how easily they could become isolated, do a great deal of travelling. Thoughtful New Zealanders are thus quite well placed to bridge the gap between the human scale at which values originate and the global level at which the most important issues actually arise, and where those values may have to be applied.

Part II

Psychophysical Parallelism: In Defence of an Alternative Metaphysics

8

Subjective Reality

We are all familiar with the idea that there are objective 'facts', and that what is objective is 'real'. But are there any subjective facts? Does the subjective world have a reality?

In the following section I present a variety of examples and arguments in defence of the view that subjective experiences should be regarded as a fundamental form of reality, rather than mere epiphenomena; and that there should be recognized many subjective facts, whose existence need not rely on first demonstrating some objective counterpart.

8.1 The subjective reality of aesthetic experiences

What is 'redness'? The objectivist would define it in terms of the wavelength of light impinging on the eye, and various associated physiological processes. But this answer would hardly suffice as an answer for a colour-blind person when he asks the question (to which he really does not know the answer): 'what is redness?'

Take the redness example in detail. From our scientific knowledge of visual sensory physiology and various associated processes in the brain it is clear that a variety of objectively-defineable processes are needed before a person with normal colour vision experiences the sensation which that person calls 'redness'. These include the following. Light of a certain frequency range must strike the cones of the retina, specific groups of nerve cells in the retina are activated and send messages in the central visual regions of the brain. To be able to call the resulting sensation 'redness', a process of socially-mediated learning must also have occurred so that a particular speech sound (the word 'red') is associated with the experience elicited by light of that wavelength arriving at the eye. All of these processes can be regarded as mechanisms. Not all of these mechanisms are fully understood yet perhaps, but nevertheless we can assume quite plausibly that such mechanisms exist and are necessary before we can perceive and name the redness of objects. There is no reason to doubt that these mechanisms are actually as objective as the internal combustion engine which drives our motor cars. But when we have said that, and even if we have given the perfect explanation of that mechanism, we have not explained what redness is in terms that our hypothetical colour-blind man can understand.

The objectivist might at this stage have recourse to the idea of 'emergence'.[1] According to this concept, sensory qualities like redness are phenomena that do not go beyond what is implied by the sophisticated neural machinery, but yet cannot be derived from them, because of the limitations of inference when dealing with complex systems. But this seems to be assuming an answer to the very question at issue. Does our inability to define the subjective nature of redness depend on the limitations of inference about complex systems? Or does it depend on some other, more fundamental and categorical limitation?

Of these two possibilities, the latter seems the more plausible. Take an invertebrate animal with a much simpler nervous system than our own. Sophisticated research can (more easily than for the mammalian nervous system) provide a complete sequence of causal interactions between the visual sense organs, the internal information processing, and the eventual behavioural output. If our inability to define the subjective quality of a sensation depended on limitations of inference about complex systems, it should be easier to define sensory qualities for animals with simple nervous systems than for our human selves, with much more complex nervous systems. But the reverse is the case. Generally we deny completely that such simple animals have any subjective existence. This actually is a question which is quite unanswerable as a matter of fact. Despite this, the tendency of most people to deny categorically any subjective life to simpler creatures than ourselves most likely stems from the fact that all we can ever know of them is at the 'objective level'. And there is nothing from which we can form an intuition of what sort of subjective life they have (if any). But the common denial of subjective life to invertebrate animals is decidedly not because there is any decisive evidence against their having a subjective side to them.

P. S. Churchland suggests that it is premature to conclude that mental qualities cannot, in principle, be derived from, or reduced to states of the brain. As analogies she points out how, in the past, science has achieved other seemingly impossible 'intertheoretic reductions'. The examples she gives are the reduction of 'temperature' to the exactly equivalent phrase 'mean molecular kinetic energy';[2] or the reduction of 'light' to 'electromagnetic radiation';[3] or the derivation of the 'blueness' of water from the microphysics of its aggregated molecules. In each case she *identifies* the high-level phenomenon with the feature at the lower level to which it is reduced. Temperature *is* mean molecular kinetic energy; light *is* electromagnetic radiation; and although the derivation of subjective qualities from brain states has not yet been achieved, she sees it as plausible to suggest that those subjective states can be identified with brain states.

However, in these cases, while most of the descriptive terms used at the higher level are different from those used at the lower level to which the higher level is reduced, there are in all cases some terms in common between the two levels of description. Long before the incorporation of temperature into mainstream physics it was realized that temperature and heat were related to energy, the same energy which is a property of a moving object. Similarly both light and electromagnetism were related to energy, and so it could not have been categorically dismissed that they might have a close relation. Similarly the microphysics of water has certain implications for the preferential scattering of light of specific wavelengths, which we call 'blue'.

However in trying to derive the subjective quality of 'redness' (or blueness, for that matter) from the physiology of visual systems there seems to be no common ground between the two levels of description. This is not just a practical difficulty, but is a limitation in principle. We can say this because redness is in very essence a private experience which in a strict sense cannot be compared between subjects, whereas visual physiology is public and therefore objective. Churchland seems not to grasp this point. She notes that the preferential scattering of light of certain wavelengths affects human observers and their instruments in all the same ways that 'blueness' does. She writes: 'it is reasonable to *identify* the blueness [of water] with its disposition to scatter . . . electromagnetic waves preferentially at 0.46 micrometres.'[4] To her, there seems to be nothing else about blueness (or redness) than the wavelength of the light by which it is defined.

The point I am making is a doctrine similar to that raised against the naturalistic fallacy. Just as one cannot derive values from facts, because they are described on 'orthogonal axes', so one cannot derive subjective personal private experience from objective publicly agreed descriptions. Our inability to define redness in such a way that a colour-blind man can understand it is because of the logical independence of subjective and objective descriptions, of introspection and inspection, rather than because of limitations on our capacity for inference. These two limitations on inference (the invalidity of infering values from facts, and the invalidity of deriving subjective descriptions from objective ones) are very closely related. The naturalistic fallacy is a special case of the incommensurability of subjective and objective.

The same point can be made in many other ways. One may ask whether musicians hear the same sounds when a piece of music is played as do non-musicians? Or do artists see the same sight in a landscape they are about to paint as do non-artists? In musical and artistic education the musicians and artists are encouraged to see and hear with new eyes and new ears. Ear training for musicians really does enable them to hear what they did not hear before. Are their subjective experiences changed as a result? If we think that the artist or the musician has different subjective experiences from normal, we appear to be giving those sensory experiences some implicit reality. Admittedly those differences between the creative arist and the normal person may arise from differences in the sensory systems of the artist/ musician compared with the normal, which differences presumably result from innate gifts and from extensive training in the former. In principle those differences could be demonstrated quite objectively. In fact, in the context of an article on the theory of the symptoms of psychosis,[5] I recently proposed a precise hypothesis of the brain mechanisms which might have led to artists such as Van Gogh or Edvard Munch (both of whom had major psychiatric problems) seeing the world in a different way from normal non-artistic individuals. But we do not need such hypotheses or explanations to come to the conclusion (or at least the strong suspicion) that creative minds have different subjective experiences from the normal. Again we conclude that, if subjective experiences exist at all, our knowledge of them (as knowledge) is independent of objective facts, and is not logically dependent on facts about the nervous systems which makes them possible.

In some sensory systems it is possible to arrange the manner of stimulation so as to create strong sensory illusions. Sometimes these illusions seem to defy what we claim we 'know' to be possible. For instance, our muscles contain sense organs which inform us about position and movement of our limbs. If a stimulus vibrating at about 50 cycles per second is applied to a muscle it may distort our sense of the position of our limbs. Under some conditions, some people claim that the stimulus makes them feel that a joint of a limb is occupying a position which they 'know' to be impossible. The elbow joint may feel as if it has been straightened, and then, continuing in the same direction, bent back to a position impossible without breaking the bones. We may be able to give a physiological account of this. But do we need such an account before we take seriously the subjective experience to which the experimental subjects bear witness?

This question may seem of rather academic importance. But there are also many experiences occurring in neurological and mental illness, which can easily be disregarded by those with normal nervous systems, because there is no objective evidence for them, and no explanation presently available for how they could arise. A patient in an acute psychotic state may hear voices that no one else can hear. He may feel that his bodily movements or speech are occurring under control of some agency other than his own volition. Do we ignore such reports, because we ourselves have never had these experiences, and cannot understand the words used by a patient when he has recovered to describe his earlier psychotic experiences? Many people would ignore them, but in doing so they ignore something very real to the patient. Indeed it may add to their psychological problem that no one gives credit to the reality of their abnormal experience.

There is here perhaps a basis for the distinction between psychiatry and neurology, which belies the fact that both deal with disorders of the same nervous system. In neurology there are far more, and more precise objective physical signs than in psychiatry. Thus, for the clinician who is suspicious of subjective statements, neurology appears to have a firmer grounding than psychiatry. This possible distinction may become less tenable as research progresses. The strange symptoms of mental illnesses, however subjective their report from patients may be, may come to be given explanations on the basis of disturbed brain dynamics which are as precise as anything in neurology. Once again we would be wise to acknowledge the reality of subjective phenomena, in their own right, regardless of the objective facts about the nervous systems and its abnormalities which might give rise to these phenomena. This was the contention of Karl Jaspers, whose work attempted specifically to define the 'phenomenology' of psychiatric states.

8.2 *The singularity of a mind in space and time compared with the continuity of matter*

A related point can be made, but in a more fundamental manner, by considering the correspondence between basic physical measurements – time and space – and their subjective counterparts. Take time first.

Our immediate subjective experience is focussed at a narrow 'section' of time. Admittedly there are strong traces of the past, as well as projections into the possible future in our present experience: Events that have occurred before the current temporal focus of our consciousness are perceived (indirectly) by the faculty of memory, and those that are likely to occur later than our current focus of consciousness may sometimes be derived by our expectations or anticipations, based on previous experience of similar events. Nevertheless, apart from these indirect perceptions of past and future times, personal experience has its centre in a small 'window' of time. Cognitive psychologists have attempted to define this narrowest 'slice' of time which can be labelled 'the present'; and they find that it is not an infinitesimal moment of time, as might be supposed if one drew a precise analogy with the physicist's sharp knife which divides the past from the future. The duration of the window of time at which consciousness is most sharply focussed is, at its narrowest focus, about 100 msec long.[6] Any events occurring on a time scale much shorter than this cannot be registered as sequential events spaced along the time axis, but are blended together subjectively into a pattern in which time (subjectively) is not a variable.

For instance, pairs of clicks of sound separated by more than 100 milliseconds are heard separately and in sequence (and we also register fairly accurately the time difference between them). But if they are closer together than the interval of about 100 milliseconds they are heard as a single sound, one of whose subjective properties is pitch. Likewise, in the visual modality two brief images, slightly different in form or position and separated in time by more than 100 milliseconds, will be perceived separately. But if they are closer together in time than this, they will be perceived as a single image, one of whose subjective properties is motion. This subjective fact is the basis of the motion picture industry. Thus subjective time is not continuous, but is divided into distinct zones. Our subjective perception of time appears to have a different structure from objective physical time.

Another example of the discontinuities in our preception of time comes on a slightly longer time scale. Up to intervals of about two seconds, a regularly repeated sound is perceived as rhythmic. That is, we have a subjective expectancy of exactly when the next repetition is likely to occur. Beyond the interval of about two seconds our sense of timing decreases. We may still have an expectancy of what events are likely to occur in sequence, but that expectancy contains less accurate imformation about actual timing.[7] Despite these discontinuities of time as it is appreciated subjectively, when time is defined objectively in the various ways that have been devised by physicists since Galileo's analysis of simple harmonic motion, time is a uniform continuum. There is no identifiable or special region at which a person's consciousness is located, and no range of intervals which are categorically different from others.

There is also another difference between subjective and objective time. Subjectively 'the present time', that 100 milliseconds slice at which our consciousness is focussed, appears to 'travel' in some indefineable way. It gradually 'encroaches on the future, and discards the past'. Not so physical objective time. For the physicist time is a dimension like space. Physicists' time does not move or travel. 'Past', 'present' and 'future' are similar parts of a vast stationary continuum. The physicist would not write, in the words of Isaac Watts:

> Time, like an ever-rolling stream,
>   Bears all its sons away;
> They fly forgotten, as a dream
>   Dies at the opening day.

Nor would the physicist have written, in words spoken by Macbeth,

> Tomorrow, and tomorrow, and tomorrow,
> Creeps in this petty pace from day to day.

A better rendition of the physicist's view of time comes in an earlier stanza of Watts' hymn:

> Before the hills in order stood,
>   Or earth received her frame,
> From everlasting thou art God,
>   To endless years the same

(Note especially the clash of tenses here: The past tense, implying the temporal world, 'stood', and the present tense, capturing timeless existence, 'thou art God'.)

Of course it is somewhat unreal to separate the subjective and objective views of time in this way, but that is exactly what is implied by physicists who emphasize the stationary nature of physical time, opposing it to the illusory impression of 'flow' in subjective time. But is it illusion, or some radically different form of reality?

A similar point can also be made about a person's location in space. At present I sit typing in my living room. If I get into my car and drive to another part of the town, the centre of my 'personal space' from which I view the universe has shifted. This is a fact, an objective fact for people who observe me, but a quite subjective one for myself. My consciousness thus has a singular viewpoint upon space as well as upon time. Yet to a physicist, space (like time) is a uniform continuum, with no special places, or special viewpoints within it. Admittedly in relativistic space there may be regions where the curvature of space is so great as to produce a singularity. But this is one that can be observed or inferred from objective observations. The singularity of my location in space and time is of a different nature, arising from the fact that a tiny fragment of the physical universe (my physical body) is also the focus of a unique and distinct viewpoint on that universe, albeit subjective.

The point can again be made about matter. In material terms there is no sharp distinction between what a person is composed of and the external environment. There is no reason to think that causal processes stop or change fundamentally at the border between the environment and the matter which embodies a person. Again there is continuity. But subjectively there is not a continuity. There is a sharp division. The physical vessel which contains consciousness is a singularity. We 'know' in some sense what is 'ourselves' and what is 'outside ourselves'.

Thus there is a sharp contrast between the subjective aspects of time, space and matter at which consciousness dwells, and the time, space and matter as perceived by the physical sciences: a contrast between the singularity of consciousness in time and space, and the matter to which it 'belongs', and the uniformity or continuity of physical time, space and matter. The contrast between the singularity of consciousness versus the continuity of the physical world in which consciousness exists cannot be emphasized too strongly. Continuity and generality of all matter is readily agreed to, since it is the fundamental principle of all science. The singularity of mind is also obvious once it is pointed out. We all readily accept the generalizability of space, time and the properties of matter. Yet we also would have difficulty in denying the singularity of our own mental processes. To do so would appear to be denying our own existence. (This statement is as simple as a classical syllogism.) Despite these two universally accepted items of belief, it is surprising how many people there are who cannot recognize the lack of congruence between these two viewpoints. *This lack of congruence seems to imply some sort of rather fundamental dualism.* Possibly it is this major metaphysical implication which is the stumbling block for so many people in giving recognition to a conception of realities which, to many other people, is as obvious as the daylight.

8.3 The subjective reality of pleasure, pain and suffering

The previous sections developed the argument with examples of components of consciousness which were 'value-neutral', providing information about the surrounding world and the position of consciousness within space and time. Now let us undertake a similar analysis of components of consciousness where aspects of valuation are prominent. The examples we choose are subjective experiences of pleasure and pain, of profound comfort or deep distress and suffering. Take a simple example of a person experiencing the consequences of an elementary 'painful' stimulus. The objective features of the painful stimulus and the body's response to it can be defined easily. There is likely to be some sort of immediate reflex withdrawal response of the part of the body stimulated, involving neural pathways which neurophysiologists have analysed with some success. More globally the animal, if it is free to move as a whole, may respond by trying to escape from the situation in which the painful stimulus is delivered. If the painful stimulus is delivered a number of times, and signals are given from which the animal can predict the likely future occurrence of the stimulus, it will acquire new responses (that is it will learn) and will thus manage to avoid painful stimuli which would otherwise be delivered. Escape responses and learned avoidance responses are far more difficult to provide clear explanations for than are reflex withdrawal responses. But in principle there is little reason to doubt that they can still be explained as a mechanism involving learning (i.e. functional change of the brain), or can be simulated with varying degrees of realism in a computer programme.

But these scientific analyses leave completely out of account the subjective side of the experience of pain, which in this case is also one which brings into account our scale of values.

Some people distinguish between pain and suffering, the former being momentary, the latter having longer term impact. These differences can also be derived from quite plausible mechanisms, which can convert a momentary pain into enduring memories of pain and corresponding lasting aversions or phobias. A recent experimental paper[8] has given evidence of the exact portion of the brain from which 'suffering' as opposed to short-term pain arise. Again, to express this just in terms of mechanisms, valid though it may be in its own terms, may leave completely out of account the subjective values we place on suffering.

Whether we concentrate on the short-term experiences of pain or the protracted experiences we call suffering, are they real or illusory?

Certainly in many practical situations it is wise to disregard apparent adverse subjective experiences. I am reminded of an episode which occurred in a girl's school I knew, when there was an outbreak of faintings. Many of the teachers were alarmed at this and thought a serious epidemic of some sort was breaking out. Not so the wily headmistress. She decreed that if anyone fainted thenceforth, they were to be left on the floor where they had fainted and *she* (the headmistress) was to be sent for. The faintings stopped instantly. Any wise and loving parent will have learnt a similar lesson with regard to some of the apparent sicknesses of their potentially manipulative children. There are many more serious and difficult examples of the same manipulative behaviours in various psychiatric illnesses. In many of these cases the apparent suffering of the individual concerned covers up some hidden source of reinforcement (even consciously admitted 'reward') resulting from the difficult behaviour. The wise approach to adopt in these cases may owe more to the mechanistic approach explained by learning theory than to a sympathetic assessment of the degree of suffering involved.

Such examples, however, tell only part of the story.

Experimental neurophysiologists sometimes carry out recordings from single nerve cells in unanaesthetized animals, an approach which has many advantages from the scientific point of view over recordings in anaesthetized animals. The most precise information is provided by a technique in which microelectrodes are inserted actually within the single nerve cell. This is a very difficult technique, and to accomplish it, it is essential to ensure complete mechanical stability, and freedom from the slightest movements, jolts and jars of the animal. This has generally been accomplished by using drugs which paralyse the animal, that is to prevent the normal function of the animal's own muscles, which produce movements. Associated with this it is also necessary to keep the animal's breathing going by artificial respiration. The animals are then fully conscious, and no doubt capable of feeling pain. Any surgical incisions or other points from which pain can arise are therefore infiltrated with local anaesthetics rather than general anaesthetics. However, since the more obvious behavioural signs of pain have been abolished by the drug which induces the paralysis, it is difficult to be quite sure whether or not the animal is in pain. The experimental animal will in any case be killed at the end of the experiment (one expects quite painlessly) to provide further information of use for the experimental analysis. However, this technique has long been outlawed in some countries (such as Britain) and in recent years a growing number of scientific journals have refused to publish results using this technique. The crux of the issue would seem to be that whereas a free-moving animal can give a clear indication of its response to pain, which can guide the experimenter to limit the pain, no such indications are available in the paralysed unanaesthetized animal.

This is just one of the more pointed examples of the ethical issues involved in experimental brain research. Others could easily be found. The question is this. Why is it objectionable that an animal, which will in any case be killed, should be freed from pain or suffering in the hours of the experiment before its death? One could easily say that animals are, in any case, incapable of suffering, so such experimental methods have no ethical implications. This is the view which would follow from the hardline materialist position. It is not a view accepted by any committee responsible for ethics of animal experimentation, nor by most scientific journals nowadays. An alternative view about experiments on paralysed animals is to say that once the animal's death has occurred, there is no longer any pain or suffering, and the slate has been wiped clean. Again this argument would legitimize experiments in unanaesthetized, paralysed animals.

This second argument is interesting. Let us put it as powerfully as possible. Let us ask the following question, not now about animals but about our kith and kin, other human beings. Compare two human beings, one of whom has a happy and a fulfilled life, beautiful relationships, healthy children, no hardship and a peaceful death. The other has a lifetime of intense struggle which ends when he dies miserably as a result of months of torture. The question is, once they are both dead, has the manner of their death any lasting meaning that we must take into account; or is the slate wiped clean?

A few catch-phrases are perhaps needed to pinpoint the issue, on the subject of the pleasures and pains of human love: ' 'Tis better to have loved and lost, than never to have loved at all.' This implies that short lived pleasure has an enduring impact. In a French version on the same theme we see both sides of the issue: 'Plaisir d'amour ne dure qu'un moment; chagrin d'amour dure pour toute la vie.' Relevant as these sayings are, the real issue is not quite the same. These quotations are talking about whether there is any enduring impact of pleasure and pain *within the span of the memory of a human being*. The real issue is actually a more metaphysical one, of whether the infinities of pleasure and pain endure in some sense regardless of the span of human life or even of social memory.

A hardline materialist would in any case deny that suffering exists. A more sophisticated materialist might adopt the second of these two positions, arguing that suffering exists at the instants when it is occurring but has no lasting reality. He would argue that pleasure, pain and suffering were properties emerging from the material aspects of our existence, and cease when that material existence ceases.

This is similar to saying that the 'pain' suffered in a frightening nightmare ceases when we awake, and the memory of the nightmare fades. The only difference appears to be that the memory of a nightmare is usually quite short, while that of severe mental torment of the torture victim is life-long. But in either case, our more sophisticated materialist would assert that the slate *is* wiped clean when the corresponding memory (whether short or long term) is erased, or for other reasons can no longer be retrieved.

This is a feasible method of argument, but consider also what follows from this view. The end will always justify the means. The most trivial end will justify any extent of cruel means. If the negative value of an animal's experience is wiped off the account at the end of the experiment, or when the human torture victim eventually dies, but the pleasure of the survivors (who might be the perpetrators) remains, because they are still alive, the end of gratifying those survivors would justify any imaginable holocaust (as well as unimaginable holocausts).

In chapter 10 we will return to this issue, and suggest another way of thinking about the reality of pleasure, pain and suffering, which may provide a surer foundation for value systems.

9

Psychophysical Parallelism

9.1 Dualism of the subjective and the objective

The word 'metaphysics' is defined as 'theoretical philosophy of being and knowing'. In adjectival form the word 'metaphysical' can mean 'incorporeal' or 'supernatural', and was used to categorize a school of poets who flourished in England in the seventeenth century. Nowadays metaphysics as a branch of philosophy is still studied, but the adjective is often used in a somewhat pejorative sense. Russell[1] identifies David Hume as the orignator of this anti-metaphysical trend, notable in the British empiricist tradition, and contrasting with the tradition on the continent of Europe. The divergence of traditions continues to this day. Indeed it was possible for Cupitt[2] to write a book on theological questions which was intended to be 'post- metaphysical'. However, any account of reality, even the most hard-headed materialist one, must make *some* metaphysical suppositions about the nature of reality, albeit very different from traditional Christian ones to which Hume was reacting. In this section I want to argue in favour of those philosophies that held that being and knowing actually do involve realities that are insubstantial ('incorporeal'). I will try to dispel the cloud of disapproval that goes along with the term 'metaphysical' in modern times.

Specifically I want to suggest that the subjective qualities and intuitions which are contained within our consciousnesses should not be ignored as epiphenomena. They are so important that we should recognize them as representatives of a fundamental form which reality takes. Since they cannot be derived from objective facts about the world, we are then led to a form of dualism. However, this dualism is one in which two totally different worlds move about in parallel, always with perfect synchrony and correspondence. This then is *psychophysical parallelism*, a philosophy which I have also attempted to explain in another work.[3]

I am not advocating the form of dualism where both mind and matter have causal efficacy, and as independent forces can influence each other. This is the position advocated by Descartes, and more recently by J. C. Eccles,[4] discussed later (section 9.4). Accordingly I propose that neither can mind causally produce changes in the brain, nor can the brain causally produce changes in mind. (The explication of this curious statement is given in section 10.2) Thus there can be both subjective and objective facts, categorically quite separate, but (on the rare occasions when we see glimpses of both at once) corresponding exactly to each other. Philosophical idealism accepts only the former even though subjective impressions without a physical world to see and a physical brain to do the seeing are impossible. Materialism accepts only the latter, even though objective facts are always dependent on subjects to appreciate them, and subjective experience to derive them. In fact it is obviously true that the two, subjective and objective, mind and matter, are always interdependent.

To explicate the parallel relation between mind and brain it is helpful to think in terms of analogies and metaphors. We must realize, of course, that a particular analogy will not be accurate in every respect. Polkinghorne[5] has pointed out that metaphors are valuable exactly because they are imprecise. They are a less-than-explicit way of suggesting a description for something not experienced or explicated before. They are thus the natural way for us to extend meaning from familiar to novel territory. The several metaphors used below lead us gradually to refine the description of the parallelism postulated between mind and matter, and to recognize some of the fallacies that come from too-close identification of the problem with a particular single analogy.

One analogy which comes to mind is that of a coin. It has two sides, with different images embossed on each side. We can study one side at once in detail, we can get a good idea that the two sides are inseparable, but because they face in opposite directions we can only get an approximate idea of the correspondence between parts of the image on one side with those of the image on the other.

However, this analogy should not be taken as valid in all respects. The two sides of a coin are similar not only in that they are in close correspondence; they are also both objective aspects of the coin. The subjective and the objective worlds, though likewise in correspondence, are categorically different in a profound way, which is not captured by the analogy with a coin.

ilar, though more technical analogy has been made by rne.[6] He refers to the alternative descriptions of light, as either waves or particles. These contrasting models can be regarded as complementary, both being applicable but without any contradiction. Contradiction is avoided because the circumstances in which each description applies are mutually exclusive. Polkinghorne regards such complementarity as a good analogy of the relation between brain and mind. Certainly the mental (inner) and physical (outer) descriptions of the mind/brain inform us from mutually exclusive perspectives, just as do the opposite faces of a coin. However, like the coin analogy, wave and particle descriptions of light are both objective. In this respect the complementarity analogy, like that of the coin, breaks down.

9.2 The mind/body problem: origin in confusion of levels of description?

Paul Davies points out another inadequacy of this analogy: that mind and brain are entities at different levels, the one a deep abstraction, compared with the other. As an example of such abstractions he mentions:[7]

a person's nationality [which] cannot be weighed or measured, it does not occupy a location inside their bodies, and yet it is a meaningful and important part of their make-up . . .

In similar vein Ryle[8] suggests that a muddle between the concrete and the abstract categories gives rise to most of the confusion about the relation between mind and body. His example to illustrate this confusion is that talking about mind/body relationships is like talking about a discourse between the British House of Commons and the British Constitution. In similar vein, John Searle, in his Reith Lectures,[9] suggests that the 'mind/body' problem is really no different from the 'digestion/stomach' problem. Since the latter is not a problem, neither should the mind/body problem be one either. The point that all writers are making is that mind is 'holistic', a high level abstract derivative of the body, like the relation between the plot of a novel, and the letters of the alphabet in which it is written. All authors suggest that by correct unravelling of this easily-confused point we are capable of solving the mystery of the mind/body problem. Is it really so straightforward?

I think not; but of course this really depends on how one defines mind. It has already been mentioned that mind can be defined 'objectively' as the sum total of the strategies of information processing displayed by the working, intact brain; or alternatively as the sum total of the subjective qualities, impressions, and intuitions experienced by a person with an intact, working brain. With either definition, mind is indeed a holistic entity. However only the former definition of mind corresponds to what Davies and Ryle refer to as mind. A 'strategy of information processing' *is* like the plot of a novel, and can be related to the brain in a manner somewhat similar to the way the plot of a novel can be related to the collection of symbols in which it is written. For such a definition of mind one can readily accept the point Ryle makes about confusion of categories; and with careful use of language one can avoid the confusion of high-level and low-level categories, to which Ryle refers.

But this has not unravelled all the perplexity about mind/body relationships. Whether we are explicit about it or not, most of us think of mind not only as objective strategies of information processing, but also as a collection of subjective experiences. The relation of *those experiences* to the brain with which they are associated is not merely one of levels of abstraction. Possibly a better analogy might be between the written symbols which make up a novel (as equivalent to 'brain') and the plot of that novel which happens also to be the autobiographical story of one's very own life, written by oneself (as equivalent to 'mind').

The point of this new analogy, a point which appears to have completely escaped both Davies and Ryle, is that the holistic entity we call mind is actually the intimate centre of subjective personal being for someone, not just a high level (but still objective) derivative of his physical being, like nationality (or even 'personality'). An essential part of the conundrum about mind/body relations is therefore the contrast between a description of a physical entity from the outside, and the description of how it 'feels to be' that very thing from which outsiders make their objective descriptions. No amount of juggling of levels of description or abstraction can, in itself, unravel this central core of the age-old philosophical problem.

9.3 *The mind/body problem: origin in the paradoxes of self-referring statements?*

Another argument used by Paul Davies to make the mind/body problem seem less metaphysical and mysterious concerns 'self-referring statements'.[10] We are familiar with the paradox which the ancient Greeks invented, when they conceived the idea of a Cretan who said 'All Cretans are liars'. Such a statement is paradoxical because it is impossible to decide whether it is true or false. As a generality, such paradoxes tend to arise when a statement refers to itself (e.g. 'This statement is false.') The most detailed formal analysis of this situation is the Incompleteness Theorem of Kurt Gödel, which proves that for any self-contained set of axioms, there are always statements which can neither be proved true nor proved false. These are the self-referring statements from which the paradoxes arise.

Paul Davies points out, correctly, that all our language about mind consists of self-referring statements. When we talk about mind, or consciousness, or their contents, it is like a computer programme which refers not only to something defined in the programme, but also to the computer itself, or even its power supply (for instance). In the case of computer programming, a basic principle is that it is hierarchical – that is, when it is required to undertake a *large* task, the task is progressively broken into smaller tasks, and yet smaller sub-tasks. At the small-scale level of the sub-task, it is not allowed to refer to tasks higher in the hierarchy than just those specified for that level. If one does, indecision, paradox, or confusion results. Davies suggests that some confusion of levels similar to this underlies our inability to understand mind. He writes that [Gödel's theorem] 'has been taken to imply that one can never understand one's own mind completely',[11] and that 'in . . . these attempts to grope towards a better understanding of the self, is the convolution of hierarchical levels'.[12]

But this misses the point again. If the enigma of the mind/brain relationship arose simply from the self-referential aspect of our language about mind, it would be confusing, but once the confusion had been properly dissected, would be no more puzzling than a badly-written computer programme, or one of the well-known paradoxes to which Davies refers. But I assert that the subjective qualities such as redness exist in some sense whether we refer to them or not. Otherwise one would have to deny that a dumb person, who never learned to speak of colours, could ever have the experience of redness. Once again the real confusion lies in the assumptions implicit in the definition of mental terms. That is, does the definition assume from the start that mental qualities are objective (namely, strategies of information processing, in this case, self-referring strategies)? Or does the person making the definition 'bite the bullet', and recognize, firmly and explicitly, that what is referred to is, in its very nature, subjective?

This is the real point of the arguments in favour of a dualism of subjective and objective. In proposing such a dualism, I am not suggesting, as Davies does, that we should actually try to understand the relation of mind to brain, in the way we understand the causal interaction of two events in the objective world. That relationship is, to me, an unfathomable metaphysical mystery, the most fundamental of all miracles. All I am proposing is that we actually accept that there is such an internal world of subjective qualities in each of us, whether or not we can understand that world in terms of our comprehension of the material world; that we accept this as a fact, a subjective fact.

In the discussions I have had with various scientific colleagues on this topic, a total impasse frequently results. This, as noted earlier, may be because we have now such limited language for subjective realities. But I also suspect that there is even an element of active denial of the primary facts of that subjective world, simply because it cannot be comprehended in materialist terms.

9.4 *Conscious awareness: origin in human language functions?*

Another way of giving a tangible account of mind and consciousness is to emphasize the close relationship of these to human language, and the related social environment in which language is acquired. This link is presented in a variety of ways by scholars of quite different orientation. B. F. Skinner, as mentioned earlier, believed that '"the mind", "consciousness", "self-knowledge" or "awareness" are no more than metaphors or constructs which became possible only when the species acquired verbal behavior . . .' Arguments against Skinner's rejection of any terminology which smacks of mentalism have already been given and will not be reiterated.

From an entirely different perspective, Alexander Luria[13] also suggests that mind originates in society, the most profound social influence being language and the abstractions and generalizations it embodies. He and his colleagues supported this view by interview and semi-formal testing of various groups of people in Uzbekistan, shortly after the 1917 revolution. From comparisons of people varying in their degree of socialization, education and literacy he came to the conclusion that many of the habits and forms of thought which we take for granted, apparently as universal norms, arise as a result of the social environment. For instance, illiterate Uzbek peasants are unlikely to name geometrical shapes as triangles, circles, etc., but are more likely to refer to them as 'a tent' or 'a plate' respectively. No doubt this result depends on the linguistic experience of the various groups Luria studied. At a higher cognitive level, Luria found that our habitual patterns of generalizing things into traditional concepts, and our habits ·of syllogistic inference, were quite foreign to these people. They were quite unable to make logical inferences in abstract, when the subject was remote from their own personal experience. These cognitive differences between the groups studied by Luria also probably depended largely on the different habits of language used, and related thought patterns in the different groups. Luria and colleagues referred to their studies as anti-Cartesian experiments: Summing up their findings, Luria considered 'critical self-awareness to be the final product of socially determined psychological development, rather than its primary starting point, as Descartes' ideas would have us believe'.[14] As quoted, this seems unobjectionable. But it should also be noted that 'critical self-awareness' is a highly organized form of subjective inner life. Luria's conclusion does not mean that the subjective inner world *per se*, even in much less highly organized form, depends for its existence on society and language. In unravelling the relationship of language (and social conditioning) to consciousness we have to distinguish organized subjective inner life from subjective inner life *per se*, that is regardless of its organization. This is a special case of the issue of definition first raised in chapter 3, where mind can be given either an objective definition, as a strategy of information processing, or can be defined as essentially subjective.

The viewpoint expressed by Luria has quite wide currency, and not only amongst scientists. The 'post-liberal' theologian Don Cupitt writes in very similar tones to Luria:

What are these beings to do with themselves? They talk grandly of freedom, but they have much less of it than they suppose. The great social facts – above all language – which have made it possible for them to become conscious beings with subjective experience, have simultaneously fixed tight limits to the range of their thought and action. They are able to communicate, and probably even to think, only by conforming to the extremely detailed requirements of socially generated communication systems, whose nature they do not fully understand. They cannot break free.[15]

Another author who emphatically asserts the close relation between language and consciousness is the well-known neuroscientist and Nobel laureate J. C. Eccles. His argument is part of a defence of the philosophical position that mind and brain are quite different and independent entities, each capable of causing things to happen, and capable of causal interaction with each other. His statements about the relation between consciousness and language derive largely from recent research on hemispheric differences in humans, especially that research which has studied patients in whom the corpus callosum, connecting the two hemispheres, has been severed. He writes:

There is . . . strong evidence that we have to associate the dominant hemisphere i.e. the speech hemisphere, with the amazing property of being able to give rise to the conscious experiences of perception, and also to receive from them in the carrying out of willed movements. Moreover, the most searching investigation of commissurotomy patients discloses that the minor hemisphere does not have in the smallest degree this amazing property of being in liaison with the self-conscious mind of the subject in respect of either giving or receiving.[16]

Eccles is even more specific than this. He identifies consciousness with just certain parts of the left hemisphere. Regarding the cortex as a repeated series of rather similar modules, like the repeated micro-circuits in a computer, he believes that only certain cortical modules accomplish the liason between neural activity and self-conscious mind. The self-conscious mind is made aware of this neural activity like a radio transmitter/receiver. Those cortical modules which have this 'transcendent property' . . . 'may be likened to a radio transmitter-receiver unit'.[17] Any interplay between the self-conscious mind and the right (non-dominant) hemisphere must, according to Eccles, rely primarily on the relevant modules in the left (dominant) hemisphere, the interchange of information from the right hemisphere being accomplished via the corpus callosum, the major pathway connecting the two hemispheres.

This view was not espoused by Roger Sperry, the neuropsychologist who did some of the most incisive experimentation on commissurotomy patients. He views the 'non-dominant' hemisphere also as having a direct role in consciousness, though the metaphysical nature of that relation is not of the radical interactionist dualist type put forward by Eccles. Actually Eccles makes several obvious mistakes. A factual mistake is that it is now well known that there are aspects of language for which the right hemisphere is dominant. Many of the more complex aspects of linguistic communication actually depend on the right hemisphere. Examples are the appreciation of prosody (the character-istic rise and fall of the voice which convey emotional tone amongst other things), and the appreciation of humour in language, or of metaphorical uses. A more philosophical mistake is Eccles' failure to accept that there can be elements of 'consciousness' which do not depend on written or spoken language. The enormous potential for communication without the more strictly linguistic forms of communi-cation can be easily illustrated by referring to the artistry of the stars of the silent films, such as Chaplin. There are also on record accounts of commissurotomy patients, who (or at least one hemisphere of whom) are deprived of access to the normal form of communication, but yet can use gestural language very expressively. Eccles spends scarcely any time dealing with this objection. Most of the evidence he refers to as showing that consciousness is related specifically to the dominant hemisphere is obtained using verbal means of responding, which naturally would be related mainly to that hemisphere. Other ways of assessing the experience of a commissurotomy patient, using non-verbal responses, are possible, and give a quite different view of this question. Thus Eccles is suggesting a dualist metaphysical relation between what, according to the views developed here, is a specific and highly organized configuration of the subjective world, rather than with subjectivity *per se*.

Admittedly it is arguable that the 'self-conscious mind' is largely reliant on the left hemisphere, because the concepts of 'mind' or of 'a person' may be closely linked to the linguistic representation of those concepts (though there are scientists who suggest that the wide integration needed to represent these global concepts can be accomplished better by the right hemisphere).[18] However, it may be rather too exact to draw a sharp distinction between 'consciousness' and 'self-consciousness', as Eccles' argument does. Certainly it seems strange to relate the metaphysical interplay between mind and brain to just the left hemisphere, and indeed to a small part of that hemisphere when, in terms of both structure and electrical functioning, the differences between the two hemispheres are apparently quite small quantitative ones rather than categorical and qualitative ones.

Moreover one may observe that to link consciousness too closely to language denies the consciousness of deaf and dumb people, and of infants prior to acquisition of language. This seems self-centered in a manner similar to the Catholic Church at about the time of the Renaissance, insisting that the only true world view was one with the planet earth at its centre.

In conclusion, the close relation between language (or social conditioning) and consciousness, emphasized by both Luria and Eccles (though in quite different ways) depends on identifying language with highly organized aspects of consciousness rather than with subjective experience in an more basic elemental form.

9.5 *Consciousness: dependent absolutely on memory?*

Paul Davies raises the relation between the facility of memory and the existence of the self. He writes: 'It is ... largely through memory that we achieve a sense of personal identity, and recognize ourselves as the *same* individual from day to day.'[19] I have no difficulty with this statement. However it does allow us to define more precisely the nature of the dualism of subjective and objective. Memory is a complex organized mechanism, enabling a complex pattern of information processing by which events of an instant leave their lasting imprint. The counterpart to this is an equally complex subjective whole, which integrates many types of subjective impressions, over a long period of time, enduring and developing over a lifetime. But the fact that there is a close relationship of the organized memory mechanism to the organized subjective integrity does not mean that the very notion of the subjective side of our dualism *per se* is dependent on the memory mechanism.

Davies refers to the 'self' in a severely amnesic person, suggesting that, in this case, 'the whole notion of *himself* as distinct from the perceived world would be chaotic'.[20] How does Davies *know* this? Both language and memory are necessary vehicles for the *outward exhibition* to other people of the subjective side of our existence. But, given that one has accepted the existence of that subjective world, it is not impossible to conceive of its existence without language and memory.

Consider a dream. One of the clearest facts about dreams is that the memory of them tends to dissipate very quickly after we awake. Very often we are left with no memory for the content of the dream, only the memory that we *had* a dream. The transience of the memory for dreams has no bearing on the subjective existence of dreams.

Consider a more extreme example. In some psychophysical experiments, a stimulus (for instance a visual image) is presented for a brief fraction of a second (typically less than one tenth of a second), and the experimental subject is asked to describe afterwards what he or she saw of this evanescent image. As a modification of this experiment, a 'masking' stimulus of a totally different nature is presented very shortly afterwards. The finding is that, for masking stimuli presented within a fraction of a second after the initial stimulus, the amount of detail which can be reported about the initial stimulus is significantly less than without the masking stimulus. Moreover, masking stimuli presented a moment later than this do not impair the report of the details of the image. Within the brief moment of less than one second, something exists, available to the experimental subject, on which he can base his description. This result seems to imply that the subjective image of the original stimulus 'exists' (and can be interfered with) for only a fraction of a second after it is presented. The duration of this 'eidetic image' is not much longer than that time-slice of about 100 msec, which psychophysicists find to be the shortest moment of perceived temporal duration. Enduring memory seems not to be necessary to imply the existence of the subjective world. Logically speaking, if one accepts this, one must accept the existence of the subjective world even when it lasts an infinitesimal moment, independent of the most short-lived of all conceivable memories.

Subjective states without language do not stretch the imagination too far. Subjective states without any memory are rather more strange. But neither of these is as strange as some of the concepts we have to accept from modern physics. There have actually been major attempts to bring the concept of mind within reach of science by reference to twentieth-century physics, especially quantum theory and the theory of relativity. These attempts have both already been mentioned. Let us consider them in more detail.

9.6   *The mind and twentieth-century physics: (a) Quantum theory*

It will be recalled that from the viewpoint of the quantum theory our picture of reality is dependent on the act of observation as much as on what might exist independent of the observation. According to quantum physics 'observable reality', at least at the level of subatomic particles, does not exist until an observation is made. Without the act of observation the position or velocity of a particle do not exist as single measures, but rather as a 'cloud' of values representing the distribution of statistical likelihoods that a particle can be detected in a particular state. An alternative way of expressing this is to envisage that a large number of different realities coexist, and the act of observation forces this cloud to 'crystalize out' upon one of the many versions of reality. This occurs at the level of fundamental particles. But one can easily conceive of amplifying devices such that, by the act of observation, a much more obvious macroscopic reality is brought into being, chosen from a cloud of alternative macroscopic realities. A particularly graphic paradox, following this line, is due to Schrödinger. He envisages a quantum event where the act of observation could create, as 'observed realities', one of two states, with each having a 50% probability. By various amplifying devices, one of these states could lead to the breaking of a vial of cyanide, which kills Schrödinger's pet cat. According to quantum theory, before the observation is made, the subatomic quantum event exists in two equally likely states. Therefore one must also conclude that, before the observation is made, the cat also exists in two equally probable states, one alive, the other dead. With this as an illustration, the argument goes that 'objective reality' does not exist. Rather, such reality as does exist, is created by the act of observation. Reality is therefore as much subjective as objective.

What are we to make of this argument? For a start, quantum theory states that reality is statistical. Thus, whether or not Schrodinger's cat is dead or alive is a statistical matter. But it is a very artificial example to chose two states having exactly equal likelihoods. In most situations the macroscopic event that occurs in practice is the one favoured overwhelmingly by the statistics. Thus, after amplification there is likely to be one overwhelmingly likely reality, rather than an ambiguous live/dead cat.

However, this is not the real issue. It is that the distinction between subjective and objective in the argument from quantum physics is not the same as the difference between these terms which has been emphasized so far in this book. By the 'act of observation' in the preceding paragraphs, is meant 'a causal interaction with a detecting device'. That device might be a physicist's elaborate equipment or, if amplified adequately, a human sense organ. But whichever of these it is, the interaction is actually an objective one, not a subjective one. The observer looking with his eye could equally well be replaced by an instrument. The actual moment when the observer takes in the subjective fact that Schrödinger's cat is alive rather than dead may be long after the actual causal interaction which crystallized that event into reality. That subjective appreciation may, for instance, be the time when he first looks at a photograph of the event taken many months earlier. And that photograph can be seen by many other people who reach the same conclusion, after studying it. Thus, in the terms in which we have so far been discussing the difference between subjective and objective, the ambiguous realities of quantum physics are all quite objective. Davies states that 'the central paradox of quantum theory . . . is the unique role played by the mind in determining reality'.[21] I believe this is a quite false interpretation, whichever of the two definitions of mind is adopted. The confusion comes from two different definitions of the word 'objective': either as 'object-like', which quantum events are not, or as 'capable of public demonstration', which they certainly are.

9.7 The mind and twentieth-century physics: (b) Relativity theory

Another way in which modern physics has been brought to bear on the concept of mind is in relation to the theory of relativity. According to this theory, various measurements, such as elapsed time and distance, are not stable characteristics of observers and objects. Their values differ according to the velocity of relative movement between what is observed, and the observer. This is not just theory; it is well attested empirical fact, though the differences are very tiny except at relative speeds approaching the speed of light. The most severe paradoxes in relativity theory come from measurements of time. In some circumstances, different observers will conclude that the sequence of two events, A and B, are different. One will see A before B, another will see B before A, while a third may see them as synchronous. However, it should be pointed out that these paradoxes only occur when the events are occurring so far away that (even with travel at the speed of light) the observer cannot influence them.

The tenor of relativity theory is to ignore the subjective notion of time which, in some mysterious way, is like a river flowing past us. Instead time is viewed as a dimension like space, in which past, present and future all coexist. The subjective viewpoint of the observer with his internal point of reference, and sense of time passing, is abolished from this viewpoint. In the actual experiments (or 'thought experiments') of relativity the timing of events is of course recorded, objectively, by a clock of some sort. But the same result would be obtained if one were to rely on subjective, introspective timing (e.g. such as Galileo must have been aware of it when he timed, with his pulse, the swinging candelabra in the church in Pisa). The relativistic space traveller would have aged less (subjectively as well as objectively) compared with his twin brother who remained on earth, just as the clocks he took with him on his voyage would have registered less time than those on earth.

Thus the implications of relativity theory are the same for objective as for subjective time. This is perhaps not surprising, since the 'flow' of both subjective and objective time derives from the same, most fundamental of physical laws, the law of increasing entropy. This can be suggested because this is the only physical law which is asymmetrical with regard to the direction of time. All clocks we have can thus be regarded as charting, objectively, the increase over time of the entropy of the system that makes up the clock. Likewise, our subjective sense of time passing can usefully be regarded as deriving in a parallel manner from the increase of entropy in the system which makes up our brains. Relativity theory has the appearance of emphasizing the objective view of time, as a dimension like space. The subject apparently has no necessary location or movement in this dimension. Nevertheless, since the time paradoxes of relativity theory apply as much to subjective as to objective time, they are compatible with the parallelistic view of subjective and objective time from the ideas and experiments of relativity. In other circumstances, however, as discussed in section 8.2, the structure of subjective and objective time are not identical. One is a transformation of the other rather than being strictly congruent with it.

9.8 The mind and twentieth-century physics: (c) Penrose and the incomputability of consciousness

Penrose's essay on the relation between mathematics, physical reality and the mind[22] has at its heart two main intuitions. One of these is a mathematical idea deriving from the Incompleteness theorem of

Gödel. One way of expressing this is that within any set of axioms, there are always true statements which actually cannot be proved true. The other intuition is an entirely subjective one of Penrose's (referred to above) that a mathematician's insight into a problem is often more decisive in discovering a mathematical truth than is the slavish following of an algorithm. From these two, Penrose suggests that consciousness itself is not computable, and cannot, even in principle, be realized by any conceivable algorithm carried out on a computing device. Instead, Penrose speculates that consciousness may be the product of fundamental physical principles which are at present entirely unknown to scientists.

Penrose clearly recognizes the centrality of subjective processes for consciousness; but by suggesting that consciousness can in principle be given a rational explanation in terms of physical principles (even if they are quite unknown at present), he fails to make the metaphysical distinction between the world of subjectivity and objectivity. He fails to realize that there is a sharp and irreducible dividing line between external objects and the subjective entity one actually *is*. I believe that inferences about one or the other should be kept separate. As already mentioned (section 9.3) I believe that the quite miraculous dualism between subjectivity and objectivity is one of the given premises we should just graciously accept. We cannot explain it.

10

'Epistemological' Dualism: The Nature of the Independence of Mind and Brain

We are now ready to confront the nature of the relation between the subjective and the objective as a generality. I have suggested once or twice a fundamental dualism between these two, between mind and brain, between the private subjective process of 'introspection' and the publically verifiable process of 'inspection'. There appears to be some sort of independence of the two sides of this dualism. Can we define this independence more precisely?

10.1 Epistemological independence of introspection and inspection

In what sense are introspection and inspection 'independent'? Certainly introspection is not independent of the physical brain which embodies those experiences available to introspection. But introspection and inspection appear to be quite independent as methods of knowing reality. Does independence of the means of knowing reality mean different realities? It could be argued that if there be any reality to grasp, it is not affected by the method we use to grasp that reality. Alternatively, it could be argued that we cannot hope to know the essence of such a fundamental reality, but only how it appears by a particular means of knowing.

Let us take some concrete examples. When an object moves towards us, it may first of all be seen in the distance, and eventually come within our reach, so that we can grasp it in our hands. In this case we co-ordinate information from two different sense organs, sight and touch, and invariably (except in small infants) reach the conclusion that the object we initially could only see was the same one we soon came to grasp with our hands. It could be said that this co-ordination of impressions from different senses is similar to the multivariate statistical computations used to validate the various constructs used in social science. The construct is said to be valid because a variety of independent measures intercorrelate. But when we discussed this earlier (section 4.4) we found the method was commonly found to need revision, and was also flawed in principle. The preferable way of validating a concept was to show the logical relation between the different ways in which we come to know of it. In the case of the approaching object we do acquire, as we grow from infancy, a logically coherent way of describing space, the permanence of objects in space and the characteristics of movement of objects in that space. With this theory of movement in space, it is possible to deduce that an object in the distance, moving in a certain direction, may come within reach of our own hands. This is a far tighter epistemological structure than merely the correlation between a moving visual image and, a moment later, the tactile impression it makes on our hand. Such a tight logical structure allows us to postulate the existence of the object in a far more solid way than mere correlation of impressions received by different senses.

Take another example. Physicists have taught us to believe in a potent but intangible force called gravity, generated between massive objects, in proportion to the product of their masses, and in inverse relation to the square of the distance between them. We can know about gravity in many ways, for instance from the movement of the moon, or from the daily and monthly fluctuation of sea levels we call the tides, or from the fall of heavy objects to the surface of the earth. If we had just the first two of those pieces of correlated information, we could not postulate the concept of gravity. Indeed the correlation between the tides and the movement of the moon was well known to the ancients, although the concept of gravity was quite unknown to them. Gravity became a concept to be reckoned with only when, following Newton's assumption that it had the properties mentioned above, the relationships between mass, distance and forces of attraction could then all be derived by logical inference. If correlation alone was to allow us to decide on the reality of natural concepts, we might be tempted to include the periods of a woman's menstruation in our definition of such concepts, because they might often correlate with the timing of the tides, or the movements of the moon.

Now take the more global case of the problem of the mind-brain relationship, and its bearing on the fundamental nature of reality. We appear to have two ways of knowing reality, introspection and inspection. In a number of instances, which vary in precision, we can establish correlations between what we know by introspection (e.g. the quality of 'redness') and by inspection (visual pigments in the retina sensitive to a particular range of light wavelengths, and activating certain pathways in the brain necessary for colour vision). But we are totally incapable of explaining the subjective quality of redness in terms of the information we have revealed by inspection of the eye and the visual pathways. The subjective phenomenon of redness is logically independent of the visual physiological processes despite the fact that they correlate with that subjective phenomenon. Many other examples could be given corresponding to the cases discussed previously. Since all we have are correlations, we are poorly placed to assert that introspection and inspection are different ways of knowing about mind/brain as a single reality. Monism – the belief in a single reality – is therefore by no means compelled by the correlations of information from different sources which we have at our disposal. A form of dualism is at least plausible.

The insistence that the two metaphysically different ways of knowing reality are still both telling us about the same single reality, might be justified by 'Occam's razor', the principle of philosophical parsimony. Such insistence is also a strong way of combatting the interactionist form of dualism such as espoused by J. C. Eccles, in which mind and brain are separate to the point of being independent causal prime movers. But such monism does obscure the profound dualism of ways of knowing. As we have seen, this has led to the neglect of the subjective, conceptual side of our intellect, leading in the extreme, to a raw and naive materialism, cut off from the subjective roots from which, historically and in the development of each individual, that side of our intellect grew. The choice between these two versions of metaphysics would seem to be a free choice, which we can make according to what we want to emphasize. There are advantages of both choices. I have emphasized a form of dualism which stresses the great differences between ways of knowing, to the point of saying there is no way of proving that they tell of a single reality. One is reminded of Marshall McLuhan's oft-quoted remark: 'The medium is the message.' This was originally a comment on the way in which technologies of mass communication determine the style in which most of us become constrained to think. Perhaps it could apply also to metaphysics. Mechanistic forms of communication encourage us to think there is nothing other than mechanism. The 'way-of-knowing' is the most important part of 'what-is-known'.

Jacques Monod, despite his clear statement of the scientific postulate that 'nature is objective' also, when arguing at a deeper level, realizes the hold of such dualism on human thinking. He writes:

Brain and spirit are ideas no more synonymous today than in the seventeenth century. Objective analysis obliges us to see that this seeming duality is an illusion; but an illusion so deeply rooted in our being that it would be vain to hope ever to dissipate it in the immediate awareness of subjectivity, or to learn to live emotionally and morally without it. And besides, why should one have to? What doubt can there be of the presence of the spirit within us?[1]

At present we should call this dualism 'epistemological dualism' because it is a dualism of ways of knowing reality. However, I do not want to overstate the case for epistemological dualism too strongly here. I have already suggested (section 4.2.) that, in the initial attempts at describing a completely new realm of phenomena, there are no *a priori* rules governing which aspects of what we observe should be emphasized. Thus, this preference of mine is possibly a semantic choice, rather than one forced by strict logical considerations.

P. S. Churchland provides an example. She writes: 'It is doubtful that the generalizations and categories of folk psychology . . . carve Nature at her joints'.[2] This concise analogy confuses the issue, and begs the question: How should nature be carved? How should one formulate one's most basic descriptive language? If one is talking about carving joints, it may seem natural, at the Sunday dinner table, to separate bone from bone, carving nature at the joints in such a manner that the joints lose their integrity. But the Designer of Limbs spent far more effort on the details of those joints than on the lengths of bone which connect them together. From the viewpoint of design of the locomotor system, it might seem more natural to preserve the integrity of the joints and divide the bones.

When there are no guidelines at a more fundamental level, the person describing the phenomena has a completely free choice. The validity of the manner of describing the world then comes to depend *a posteriori* on the uses we can demonstrate for that form of description. This basic principle ('If it works, use it') must be applied not only to choice of descriptive languages in the more descriptive aspects of science. It must also be applied to metaphysical descriptions of the nature of reality, because certainly in this case there are also 'no more fundamental guidelines'. Thus, while I make my preferred choice of the basic constructs for describing reality, I am tolerant of those who would prefer a monistic description of the mind/brain entity, provided that they admit that their choice is also a preference, rather than something that is strictly forced by evidence and logic. We all have our agendas, hidden or otherwise, and the emphasis given by monism has some associated advantages, as mentioned above.

It is worth recapping some of the examples by which the epistemological dualism was explicated. On one side of the dualism, mind consists of a collection of subjective qualities and impressions. On the objective side this corresponds to strategies of information processing (which can be displayed by behavioural experiments) and to underlying brain processes which have formal similarities to these strategies. The unravelling of the relation of behavioural observations to brain mechanisms is no different in principle from the rest of science (e.g. the relation of the behaviour of gases to the dynamics of the atomic and molecular behaviour). But the relation between the subjective qualities and impressions, and brain mechanisms is something totally different. Correlations may be established, but these cannot be rationally explained. The quality of redness cannot be defined or explained no matter how much visual physiology we learn. The values we place on experiences of pleasure and suffering cannot be validated from physiology, no matter how much we know about the escape reflexes and avoidance learning mediated by painful stimuli. We may be able to explain from knowledge of brain processes why the subjective present lasts only about 100 msec, but we will not be able to explain why our existence appears to be so highly focussed at a particular region of the vast time continuum.

Thus we have seen that subjective qualities such as redness exist in some sense 'independent' of the objective world. We have seen that subjective qualities such as redness are not logically derivable from the objective world but are logically independent of it. They also may not be dependent for their very existence on the organization of the material world, since the subjective world can exist without influence of the cerebral organizations underlying the obvious functions of either language and memory. (Cerebral organization certainly affects the organization of subjective reality, but there is no way of proving that it affects its very existence.) Can we define this independence yet more precisely?

10.2 *Causal independence of the subjective and objective worlds*

Epistemological dualism is a rather mild form of dualism, compared with the interactionist dualism of J. C. Eccles. The difference between these two dualisms seems to lie mainly in whether the two sides of the dualism are independent to the extent that they can have causal influence on each other. This issue requires explicit discussion.

Are subjective qualities such as redness *causally* independent of the objective world, such as visual stimuli or physical processes in the visual systems of the brain? That question hangs critically on the definition of 'cause'. John Stuart Mill defines a cause as 'the antecedent or combination of antecedents upon which an effect is invariably and unconditionally dependent'.[3] At first sight this seems a purely empirical definition of cause, which could be established just by making appropriate observations and correlating them. However, as is often said, correlation does not imply causation. Mills explains carefully that his definition of causation requires more than mere correlation, however consistent it be, otherwise one would conclude that day caused night and night caused day. The key word in his definition is 'unconditionally'. By this, he means 'as long as the present constitution of things endures', in other words as long as the ultimate laws of nature hold. Thus, an slightly changed alternative definition of causation is: 'The cause of an effect is the antecedent or combination of antecedents which, by deduction from ultimate physical principles (if we could ever know them) are necessary and sufficient for the effect to occur.' This is a definition based on the coordinated reasoning within a theory of causation.

Returning to the issue of causation between brain and mind, we can establish correlations between the two; but since subjective qualities cannot be derived from objective facts about brain processes by any conceivable reasoning we cannot explain that correlation in terms of ultimate physical laws of nature. Therefore, if Mill's definition is adopted, light of a certain wavelength falling on the retina cannot be said to cause a sensation of redness, because by no means can the sensory quality of redness be inferred (by reference to physical priciples) from the fact of light striking the retina and producing a number of objective changes in the brain.

What about causation in the opposite direction, that is, mind causally influencing matter? Do subjective states have a causal influence on the objective world? B. F. Skinner argues that mentalistic terms are quite redundant in explanations of objective behaviour. He writes

A British statesman recently asserted that the key to crime in the streets was 'frustration'. Young people mug and rob because they feel frustrated. But why do they feel frustrated? One reason may be that many of them are unemployed, either because they do not have the education needed to get jobs, or because the jobs are not available. To solve the problem of street crime, therefore, we must change the schools and the economy. But what role is played in all this by frustration? . . . Since many of the events which must be taken into account in explaining behaviour are associated with bodily states that can be felt, what is felt may serve as a clue to contingencies. But the feelings are not the contingencies and cannot replace them as causes.[4]

Here I partly agree with Skinner. Relationships of causation must be established entirely in the objective world. That is, they can be established only between things that are directly observable, or securely inferable from observations, like gravity. Frustration is however an ambiguous term, like many psychological terms. The word can represent an inner subjective quality, in which case I, like Skinner, believe it has no part in a causal explanation. Alternatively it could be carefully defined as a strategy of information processing, in which case it could be securely inferred in objective terms, and could then be part of a causal chain, just as the definition of a computer programme may be needed in explaining the performance of some modern piece of machinery. Once again, the issue of whether mind is causally effective depends on matters of definition, the definition of mental terms, and the definition of cause.

The maxim has already been mentioned that 'correlation does not imply causation', and this maxim is often repeated and just as often forgotten, especially in biological and medical research. If it is true, then no amount of empirical demonstration of correlation will be sufficient to prove causality. Something more is needed than mere correlation. Thus for Mill's definition of causation to be satisfactory requires logical necessity as well as constant correlation. In framing this definition, it should be noted that one is also rejecting the vernacular usage of the word cause. What are the consequences of this choice for one's view of the relationship of subjective to objective?

Since, as we have already seen, subjective experiences are not logically derivable from objective processes in the brain (though they undoubtedly may correlate with them) we must also keep the mental events and brain processes separate in considerations of causal interaction. Thus one must conclude that there can be no causal interaction between mind and brain in either direction. Yet I have also been arguing that both are valid, complementary forms of reality. Therefore one has to conceive of a form of relation between mind and matter categorically different from 'causal'. For this relation I use the term 'parallelism'.

This may seem a very strange manner of reasoning. Let me give an example to illustrate how it might work. Take a complex piece of behaviour in which a person takes in certain information with his eyes, engages in lengthy processes of thought, and eventually emits an appropriate behavioural response. Such a sequence involves both mental (subjective) and brain (objective) events. According to the view I have just proposed, causation, in the strict sense, applies to the relation between the various physical processes in the brain – such as the stimulus, the processing of the stimulus by the visual system of the brain, the physical events (less well defined) which underlie thought, and those in the motor systems which generate the objective behaviour. But one cannot say that the physical events in the visual systems of the brain *cause* subjective visual sensations; nor that there is causal interaction between the physical events associated with thought and the subjective experience of that thought; nor that the subjective experience of volition is the cause of the behavioural response. These relations are of a type categorically different from causation, a correlation which cannot be derived logically by any kind of inference. It is this relation, which may seem quite strange because of its metaphysical implications, which is denoted by the term 'parallelism'.

10.3 The subjective world as a parallel to the physical world as a whole

At a recent conference on consciousness and the brain[5] it was noted by commentators that none of the participants were of the 'interactionist dualist' persuasion, who view mind and matter as separate stuffs causally independent, and capable of interacting with each other. There were also no overt behaviourists, though some of the participants retained some version of that philosophy. The overall consensus was that consciousness is inherently subjective, and can be accessed only by obtaining subjective reports, not from third persons, nor by observation of behaviour. This is an important trend. Part I of the present work was written exactly to emphasize this, by showing that our scientific heritage has depended, in part, on exactly that realm of subjectivity.

However, another important aspect of this conference, which can also be found in the writings of the philosopher John Searle, one of the participants, is the statement that 'mental phenomena are a product of the brain'. This seems straightforward enough. However, in his Reith Lectures, Searle gives a fuller statement, that

> mental phenomena, all mental phenomena, whether conscious or unconscious, visual, auditory, pains, tickles, itches, thoughts, indeed all of our mental life, are caused by processes going on in the brain.[6]

Note here that mental phenomena can be unconscious as well as conscious. Thus, as for Freud's view of the unconscious mind, Searle must be defining mind in part at least as a strategy of information processing, that is, as something in the objective world which need not be subjectively accessible. Note also the interchangeable use of 'all mental phenomena' and 'all our mental life'. In the statement that 'all' of 'our' mental life arises in the brain, there is a significant issue. We have already seen that Searle thinks that the mind/body problem is to be solved just by unravelling the use of high- and low-level descriptions. But in this statement he is implicitly denying that any configuration of matter other than 'our' brain can be associated with consciousness.

The reasoning of the preceding pages suggests that this might not be true. The actual overt display of consciousness depends on memory and language (amongst other faculties), and these depend on mechanisms in our brains, with language being distinctively human. But one cannot deny consciousness to someone just because they have no language; and, following the above arguments, it would be dangerous to deny someone's consciousness to someone because they have profound amnesia (though undoubtedly the 'form' consciousness must take, and its overt display, are greatly affected by this memory impairment). Thus it would be unwise to deny some aspect of subjectivity to other mammals, just because we cannot communicate with them; nor to birds, reptiles, amphibia or fishes. If we look for an animal in which there is no trace of memory, we would be looking at a very simple life form; but our argument suggests that we cannot deny some element of subjectivity to even that life form. The argument can easily be taken right back to plants, bacteria, viruses, and to inanimate matter as a whole. The general point is this: that consciousness as we know it, and communicate it, is dependent on the organization of our brains. But there are many other organized forms of matter in the universe. They may not have the properties that readily display overtly a subjective world within them; and we cannot guess which, if any, are the integrated portions of matter in which those subjectivities become focussed. But neither can we categorically deny the existence of such subjectivity in forms of organized matter other than our own (i.e. presumably human) brains. Consciousness as we know it is too limited a concept for such a profound issue. Indeed, since all matter is in some sense organized, as is the universe as a whole, one possibility is that subjectivity, in some unknown form, is also contained in the universe as a whole; and that various organized fragments of it contain fragments of a universal consciousness.

Another writer who has recently entered this discussion is Roger Penrose. In contrast to Searle, who suggests that subjective states are high level consequences of the computations occurring during brain activity, Penrose suggests that they are non-computable, though still a high-level product of physical activity in the brain. As mentioned in section 9.8, he derives the non-computability of mind in part from various arguments related to Gödel's theorem. He recognizes the problem that consciousness, being a global attribute of brains (or, apparently, certain parts or certain brains), cannot be a local product of any of its parts. In a lecture in Dunedin in April 1993 he speculated that quantum effects might be involved in unifying local events in the brain to produce the global attributes of consciousness. The aspect of quantum theory referred to here is that sometimes, at the level of sub-atomic particles, regular correlations between events may occur even though they are separated sufficiently far that no causal influence could generate the correlation (even if transmitted at the speed of light). Admittedly, most of the signal-transmitting components in the nervous system are too large to be influenced by quantum effects. However, he referred to recent evidence of the fine structure of cells. The building blocks of a structure of all cells, called the cytoskeleton, are much smaller than synapses and, Penrose speculates, interaction within those elements could be influenced by quantum events.

Once again the flaw in this reasoning is that it fails to accept the essential subjectivity of mental processes. Conceivably quantum events in a complex organized structure could give it non-local properties, global attributes of the structure as a whole. But they would still be objective properties, somewhat in the way that a cloud of gas molecules has the global property of temperature. Penrose is prepared to accept the possibility that single celled animals, such as paramecium, might have some element of consciousness ('atoms of mind'), by virtue of quantum events unifying the physical state of the cytoskeleton within that cell. But it appears that he would demonstrate such an element of consciousness by the usual physical observations rather than by 'being' that consciousness, or by logical inference from our own subjective sense of being to other beings with which we have a sympathetic 'understanding' (*verstehen* in Jasper's terminology). Penrose rejects the idea that the relation of mind to brain is fundamentally mystical, a metaphysical conundrum. He seems unwilling to admit the essential subjectivity of mind, something that cannot be directly grasped unless one actually *is* the subject. To me it appears that to combine the mathematical insight that consciousness is 'non-computable' with the admission that it is also inherently subjective, accessed directly only by *being* the subject, possessing that consciousness, is tantamount to admitting the mystical nature of mind. But Penrose will not grasp that nettle. In the words of the seventeenth-century poet Thomas Traherne:

> . . . Sure men are blind
>   And can't the forcible reality
> Of things that secret are within them see.[7]

Again, I stress that the viewpoint of epistemological dualism which I advocate is not obligatory. It is one way of answering a puzzle, for which there is probably no absolute answer. In Part III we shall consider this class of puzzle more explicitly. For the present, I reiterate that for this class of question there is some merit in deciding the answer not by deduction *a priori* (which gives us no definite answer, because there is no certain initial premise), but by working out what are the logical and psychological consequences of particular viewpoints, and making the decision *a posteriori*.

10.4 An advantage of epistemological dualism over monism with regard to value systems

In section 4.2 I wrote about biological descriptions: 'Rendering the complexity of what strikes the eye into a meaningful description for others to read involves always a selection of detail. *A priori* there are no rules for such selection. They are the subjective choices of the investigator. The selective process is validated more slowly, and by more complex processes than the actual visual images recorded by the observer. In general a principle of selection of which data are relevent is validated only when the data included by the selection can be encompassed and accounted for in terms of some rational, probably explanatory framework.' In this case the selection of data relevant for a description is ultimately sanctioned *a posteriori* by its usefulness. If we go from the detail of such scientific descriptions to the choice of descriptive language for reality as a whole, we again must be guided by what actually turns out to be useful, because there can be no *a priori* guide.

It is admitted that there are advantages to a monistic metaphysics. For strictly scientific purposes we do not need psychological terms that have mentalistic implications, if we take them as implying the existence of an inner subjective world. We may however need many closely related terms which contain implications about strategies of information processing which are objectively identifiable. But, apart from these considerations, there is a great advantage, not yet mentioned for the form of psychophysical paralellism I have called epistemological dualism. In the end this is decisive in determining my preference for that variety of metaphysics.

In chapters 5 and 8 attention was drawn to the difficulty of building value systems upon a materialist framework. However, there seemed to be a link between subjective experience as such and our value judgments, because in the end all value judgments can be traced back to primary experiences with an evaluative component, pleasure, contentment, pain and suffering. Therefore, if we are going to claim that any of our schemes of values are something more than just personal choices, modifiable according to time and place, we do need to assert the reality of subjective experience, and therefore claim the validity of the subjective mentalistic implications of some psychological terms. However, for our scientific endeavours we cannot allow such mentalistic concepts to have causal efficacy, because this introduces unruly and unfathomable uncertainties into our thinking where our prime objective is to discern the regularities of nature. Hence, to preserve the possibility of building a rational scale of values it is an advantage if our fundamental framework for description becomes dualistic. The world of cause and effect, and the scientific study of it, is kept quite separate from the world of values, and the logical and other processes by which we develop them.

To sum up, there are two worlds, that of subjectivity and that of objectivity, moving in parallel. The two are utterly different ways of apprehending reality, with quite different implications. The objective world is the world in which we can undertake scientific study of the regularities of nature, but is value free. In contrast, a major implication of the subjective world, which cannot be derived in any way from the objective world, is that values actually exist, in an absolute rather than a relative sense. We may not have a precise way of knowing the completeness of that scale of values, but we can approach it in the belief that it exists in some firm absolute sense, whether or not we can ever know it. This dualistic framework, in which we can retain the merits of both the scientific enterprise and the specific subjective qualities, including those from which we derive our values, can be sustained only if first we assert the metaphysical reality of both the objective world and subjective experience as generalities. This is an assertion of metaphysical dualism.

10.5 Psychophysical parallelism and theistic belief

The relation between psychophysical parallelism and theistic belief was mentioned in the chapter 1. How does this relationship come about?

To try to answer this question it is appropriate to quote R. W. Sperry:

> Can conscious experience exist apart from the brain? Dualism, affirming the existence of independent mental and physical worlds, says 'yes' and opens the door to a conscious afterlife, and to many kinds of supernatural, paranormal and other-worldly beliefs. Monism, on the other hand, restricts its answers to one-world dimensions, and says 'no' to an independent existence of conscious mind apart from the functioning brain.[8]

The dualism referred to in this quotation is, of course the interactionist dualism advocated originally by Descartes, and also by Eccles and Popper. It should by now be clear that their philosophy is very different from that advocated here. Hence it is necessary to spell out the implications of the present philosophy for the questions referred to by Sperry.

To do this it is neccesary to point out that the relationship of mind to brain (parallelism) in the philosophy I advocate might be a specific example of a relation between mind and matter in a more general sense. One may ask whether there is any suggestion of mind associated with entities other than the human brain.

That question might refer to subhuman animals. One knows about the consciousness in another human being because humans are social animals, with the faculty of language by which they are able to reveal their inner world. This is a necessary prerequisite for detecting that they have an inner world. Therefore, one cannot exclude the presence of an inner subjective world in subhuman animals, unless they really have the same abilities at communication and the same motivation to communicate as do humans. Since they do not, one cannot exclude the presence of that inner world. Once one admits that subjectivity may exist without language or memory, the distinction between the information processing paradigms which in humans subserves their consciousness, and the information processing paradigms which exists in other animal groups (non-human mammals, lower vertebrates such as fish, octopus, insect, bacterium etc) becomes arbitrary.

One could ask the same question about a group of humans (a 'committee'), about a computer, about the non-neural parts of the human body or about those parts of the human brain (such as the cerebellum) which appear to have little to do with consciousness. No doubt the manifestations of the subjective inner world in humans is closely related to the organization of the human brain (or at least the human forebrain). Parsimoniously, one would expect that the subjective inner world of any other animal, if it could be revealed, would also bear close relation to the organization of its nervous system. The same could be said about a committee or a computer or the non-neural parts of our bodies. Do they have any corresponding consciousness? We cannot know, because, for the most part, they are not part of the organization to which the human communication faculties have access. We cannot exclude these possibilities.

It might be suggested that what we are conscious of corresponds to only a minute fraction of the organization of our material aspects. This could lead to Sperry's suggestion that consciousness is not a property of all matter. But this argument is flawed. What 'we' are conscious of (i.e. what can be identified by us as part of 'us', our person) is only a certain part of the organized matter associated with our bodies. But there may well be consciousness associated with other organized parts of our bodies (e.g. individual white blood cells), but because their physical organization is largely independent of the parts of our brain which subserve 'our' consciousness, their consciousness is not incorporated into the personal identity we more orthodoxly refer to as 'our own' consciousness. In a similar way, my own consciousness is separate from that of other people, this being related, no doubt, to the fact that our physical brains are also separate.

One could ask the same question about the physical universe as a whole. From the principle of parsimony it is plausible to extend the parallelism between mind and human brain to other brains, other organized matter, indeed to the material universe as a whole. In every case the same answer can be given, in terms of psychophysical parallelism.

Some find this difficult to accept. Polkinghorne, in discussing consciousness in a cosmological context (the 'anthropic principle' see below, chapter 14), considers whether consciousness could occur in parts of the universe where there is no carbon-based life. He suggests that this is like

> drawing a very large intellectual blank cheque on an unknown account . . . When one considers the physical complexity of the human brain (far and away the most intricately interconnected physical system we have ever encountered), it is difficult not to believe that this degree of structure is necessary as the physical substrate sustaining self-consciousness, and it is very hard to believe that there are many radically different ways of realizing naturally such a necessary complexity.[9]

Obviously my own version of psychophysical parallelism permits such alternative means of realizing consciousness, though there is plenty of room for debate here. In one respect, however, Polkinghorne must surely be wrong. How can the human brain be 'far and away the most intricately interconnected system', when it is clearly also a small component part of an intricately connected human society; and that society a tiny fragment of the immense cosmos in which it is located?

The derivation of the Deity is thus as follows. The sum total of the subjectivity in the universe would seem to correspond to a global mind, just as the sum total of subjective experiences of an individual person constitutes his/her individual mind. The universal mind or 'great consciousness' is seen as the equivalent of the traditional concept of God. Since subjectivity is the hallmark of a person, it is quite natural to personify this universal subjectivity, and to regard God as in some senses akin to a person. When we die, our brain disintegrates. As it loses its highly organized structure and function that individual mind disappears, and loses its collection of memories and other impressions gained during life. But the great consciousness continues, and possibly the fragments of the individual mind somehow merge back into it.

Few scientists now believe in an afterlife. However, many religious persons concerned with pastoral care (for instance of the dying) often regard the traditional Christian doctrine of the afterlife as critical to their ministry. This is because there is no real way in which comfort and hope can be offered to those whose life is in the process of ending, if all that can be expected is annihilation and nothingness. On the other hand, hope and comfort can realistically be offered if there can be an expectation of some sort of continuity after death. The view of God just offered is not the traditional Christian one, but nevertheless allows hope to be conveyed to the dying, in a similar way to that allowed by traditional Christian doctrine.

This concept of God does not conflict at all with scientific knowledge and laws concerning the regularities discernible in the behaviour of the natural world. In this respect it is quite different from the interactionist dualism of Eccles and Popper. Apart from these two writers, it is quite common in modern culture, as noted in Part I, to regard science and religion as implacably opposed. There are plenty of historical grounds for this belief, if one thinks of past battles between science and the established churches. But there is no necessary conflict between the views developed above about religion and the corpus of scientific tradition and knowledge.

Paul Davies[10] argues that science (and in particular physics) is now giving answers to questions that were confined to the realm of religion. My own view is that this is not so. The experiential evidence on which a religious viewpoint can be based is not technical or scientific. It is available to almost anyone, if they accept their personal existence at face value, without the distortions coming from the language adopted in a culture now dominated by science and technology.

Davies' book is concerned with the objective case for the existence of God.[11] However, this seems all beside the point for the concept of God which I have developed above. This is because nothing said so far suggests that God has an objective existence. On the contrary, God is the principle of subjectivity in the universe. Subjectivity then is the ultimate miracle. Likewise, all the traditional 'proofs' for the existence of God[12] – most of them invented by mediaeval philosophers – seem tortuous, indirect, contrived, and thoroughly unconvincing. Those arguments also are trying to establish the objective existence of God. But I believe we should be looking for the decisive evidence on that question within ourselves. From that source the case can be made simply and directly; and, once the basic conceptual jump has been made, it can be made far more convincingly.

The aspect of the traditional view of God which is most easily compatible with the viewpoint developed here is that of 'God the creator'. God in this sense is 'responsible' for initiating within time the universe with all those regularities we observe. The notion of God the creator sometimes also includes the idea of God 'sustaining' the universe by continual control. Thus God can be seen as necessary for the *continued expression* of those regular patterns of natural behaviour in the universe. As far as psychophysical parallelism goes, we have in principle no way of explaining them in rational form. We have to accept them as unexplained miracles. But one can include the miraculous synchronization of events in the subjective world of our minds with those in the objective world of our brains by the same continual sustaining action of the Deity. (But note that in Part III of this work, a quite different role is put forward for the Deity in her sustaining power.)

However, it should also be noted that the concept of the Deity worked out here has no necessary relation to the Christian concept of God. In particular, there is one aspect of the traditional Christian God which many regard as a blatant self-contradiction. This is the belief that God is both all-powerful and all-loving. Nothing has been admitted so far which leads us towards such a contradictory combination of omnipotence and benevolence. Indeed, the philosophy developed so far would be quite compatible with a theology that is quite heretical as far as Christianity is concerned. This is the belief that there are two independent Gods, one of whom is the symbolic personification of all our values, but who has actually no power to change events in the world; and the other who is all-powerful, but who is totally amoral, quite neutral where matters of human value are concerned.

This is one possibility. There is another way, however, in which the idea of a God who is the personification of good, but with little or no power, can be incorporated into some of Christian mythology. This is dealt with in Part III, where the role of mythology is discussed more fully.

10.6 *Epistemological dualism, theology and value systems*

There is one other aspect of a God derived in this way which needs to be pointed out, referring to the possibility of an absolute scale of values. Since subjective experience contains both value-neutral and value-loaded experiences, the 'god-mind', which is derived from the principle of subjectivity in the universe, must contain both. Thus the god-mind is in a sense the repository of our own fundamental sense of value. To say this is not to make any simplistic assertion that God is the source of specific commandments. Obtaining answers to specific questions of morality is related to the absolute value scale which resides in the Deity in only a very indirect way, not least because we do not have assured knowledge of that absolute scale.

Notions of God usually include the eternal or timeless existence of the Deity. This also follows from the reasoning given above. If the Deity is derived as the subjective side of a metaphysically dualist universe, which is both material and spiritual, that Deity could well be eternal, or at least as eternal as the physical universe. This idea is helpful in giving a firmer possible foundation to a scale of values.

It is of course very difficult to work out a scheme of values which can be applied in a fully consistent manner. In section 5.2 we saw that value schemes relying entirely on factual statements about what is supposed to be 'human nature' provide no real constraints to one's thinking when one really is on the horns of a difficult ethical dillema. Likewise, we found that 'relative value systems' are no more solid than quicksand. In chapter 5 we explored the idea that aesthetic and moral value systems could be based on the primary evaluative aspects of some universal experiences of pleasure and contentment, of pain and suffering. But none of these experiences endures permanently, and it is easy to argue that when the experience stops (which may mean when the person with a powerful and painful memory dies) the slate is wiped clean, and there is no trace of the former suffering. It appears that, without a metaphysical foundation for values, it is quite impossible to work out a satisfactory and consistent scheme of values; and it becomes easy to point out contradictions in any attempt.

Therefore, I want to assert the reality of the evaluative side of these experiences on some eternal scale, 'independent' of time, place and human existence. Only if that is done can one have a satisfactory metaphysical foundation for one's scheme of values.

In physics, conservation laws are statements on such an eternal scale. These are statements like: 'Matter cannot be created nor destroyed, but only transformed.' Conservation laws are the strongest way science has of asserting the reality of some entity. No doubt such a conservation law is outdated in the strange world of contemporary physics, but the principle of a conservation law, as a statement of the reality of some entity still survives.

If pleasure or pain and suffering are to have sufficient reality to give life any moral seriousness, we have to regard them as in some sense eternal, or subject to a conservation principle, and not just symbols on a blackboard to be wiped clean when life ends. In section 9.6, we considered the form which subjectivity might take in the absence of memory to connect experiences at different times. In a similar context, but with reference to the eternal dimension of human subjectivity, the following quotation is fitting: 'We almost touch eternity when we live in the present.'[13]

Cosmologists discuss the beginning and the end of the universe, and some of them consider that, in so doing, they might be able to give definitive answers to age-old theological questions. However, if subjectivity is so metaphysically different from the objective world that it 'touches eternity', and if that subjectivity is the direct approach to the Deity, such actual events in the history of the universe would seem to be irrelevent to the theological issues.

If there really is this eternal dimension to subjective experience, we must envisage some sort of influence of the subjective world of the individual human mind upon the Great Consciousness which is the Deity. There is no way of confirming that this is true, and how it could come about is also unanswerable, because the only reality which we can study scientifically is the objective one. These imponderable questions lead us on to mythology, a topic dealt with in detail in Part III.

10.7 Summary

For readers who have followed the argument so far, I cannot do better, by way of summary, than quote in full the poem by Thomas Traherne, already quoted in part, which captures the essence of the philosophy I have tried to develop, but with an elegance and conciseness which I cannot match. Readers may note especially the final couplet: 'Thoughts are the real thing, from which all joy, all sorrow spring.' This was undoubtedly closely related to Descartes' maxim 'Cogito ergo sum', but the tone is quite different, and seems to fit the parallelism I espouse better than the interactionism of Descartes.

Dreams

'Tis strange! I saw the skies;
I saw the Hills before mine Eys;
The sparrow fly;
The Lands that did about me ly;
The reall Sun, that hev'nly Ey;
Can closed Eys ev'n in the darkest Night
See throu their lids, and be informe'd with Sight?

The Peeple were to me
As tru as those by day I see;
As tru the Air,
The Earth as sweet, as fresh, as fair
As that which did by day repair
Unto my waking sense! Can all the sky,
Can all the World, within my Brain-pan ly?

What sacred Secret's this,
Which seems to intimat my Bliss?
What is there in
The narrow Confines of my Skin,
That is alive and feels within
When I am dead? Can Magnitude possess
An activ Memory, yet not be less?

May all that I can see
Awake, by Night within me be?
My Childhood knew
No Difference; but all was tru,
As reall all as what I view;
The world its Self was there. 'Twas wondrous strange
That Hev'n and Earth should so their place exchange.

Till that which vulgar Sense
Doth falsly call Experience,
Distinguisht things:
The Ribbans, and the gaudy Wings
Of Birds, the Virtues, and the Sins,
That represented were in Dreams by night

As really my senses did delight,

Or griev, as those I saw
By day: Things terrible did aw
My soul with fear;
The Apparitions seem'd as near
As Things could be, and Things they were:
Yet were they all by Fancy in me wrought
And all their being founded in a Thought.

O what a thing is Thought!
Which seems a Dream; yea, seemeth Nought,
Yet doth the Mind
Affect as much as what we find
Most near and true! Sure men are blind
And can't the forcible reality
Of things that secret are within them see.

Thought! Surely thoughts art tru
They pleas as much as Things can do:
Nay Things are dead
And in themselves are severed
From souls; nor can they fill the head
Without our Thoughts. Thoughts are the reall Things
From whence all Joy, from whence all Sorrow springs.

11

Organized Religion and its Relation
to Metaphysics

The previous chapter developed arguments in favour of a form of psychophysical parallelism otherwise referred to as 'epistemological dualism'. Part of this line of reasoning was related to some varieties of religion, and in the last part of the chapter, a concept of God was derived from the basic philosophy. At this stage it is appropriate to consider briefly how that way of thinking about religious issues might relate to actual religious organizations, especially the established Christian churches, the organizations with which I have had most contact.

11.1 Roles of religious organizations

Religious organizations serve many purposes for the individuals who adhere to them, amongst which are the following:

1. At the intellectual level, religious organizations cater for mankinds' perennial concern about insistent though insoluble metaphysical and philosophical questions. The three central questions with which religions deal are: Where did we come from? Where are we going to? What are we here for? The first two are questions about existence ('ontological' questions) and have many features in common. The third question, about human purpose, raises rather different issues.

2. Religious organizations are commonly expected to provide authoritative prouncements about moral issues of the day. This is of course closely related to the third of the above questions. It is not to be brushed aside. Many people nowadays comment on the fact that moral consensus about acceptable behaviour has in the last generation been mainly eroded. There are no rules now; anything goes; there is no other authority to appeal to than 'whatever turns you on'. Churches and other religious organizations can fairly be seen as bulwarks against the ensuing chaos.

Liberated educated (and well-heeled) spokepersons may decry the arbitrariness of the authority of the churches, but they are perhaps not sufficiently aware of the void that opens up if there is really no consensus and no authority. Indeed, of the three great religious questions mentioned above it is clear that the third is the one of most immediate practical import. We may find it fascinating to follow the astrophysicists' arguments for the 'Big Bang' theory of creation, and the events occurring in the first fractions of a second after this event, and we may try to absorb the prediction that the planet we dwell on is ultimately doomed to become uninhabitable. If we have been brought up to regard the Bible as the word of truth, we may gain comfort from the fact that the modern scientific view of the origin of the universe bears some resemblance to the Genesis story of creation. But the real heart of religion (and this applies whether we belong to an established church, or are part of the amorphous mass of agnostics and atheists outside the churches) is not the answer provided to these ontological questions, but that provided for the question 'What do we live by?' This question, which forms a central focus in Solzhenitsyn's book *Cancer Ward* is one we cannot dodge. In the sense that we all have our own answer to this question, we all have a religion. If we are unable to arrive at a decision by ourselves, many of us seek an external authority.

3. Churches provide a power structure within society as a whole by which leverage can be exerted on the political masters of a country. It may legitimately be asked why the churches have greater leverage than the equally numerous persons with no affiliation with organized religion. However, it is not clear that churches now have greater leverage than other non-religious organizations of equivalent size. Today, pressure-group politics are important in many Western-style countries. It is possible that, within Britain, the Church of England may be disestablished within a few years.

4. At the community level, churches can provide a social structure for development of relationships, providing a sense of belonging, or community, in otherwords providing 'fellowship'. This is important because there are few other organizations that provide a stable social network which can form a basis for development of relationships and nurturing children. Educated, liberated critics may again decry this. But they have many advantages in their lives. For instance for the fortunate, the workplace provides the basis for a lot of social contacts, and fellowship which can replace the churches. But consider the situation in small-town New Zealand. Few people have much education and social

horizons are very limited. The hard choice, now as ever, is often between the church and the public house. In some churches (especially nonconformist) valuable lessons in democratic processes are learned and can have major influence on the style of future politicians.

5. Religious organizations world wide have been the inspiration for some of the finest works of art mankind has produced, in the fields of visual arts and music. Historical religious writings such as the Bible or the Koran can in part be seen as religious works of literary art, containing poetry, parable and myth. Church symbols and rituals may also be regarded as a form of art in which believers are participants in worship rather than passive onlookers. Polkinghorne regards the continuity of tradition in these matters 'week by week, and month by month on a hundred thousand successive Sundays'[1] as a vital part of the structured freedom which churches provide. Religious art and music, religious writings and ritual often are closely related to the intellectual foundation of religious thinking, and the concepts provided as answers to the three central religious questions. While the intellectual arguments for a particular belief structure are explored by the intellectuals within a church, the same ideas can be explored in terms of the symbolism of religious art, music, writing and ritual, in which form they may have a wider appeal.

6. Many religious organizations give validity to a variety of forms of psychopathology. A few examples should be given. 'Hearing voices' can be interpreted as hearing the word of God, though in a different context this can be regarded as a symptom of a major psychotic disorder. Asceticsm within religious organizations may actually be related to clear psychopathology, for instance of eating disorders such as anorexia. Pathological relationships of power and submission are a part of some religious organizations. Some prayer rituals may be seen to be on the verge of an obsession.

11.2 Comment

The first two items of the above list are probably those which are dealt with most seriously in this book. However, all of these functions of religious organizations can perhaps be linked together, sometimes for better, sometimes for worse, as a network of myths and symbols. Mythology forms the main theme of Part III of this book. Here it is sufficient to point out that the complex philosophical and metaphysical issues which the intellectuals in religion think about cannot be critically evaluated by everyone in those churches. But they can nevertheless be communicated by the use of myth and symbol. Religious organizations, religious ritual and art are very much concerned with the communicative power and influence of these symbols.

Any actual religious organization is its own distinctive mix of these various factors, some achieving a socially useful blend, others a more malevolent one. But the important thing is that would-be adherents to a religion are often unaware of the interweaving of different threads that a religious organization offers. They are offered a package, and have to choose to accept it or reject it as a package. The tragedy of this is that religious thinking as such may be rejected because the package as a whole was not acceptable, or that the particular symbols are inapropriate or out of date. Furthermore, many modern educated persons, particularly those educated in the sciences, may reject religion in part just because it deals in the implicit language of symbolism, when they would prefer a statement of belief in more explicit terms which suggest empirical ways of testing the belief. However, as Polkinghorne[2] points out, the language of symbols is the natural language with which to convey religious truths. No other language is sufficiently open-ended, and capable of communicating so widely as is the language of symbols.

Were it not for these difficulties, there might have been elements in the package which, by themselves, and if pursued seriously, would be more acceptable to many scientists. The stumbling block may be the 'package deal' offered by a religious organization. Were it not for this stumbling block, parts of the package could have a major beneficial influence on the persons involved, liberating or empowering them.

Paul Davies (like many others) criticizes the dogmatic attitude of many organized religions to the truth of their pronouncements, and contrasts this with the traditional scepticism of scientists, who (collectively, if not always individually) are always willing to change previously cherished beliefs, if the evidence makes this necessary. This criticism of organized religion is only partly true in my view. It is also somewhat an idealization of science to think that its scepticism leads to steady rational progress. There are many fads and fashions in science, some of them both enduring and dangerous. With regard to religion there has been and still is plenty of dogmatism and bigotry. But other people within the churches have a more flexible attitude to truth. As just pointed out, much of religion is concerned with the language of symbol and myth. The symbols and myths by which religious truths are expressed change over the generations, while many of the basic truths remain the same. Most of the trouble comes from misinterpretation of symbols and myths as factual statements. No doubt many religious leaders fail to make clear this distinction, clinging to outdated symbols, and to their literal truth, over the centuries, as if they were immutable factual statements; and it is this which arouses the ire of their critics outside the churches. But other people within the churches recognize the myths and symbols for what they are – flexible vehicles for expressing deeper and more difficult truths, and they are quite prepared to change the symbol or myth to suit time and place. Curiously, the charge that the churches are guilty of dogmatism and bigotry is levelled more against the use or misuse of symbol and myth rather than at the underlying truths.

In the above list, the first item mentioned the three great religious questions. Let me say a little more about the first two of these questions, because they are most closely related to the metaphysical questions of the previous chapter. (The third of the religious questions is more difficult, and is central to all the remaining sections of this book.)

The first two of the great religious questions are about the origin and end of existence, especially human existence. They ask 'Where did we come from?' and 'Where are we going to?' Physicists such as Paul Davies[3] provide answers to these questions from cosmology and astrophysics. Evolutionary biologists provide answers relative to the past and probable future duration of life on the planet earth. But these answers may be making a mistake by giving a scientific answer to a question that is really metaphysical, not scientific. Psychophysical parallelism provides a different sort of answer to these two of the great religious questions, a metaphysical answer to metaphysical questions.

As we saw in the previous chapter, the parallel between our own mind and the matter of our brain can be extended. We can hypothesize that other humans than ourselves have subjective experience, that other creatures than humans have also subjective experience. There are no valid reasons for drawing borderlines between those living things which have, and those which do not have some form of consciousness. In the end there is no reason to deny that there is a mental parallel to the whole of the material universe. This, as we saw, is a possible way of defining the Deity (though as we will see later, this definition is only a part of the symbolism for which the word God is used).

This definition of the Deity is a sort of answer to the first two of the above questions. 'Where did we come from?' 'Where are we going to?' The answer is that 'we' (i.e. our conscious beings) are derived from the 'great consciousness' which is the Deity and, at our death, will rejoin that great consciousness. Defined in this way, that great consciousness has some similarity to what Christian theologians call 'God the creator'.

The merit of this way of thinking is that it allows us to retain the reality of subjective experience and the aesthetic values derived therefrom. We do not need to postulate a mental category which can interfere causally in the material world. The mental world is parallel to the material world, logically and causally independent of it, yet correlated. So our analysis of the causal mechanisms of the material world by normal scientific enquiry is not undermined by admitting the parallel reality of the mental world.

Another merit of the philosophy of psychophysical parallelism philosophy is that it does not draw an arbitrary distinction between humans and animals (just as it does not rely on language as a definition of consciousness). This has been a stumbling block for many people when considering the Christian view of mankind. In a recent letter in *The Lancet* the writers observe:

> This artificial separation of man from nature (giving man a categorical spiritual dimension) which is alien to many Christians is an important reason why some scientists have disowned the Christian cosmological view.[4]

In this chapter I have dwelt briefly on the strengths and weaknesses of religious organizations. In previous chapters I have argued as strongly as I can for the merits of a metaphysical approach called, alternatively, 'psychophysical parallelism' and 'epistomological dualism'. But I am also severely aware of a weakness in this approach. We come to these next.

Weakness of Psychophysical Parallelism: Confronting Neural Determinism

Psychophysical parallelism, as explained in the above chapters, was framed with a particular aim in mind, that is to reconcile two very important needs for human existence, one very old, the other of more recent appearance. Firstly it is necessary to retain the possibility of constructing a solid scale of human values. But second, in the modern world, where science has brought about such immense practical changes, this has to be done without undermining the scientist's quest for the underlying regularities in nature. Included amongst these regularities of nature are those within the human brain which determine human behaviour. The result of that discussion was two conclusions: I. We must retain the belief that brains, including human brains, are a mechanism. 2. The subjective side of human existence (and, by extension, of animal existence), from which ultimately we derive any scale of values, must be counted as an independent and equally valid form of reality. That subjective side is in no way an epiphenomenon or derivative of our material brains; and, in terms of cause and effect, it is neither the master nor the servant of our material brains. Instead, it has been conjectured that this subjective form of reality pursues a course miraculously in parallel with the physical side of our brains. By emphasizing the independence of subjectivity from objective existence, it is possible to retain the subjective origin of value systems, as valid in itself and not a mere epiphenomena associated with our objective existence.

The problem is that this derivation of values gives validity to only one type of value. It validates the value decisions that one form of experience is good, and another bad, and that the difference is not mere illusion. This is very important, and a necessary condition for the construction of any solid value system of a more comprehensive nature. But in practice it is not enough. The really important decisions we sometimes have to make are of a different form. They involve not so much the choice between different experiences which we, as passive subjects, would prefer (or prefer not) to experience. Rather, they involve the choice between different strategies and principles of action which, as alternatives, we can bring about as active agents, with ourselves as 'prime movers'. To put our decisions about matters of value in this perspective inevitably raises the third of the great religious questions, 'What are we here for? What should we live by?' It does so in a more incisive way than does an expressed preference for one sort of passive experience over another.

To raise the third of the religious questions in this manner confronts the philosophy of psychophysical parallelism in a most profound way. If the behaviour of our brains is deterministic, like any other physical mechanism, how can there be any real choice, as implied by these questions? If the behaviour of our brains is deterministic, how can this most difficult of religious questions mean anything? Yet on the other hand, how can we live without providing some sort of answer to that third of the great religious questions? These conundrums appear to present difficulties far more immediate and far more profound than the first two ontological questions with which religions have to deal.

Paul Davies, in his book *God and the New Physics*, entirely avoids this class of question. He deals with the issue of the origin and end of the universe in relation to religious questions, but not the question of 'What we are here for?' 'What do we live by?' Only once does he engage with this, the most immediate and difficult of the three great religious questions.

> Much has been written about the relationships between free will and the question of blame and responsibility for crime. If free will is illusory, why should anyone be blamed for their acts? . . . Could not the felon plea that at least one component of his multi-self is obliged by the laws of quantum theory to commit the crime? We must however turn aside from this minefield.[1]

It might be argued that the issue of determinism versus free will is of little importance because, even if our behaviour is actually determined by the mechanism of our brain, that mechanism is so complex that we are never likely in practice to be able to predict human behaviour. To do so we would have to have vast knowledge about both the hereditary and environmental influences which shaped a person's psychological makeup. In obtaining that information there is a sort of psychological indeterminancy principle: One cannot obtain even the most elementary parts of the necessary information without changing radically the person whose behaviour one wants to predict. Thus the person under study (just like one of Heisenberg's elementary particles) is changed in unpredictable ways by the very act of observation. In practice therefore, prediction of human behaviour becomes impossible, and it could be said that to all intents and purposes, we have 'free will'.

However, this argument, even if true, does not allay the anxiety of thinking people considering their own sense of freedom. If we accept the premise, which seems to be fundamental to the scientific view of the world, that all nature is regular and lawful, then it follows with impeccable logic, that our own behaviour is determined by such natural laws. Such an inference is not at all affected by considerations of whether our physical makeup is simple enough to make predictions in practice. We do not attribute 'free will' to a computer just because we do not understand fully its inner workings, and cannot predict the output it delivers from a given input. We believe it to be a mechanism because all its component parts are a mechanism, designed and constructed in order to perform regularly in specified ways. We can use almost the same argument for the human brain. Although we do not understand, and cannot predict the working of the integrated brain, we do know a great deal about the individual cellular components, the biochemistry, and principles of connection and interactions between nerve cells. From such information we have no scientific reason to doubt that all the component parts act as mechanisms. From this, there is also no scientific reason to doubt that, in principle, the integrated human brain also functions as a quite deterministic mechanism. When questions are raised about the possibility that humans might have freedom or responsibility, or that moral decisions should be taken seriously on their own merits, regardless of our physical brains, it matters little whether we consider that determinism in the brain is something demonstrable 'in practice' or merely inferable 'in principle'. The assumption of freedom and responsibility, basic to any moral argument applied to human behaviour, is quite antithetical to the assumption of natural law, and this is basic to attempts to understand and explain the workings of the brain which generates that behaviour.

However, although strictly it matters little whether determinism is demonstrated in practice or merely inferred in principle, the anxiety provoked by the idea of neural determinism is certainly more immediate, and more easily grasped if one has concrete examples where the idea appears to apply in practice. Modern neuroscience is beginning to provide such examples. In the paragraphs below a number of cases are described of human behaviours where our initial, almost instinctive reaction is to form a moral judgment that the behaviour is objectionable; and yet each, when looked at in the cool light of modern biological science, can be explained rationally from known mechanisms, where value judgments have no place at all. Generalization from these cases might lead us to doubt that any human behaviour can be judged good or bad in moral terms. This view, clearly implicit in modern neuroscience, is at least a plausible view, if not directly verifiable.

The first example I choose is asthma. The basic description of this illness focusses on periodic difficulty with breathing resulting from constriction of the airways in the lungs. However, in some cases of asthma, especially childhood asthma, there are associated psychological problems, which may even be the more important source of impairment for some patients. These psychological problems often centre around aggressive emotions.[2] Some people with asthma have great difficulty in handling aggressive emotions. On the one hand they have very strong feelings of aggression to those around them; and on the other they may also have greater or lesser degrees of insight that those powerful emotions are not reasonable responses to the emotional realities around them. This psychological problem has actually been depicted in dramatic form by Samuel Beckett in his play *Waiting for Godot*. The dominant character in this drama, the bullying tyrant called Pozzo, is also portrayed as being asthmatic.[3] In this case, no doubt for dramatic purposes, he is portrayed as having no insight whatsoever into his psychological problem. Certainly he is portrayed as an ugly character, and the immediate reaction of the audience is to judge him harshly as the villain of the piece. But Beckett's message was undoubtedly more profound and subtle than that.

One may ask how aggressive emotions become so interlinked with a disease of the lungs. Some of the literature on this question is psychoanalytic in orientation, suggesting that asthma arises because natural aggressive emotions have had to be consciously suppressed or unconsciously repressed.[4] As with much psychoanalytic reasoning, parents or other people who form the dominant psychological environment tend to be blamed for the illness of their offspring. In such reasoning the original naive negative moral evaluation applied to the patient is transferred to the parent who has been the major factor in his or her psychological development. But in either case, there is a confused mixture of objective scientific explanation with value judgment.[5]

At the descriptive level this psychoanalytic account of asthma has a ring of truth about it. However, as far as explanation goes I believe it to be a serious distortion. As with much psychoanalytic reasoning, important facts, as correlations, are grasped, but they are put together in a manner which confuses cause and effect. An alternative explanation based on elementary physiology and elementary learning theory accounts for all the same descriptive facts, and has much to recommend it as a truly scientific explanation. It does not make any value judgments, and blames neither patient nor parents for the illness. The explanation goes as follows.

The link between aggressive emotions and asthma is probably the adrenal gland. This gland is controlled by the brain. When it comes into action and releases adrenaline into the blood stream, this will instantly relax the smooth muscle in the airways of the lungs. For someone in an asthmatic attack this gives instant relief. In fact, in the emergency room, an injection of adrenaline is one of the best ways of resolving things, in the short term. However, under normal circumstances that release of adrenaline into the blood stream occurs not by an injection, but from the adrenal gland, under control from the brain. This occurs especially at those times when one has aggressive subjective feelings. At these times adrenaline release also has several other external manifestations besides its effects on the airways, such as quickening of the heart beat, flushing of the face and other well known signs associated with aggressive feelings.

Thus, one may conjecture that some asthmatic children may learn (perhaps at a very early age, and quite unconsciously) that if they become aggressive it will help to clear their lungs. When this has occurred a number of times a learning or conditioning process is set in train within the child's brain, such that a contrived state of emotional aggression is generated every time there is the start of an asthmatic attack. This may appear to be directed against parents and other major figures in the child's social life. This, however, means that a person with chronic asthma may be using aggressive emotions for two quite different purposes. Normally aggressive emotional responses are used in appropriate contexts of social interaction; but asthmatics develop a special use for this emotional response, namely to clear their lungs. When a child discovers this psychological trick it may help to keep the asthmatic symptoms in check, but there may be associated with it a tremendous cost to the social and emotional development of such children, not least because other people misunderstand the function of the display of aggression.[6]

Eating disorders such as anorexia nervosa are also a complex mixture of physical symptoms and psychological changes. In anorexia sufferers, apart from the severe problem with lack of eating itself, there are psychological traits, especially a tendency to try to control everyone around them, by complex and devious means, and in a most pathological manner. This is terribly difficult for other family members to live with, and it may be very difficult for them to be detached about it and to regard the threat to their own autonomy, which the patient represents, as the symptom of the patient's illness. More likely, such an illness can provoke anger, retaliation and a morally judgmental attitude in other family members. This type of illness is far being from understood. However, the pathological behaviour patterns are very striking. Moreover, to any detached observer, they are very counterproductive in that they undermine relationships the patient has with those persons most committed to his or her well-being. Yet these behaviour patterns can occur in highly intelligent persons, who in normal circumstances can show great foresight and benevolence to those around them. One suspects that, as with asthma, there is some internal mechanism of avoidance conditioning, such that the pathological behaviour reduces some aversive consequence of the primary features of the illness. This is at present conjecture, it needs to be said. It is not yet known what other more basic feature of the illness there might be, from which the pathological behaviour develops as an avoidance mechanism.

The third example I choose, of human behaviour which meets with general disapproval or fear, but which is likely to arise from a disturbed brain mechanism, is also from psychiatry, namely psychotic illnesses such as schizophrenia. The whole symptomatology of these illness is excedingly complicated, and involves many disturbances including sensory processes, thinking and feeling, as well as overt behaviour. For the purposes of my argument, I concentrate on one class of symptom, the psychotic delusions. Patients may harbour beliefs which most people around them would regard as incredible and bizarre, yet these beliefs are held by patients with great vehemence and tenacity, despite the fact that the obvious interpretation to be made from abundant evidence around the patient is that the belief is false. In extreme cases, where appropriate drug treatment has not been given, patients may act out their delusional beliefs, occasionally with disastrous consequences.

People who know little about this sort of strange illness have a wide variety of distorted views about it. Images of mental illness purveyed by the mass media, especially in fictional portrayals, do not help to clarify the situation. Many people are intensely frightened by the words schizophrenia or psychosis, though they do not know much about what the words really mean. Other people transfer their negative value judgments to psychiatrists, mental hospitals, or the parents of such patients, and do not fully realize how terrible untreated psychotic states can be for all who have anything to do with them. Few people realize the full extent of the tragedy of severe psychotic illness, and even fewer follow up this realization with a serious attempt to understand as much as possible about it. Scientific understanding of this class of illness has thus become clouded in the popular mind by factual distortions, half truths and adverse value judgments at many levels.

But how are we to understand the strange symptoms of such psychotic states, such as the powerfully held, incorrigible delusional beliefs? There are good reasons for believing that a disturbance in brain chemistry underlies much of the abnormality in psychotic states. This can be said partly because a remarkably similar psychotic state can be produced in quite normal people who take amphetamine or amphetamine-like drugs, especially in large doses or for long periods. In addition, since the 1950s a group of drugs have been in use which usually alleviate the symptoms of psychosis. These antipsychotic drugs, it must be admitted, are controversial for many people because of the unpleasant side effects they often produce. Undoubtedly they can cause severe problems in themselves, and have been much overused to 'control' or 'manage' difficult patients, without much thought being given to the possibility that in smaller doses they are actually a quite selective and specific treatment for a particular illness. Nevertheless, when they are used in optimal doses they are remarkably effective in reducing the more dramatic and severe symptoms of psychosis in many cases.

Since there are between fifty and a hundred medicines known with this property, it has been possible to define the biochemical properties they have in common from which their beneficial actions in psychosis derive. Almost all of the antipsychotic drugs antagonize a particular messenger substance in the brain, the much-studied chemical called dopamine. Other evidence implicates dopamine in the production of psychotic states. For instance amphetamines, which can precipitate psychoses in normal people, release dopamine in active form in the brain, and thus accentuate the normal functions of this substance. From this, and much other similar evidence, it has been proposed that the messenger substance dopamine is somehow overactive in the brains of those suffering from psychosis. Much effort has been devoted to the search for direct evidence of overactive dopamine mechanisms in the brain of people with psychosis. Most of this work has been inconclusive, and the search continues, using ever more sophisticated methods. The lack of such direct evidence (the 'smoking gun', as it were, in our search for the culprit in schizophrenia) does not detract from the weight of indirect evidence that in some form or another overactive dopamine is involved in the generation of psychotic states.

This part of the story of schizophrenia research has been empirical. But there are equally difficult questions to be investigated at the theoretical level. In particular, what could be the relationship between overactive dopamine, in whatever form it occurs, and the strange symptoms of psychosis in humans? Here we can learn a lot from experiments on the role of dopamine in the behaviour of experimental animals. As discussed in an earlier chapter, psychologists earlier this century defined the concept of 'reward', as being important in certain forms of learning. The implication of this description is that there must be an internal signal in the brain which mediates both the subjective euphoria we identify as reward, and the objective reinforcement of behaviour occurring when that behaviour has favourable outcomes.

Of course, such analysis of the chemical basis of learning in animals is a far cry from human thought processes, which become deranged in psychosis. Nevertheless many scientists believe that there are close parallels between the internal processes of thinking in human beings, and the processes governing externally-directed behaviour found more widely in mammals. Indeed it is very plausible to envisage that the thoughts we have which have pleasant or favourable consequences in the world of thinking may often be reinforced, and then are more likely to recur in one's mind, just as externally-directed actions which have favourable consequences in the external world are also reinforced, and become more likely to occur again. From suppositions like this it becomes an easy step to envisage that overactivity of the internal reward signal makes the thoughts, ideas and beliefs we may have (about favourable or unfavourable aspects or our environment of our own behaviour) become reinforced so strongly that they become incorrigible delusional beliefs. In other words, just as reward-enhancing drugs like amphetamine can be highly addictive, the psychotic state can be regarded as an addiction brought about by overactivity of natural reward mechanisms. Psychotic patients become, so to speak, addicted to certain of their own thought patterns.

To express the same thought in terms of the electrical activity in nerve cells, one may postulate that there are groups of active nerve cells forming stable patterns of activity, and these correspond to (and represent) normal beliefs. Usually, in contemporary neuroscience, configurations of active nerve cells which collectively represent the meanings of stimuli, responses or internal thoughts are called cell assemblies. When dopamine is overactive, the stability of these cell assemblies can be envisaged to become complete. Configurations of activity in nerve cells then endure despite any external influence which might be expected to shake their stability, because of the overactivity of dopamine as an internal reinforcer. Granted, this is at present a slightly metaphorical explanation of psychotic delusions, but only slightly. Research is currently in progress to try to express some of these ideas as computer simulations, using, as far as possible, accurate assumptions about known processes in real brains.

Admittedly, this account of the delusional symptoms of psychosis accounts for only some of the symptoms. A more complete theory of psychotic symptoms would have to be considerably more complex. For instance, it would have to take account of the fact that, even limiting oneself to the acute stage of schizophrenia, much of the symptomatology of psychosis (as of drug induced psychosis) is very *un*pleasant rather than euphoric (as implied by the previous paragraphs). Nevertheless there are a number of features of psychosis which recommend this hypothesis as a starting point. For instance, many psychotic patients, at some stage of their illness, will express a preference for their symptoms as opposed to the treatment given for them. Furthermore, a large proportion of psychotic delusions are about subjects with strong evaluative components (ranging from heaven to hell), rather than about value-neutral matters. These are the subjects which are most likely to invoke the reward and reinforcement mechanisms because, in normal circumstances, those mechanisms are controlled by motivationally significant information.

In each of the above three examples – asthmatic psychology, the psychology of eating disorders, and the psychological disturbances of psychosis – there has been a distortion or exaggeration of the processes which reinforce or 'stamp in' patterns of behaviour or thought. It may be denied that one can make any philosophical point about freewill or determinism in normal human behaviour from such examples of severe abnormality. But reward processes operate just as much for normal human thought and behaviour as in abnormal cases. It is likely to be similar processes that make a particular colour scheme attractive to an artist, or a particular combination of sounds persist in the mind of a composer. The subjective attractiveness of certain ideas which motivate the activities of philosophers, and that of certain character profiles which motivate the novelist, in all probability has a similar mechanistic basis to the attractiveness of delusional ideas in psychosis. At a more mundane level, it is the internal reward systems of the brain which, in different ways in each individual, provides the personal ambitions and satisfactions we all pursue. We credit our own subjective feelings about these goals and ambitions with a primary reality or validity. The psychotic patient gives the same sort of validity or reality to his systems of delusions. As far as the philosophical issues are concerned, there is no reason why the determinism we attribute to a deranged mind in mental illness cannot also be applied to normal human decisions and behaviour. No doubt thought and action is more versatile and adaptive in normal human beings than it is in the mentally ill, but that is no reason to doubt that the remorseless neccessity of causal processes is still in operation in the former as well as the latter.

Of course this line of reasoning reduces all human striving to dust and ashes. If all our personalized ambitions derive from a mechanism in our brains, there is nothing objectively valuable about the behaviour which subjectively we prize most highly. It would follow that there can be no objective virtue in scientific or artistic excellence, for which prestigious prizes are given, nor for political courage in the face of enormous odds. Neither is there anything objectively wicked about the mass murderer, which would merit our punishing him for his wrongdoing. There is nothing morally good or bad about any of these. These actions, for better or for worse, occur merely because particular cell assemblies in the brains of these individuals are fullfilling their individual destinies. Cell assemblies, whatever they are, are a mechanism, which can be neither good nor bad.

Most destructive of all, this line of reasoning found within modern neuroscience undermines one of the most important premises for our social existence, the concept of a person. To describe how this happens let me counterpose modern neuroscience with a biblical parable, the parable of the talents. In this story we are encouraged to believe that whatever faculties we have should be used to best advantage; we have no grounds to complain that the faculties we have been given to start with are limited if, at the end of the day, we have made no use of them such as they are. This is a very powerful story. It emphasizes that we have only one life, and that we are responsible for putting it to best use. Above all it assumes that there is such a thing as a person, who has personal responsibility for whatever achievements he or she produce or fail to produce during their lifetime.

But are there such entities as persons? Remember Skinner's belief that 'the mind' or 'consciousness' is a no more than a metaphor or a construct, that self-awareness of ourselves as persons has no more fundamental basis than our capacity for verbal behaviour.

What criteria do we adopt to know of our personal existence?

For some people our *inner emotions* are proof of our personal existence. But it has long been known that emotions or, at least emotional behaviour, can quite consistently be produced by stimulation of a certain part of the brain (hypothalamus and amygdala) in what appears to be a quite mechanistic fashion.

For other people the *pleasure and pain of life* are the proof of their existence. Yet stimulation of other brain regions elicits behaviour apparently designed to ensure the repetition or avoidance of that stimulus. Since the brain appears to be able to adapt itself so as to bring about further repetition of the stimulation, we may say that the effect of the brain stimulus appears to be pleasurable. This has been shown in both animals and in human beings.

For yet other people, the *experience of conscious exercise of free will* proves to them their own existence. But even our most deliberate and cognitive decisions about which behaviours we perform can be related to a mechanism in the brain, albeit using different nervous circuitry than the autonomic or endocrine control mechanisms.[7] Libet[8] has shown clearly that when a so-called voluntary act is performed, the electrical signs of the impending act start to develop in the brain a small but significant time before the person will report the conscious experience of volition. Volition appears not to be an uncaused cause, but is all part of the causal machinery of the brain, albeit in part unconscious.

For René Descartes *thought* was the criterion of personal existence, as captured in his famous phrase 'Cogito ergo sum'. Yet we know quite clearly that the vigour and creativity of thought processes can be abruptly reduced in normal people by certain psychoactive drugs (especially those used to treat psychotic illnesses), and that the abnormalities of thought in psychosis are also radically changed (normalized) by such drugs.

Cupitt gives us both sides of this issue, wearing in turn an 'objective' and a 'subjective' hat. As an objectivist he writes:

> What are we? Let us be objective, you and I, and look at ourselves as if from a public standpoint, beyond the narrow sphere of our own subjectivities. What do we see? We see that we are biological organisms who live within narrow physical limits and move from birth to death over about seven decades. To one such being it may seem to matter greatly whether for him it is a case of two down and five to go, or five down and two to go, but from an objective point of view such differences are not significant. We are all in the same boat. Every individual is alike ephemeral, and that is that.[9]

Wearing his subjective hat he writes:

> Within the field of subjectivity my life is boundless. I see neither its beginning nor its end: it is only from society that I learn of my finitude. From within, my subjectivity is a complete world that includes not only the relatively little that I personally do and undergo, but also the far vaster regions that thought traverses; and the spotlight of consciousness, the *I think*, ranges over all these inner spaces like a god ... The *I think* appears to be what was meant by talk of our immortal soul. For if any feature of my subjective life other than this were to be immortal then I might well complain that its immortality is not truly my own immortality; whereas if the *I think* is immortal, then surely I am. So the *I think* is the immortal soul.[10]

When one reads the whole of Cupitt's book it becomes clear that the objective view of humankind is closer to his own leanings. And from the standpoint of neural, rather than social determinism, Cupitt's *I think* becomes no more remarkable, metaphysically than the workings of a computer.

Where amongst the mechanisms of that neural computing machinery is the person to be found? Modern neuroscience, by implication, can dispense with the concept of a person. For all these apparent evidences of personal existence, the subjective experiences could be regarded as mere epiphenomena, with strictly causal mechanisms constituting the more solid underlying reality. Rather than Descartes' 'I think therefore I am', we should say 'The thoughts I experience come from a neural mechanism, not from *me* (whatever that is). Therefore I do *not* exist.' Modern neuroscience would give greater reality to the cell assemblies underlying thought or action than to the *person* who some would suppose to be 'responsible' for the good or bad thoughts or actions. As far as scientific explanation goes, the concept of a person is quite redundant. The language in which scientific explanations of human behaviour must be couched is the language of cell assemblies, not of persons. When the mathematician Laplace met Napoleon, and was asked about what the science of their day had to say about the nature of God, Laplace replied, 'I have no need of that hypothesis.'[11] Clearly he had no notion of the miraculous nature of his own subjectivity. A modern day Laplace, schooled in cell assembly theory, might be asked what modern neuroscience has to say about the nature of a person; and he also would have to reply, 'I have no need of that hypothesis.'

Admittedly, few of even the most ardent materialist neuroscientists would actually assert this belief in explicit fashion. But nevetherless this belief is quite clearly implicit in many of the ideas of modern theoretical neuroscience, and much else of the philosophical package it offers. The remorseless logic of modern neuroscience is coming close to explaining neurological and mental disorders, as abnormal patterns of activity in complex combinations of nerve cells. But these assemblies of nerve cells appear to have greater reality than the person to whom they belong. Once pointed out, the disjunction between these scientific ideas and the concept of a person, so fundamental to our social existence, stands out as a glaring inconsistency. Yet many highly intelligent persons live without confronting this fact. Take Cupitt again. He writes:

> While it is possible . . . to learn to look at animals and plants and see them simply as natural products of chance and time, variation and selection, it is more difficult consistently to think of one's own thinking as mere natural process and a product of evolution. There are horrors ahead here with which few of us have yet grappled.[12]

Like many liberal religious thinkers, his theological position is defined more by the need to defend against what is seen as the loose thinking of fundamentalists, than by an acute awareness of the 'void' which opens up when all contact with religious thinking is lost. In this respect the agenda for the thinking of such persons has been set by the fundamentalists rather than by an awareness of this void, and the perennial religious questions which confront us when we escape from the influence of institutional religion. I hope that this book focusses on those basic questions rather than on the peripheral issues brought to our attention by the more simple minded approach of certain religious groups.

Overall, we find again, as we found in Part I of this book, that the encroaches of scientific materialism and the scientific way of thinking destroy implicitly many of the fundamental beliefs that have underpinned that delicate plant, the human capacity for social life. The tendency to destroy by objectivizing strikes deepest and most powerfully in the biological sciences. In the neurosciences, an enormous amount of brilliant and elegant experimental studies are progressivelly unravelling the mysteries of the brain, including the human brain. It becomes gradually easier to consider that mental processes are a biproduct of a very complex but nevertheless ultimately quite comprehensible mechanism. I am well aware of this from my own work. I contribute to the research going on in many countries in this area. And I sincerely believe that we are on the verge of a mechanistic understanding of human thoughts, memories and emotions. And I believe that this will soon bring dark subjects like mental illness within the reach of fully rational disease theories, and rational, humane treatment. But nowhere, as this process goes on, is any account given of what goes to make up a person.

In similar view Monod points out the destructiveness of the determinist world view, but from the perspective of evolutionary theory and molecular biology. After describing the various types of genetic mutation he writes:

> We say these events are accidental, due to chance. And since they constitute the *only* possible source of modifications in the genetic text, itself the *sole* repository of the organism's hereditary structures, it necessarily follows that chance *alone* is at the source of every innovation, of all creation in the biosphere. Pure chance, absolutely free but blind, at the very root of the stupendous edifice of evolution; this central concept of modern biology is no longer one amongst other possible or even conceivable hypotheses. It is today the *sole* conceivable hypothesis, the only one compatible with observed and tested fact ... There is no scientific position, in any of the sciences, more destructive of anthropocentrism than this one, and no other more unacceptable to the intensely teleonomic creature that we are.[13]

I have met various people who claimed they could live with a philosophy in which mankind is just another form of matter, and that the true wisdom comes from seeing ourselves with this degree of detachment and objectivity. Sometimes this intellectual stance is related to Buddhist philosophy. Cupitt, for instance, working towards Buddhist beliefs writes that 'the individual will in due course have to be demythologized'.[14] However, none of these persons I know has convinced me that they really know what they are saying. The intensities of pleasure and suffering around which our life focusses occur to individuals. The realities of suffering cannot be dismissed as an illusion just by 'demythologizing' the concept of individual selfhood. One of the more profound forms of suffering is mental illness, in which the integrity of the individual is undermined. Amongst such disorders, the psychotic illnesses are common, and can provide those who experience them with very graphic subjective knowledge that the 'I think' of Cupitt is not an immortal soul but a fallible mechanism. The erudite detachment of those who consciously reject the concept of individual selfhood is a world apart from those who cannot find that selfhood, however far they seek. Buddhists who voluntarily detach themselves from selfhood and individuality really demonstrate a very great stability and integrity of their individual selves which totally belies their expressed belief. When the sky falls in, and we face isolation, madness and death (and we must all face at least one of these) can we really accept that we are just so much dust, rather than that focus of consciousness, of hopes and dreams, pleasures and sorrows which we call a person?

The clinical psychologist Frith, specialist in the psychology of schizophrenia, has written: 'Most of us share in common the useful delusion that we have free will. Schizophrenic patients have lost this experience.'[15] This quotation illustrates just how far the process of objectivization has gone in modern culture. Strangely, it is exactly those who suffer real psychotic delusions who are brought most sharply to the realization of the fact that their own minds are a mechanism. While the philosophy of determinism may be a theoretical anxiety for some of us, for those who have experienced psychotic disintegration of the mind it is no longer theoretical. This I believe is one of the reasons why psychotic illnesses such as schizophrenia are so terribly damaging to personal integrity. There are in fact plenty of other reasons, but this single one undermines in a most profound way many people's notions of personal existence. But in less direct fashion any of us has access to evidence for the determinism of our brains, which can do nothing but provoke anxiety.

Jacques Monod utters one of the most profound and fundamental statements of the destructiveness which the scientific attitude has upon the patterns of thought on which civilization depends. The last chapter of his book *Chance and Necessity* is called 'The Kingdom and the Darkness'. By 'The kingdom' he means the style of thinking which reigned for 100,000 years, from the birth of humankind to the scientific Renaissance. This style arose presumably as a result of natural selection at the cultural level and led mankind to create a wide variety of myths and religions. These, as purportedly true statements, provided mankind with a meaning to his existence. In these constructions 'truth' has been a vehicle for allaying mankind's deepest anxieties. These anxieties, which are quite subjective, are his need for an explanation of his place in the universe; and therefore, his need to answer the third of the great religious questions, 'What are we here for?' or 'What should we live by?' But, developing since the Renaissance, the ever-questioning human mind has broken this old covenant. There has appeared the unprecedented notion that objective knowledge is the only source of real truth. In such objective knowledge there can be no compromise with man's subjective needs, nor any sympathy for his existential anxieties. Monod writes:

> Cold and austere, proposing no explanation but imposing an ascetic renunciation of all other spiritual fare, this idea [of objective knowledge] could not allay anxiety; it aggravated it instead. It claimed to sweep away at a stroke the tradition of a hundred thousand years, which had become assimilated in human nature itself. It ended the ancient animist covenant between man and nature, leaving nothing in place of that precious bond but an anxious quest in a world of icy solitude. With nothing to recommend it but a certain puritan arrogance, how could such an idea be accepted? It was not; it still is not. If it has commanded recognition, this is solely because of its prodigious powers of performance. In the course of three centuries, science, founded upon the postulate of objectivity, has won its place in society – in men's practice, but not in their hearts.

> No society before ours was ever torn apart by such conflicts. In both primitive and classical culture the animist tradition saw knowledge and values stemming from the same source. For the first time in history a civilization is trying to shape itself while clinging desperately to the animist tradition in an effort to justify its values, and at the same

time abandoning it as the source of knowledge, or *truth* . . . All these systems rooted in animism exist outside objective knowledge, outside truth, and they are strangers and fundamentally *hostile* to science, which they are willing to use but do not respect or cherish . . . The divorce is so great, the lie so flagrant, that it can only obsess and lacerate anyone who has some culture or intelligence, or is moved by that moral questioning which is the source of all creativity.[16]

In comparison to this powerful and eloquent statement of mankind's agonizing position, Monod's suggestions of a way of escaping from the impasse, presented in the last few pages of his book, seem rather lame. He refers to the 'ethic of knowledge', as fundamental to the scientific enterprise. As such it brings knowledge and values simultaneously into play.

Where then shall we find the source of truth and the moral inspiration for a really scientific socialist humanism? Only . . . in the sources of science itself, in the ethic upon which science is founded.[17]

Why does this suggestion have such a hollow ring to it? It does not really provide any answers to the acute ethical dilemmas which we sometimes feel. If we were to follow the ethic of knowledge towards Monod's Utopian scientific state, we would still have those same anxious dilemmas. The inner world of subjective experience which, I have suggested, is at the heart of value judgments and value systems, is not openly acknowledged in Monod's answer; and without that acknowledgment any ethic is founded on quicksand.

The question of the relation between subjective and objective realities, which has been the thread uniting all the arguments presented so far in this work, thus comes to centre stage again. Can we reconcile the objectivity of scientific knowledge with the subjectivity from which our values must derive? I believe we can, but in order to do so we must recognize that certain tenets of the scientific enterprise are not objective truths, but are assumed answers to insoluble questions. They are, in all important senses, myths for the mind of modern men and women, suitable once they have abandoned the traditional religious myths of antiquity, but no more objective than them. Part III of this book explores this idea in more detail. It emphasizes that we need myths, just as much now as did the ancients. But we should not choose our myths simply as antithesises to the outdated myths of the pre- Renaissance cultures and their religions. They should have something more positive to recommend them. Nor should our myth-making lack constraints. But where questions are in principle insoluble there is some room for manoeuvre, provided we do not postulate anything which is self-contradictory or contradicts empirical observations (as do many traditional religious beliefs, including the myths of Christianity.)

In Part III I identify some common beliefs of the contemporary scientific and secular culture as myths. Most fundamental of these is the belief in determinism. However, deriving from that central belief are certain other very influential beliefs, notably those associated with the names of three thinkers who have shaped the modern world: Sigmund Freud, Karl Marx, and (make no mistake) Charles Darwin. These I believe are all destructive myths, in the sense that they have won their widespread popularity as antitheses to established religious belief, rather than for any more positive reason. By pointing out a flaw common to all these belief systems, it becomes possible to demarcate how some more constructive myths can be identified, ones which have some positive consequences to recommend them.

Part III

Reconstruction by Creation of Myths

13

The Creation and Uses of Myths

The technology which has arisen from the scientific developments of the present and past few centuries has revolutionized most of our lives, has opened exciting new opportunities for many of us and, in Westernized countries, has made life safer and more comfortable for most of us. But at the conceptual level the philosophical package which has been associated with those advances has left a trail of destruction. These advances have undermined our appreciation of what is subjective and qualitative, to be replaced by emphasis on what is objective and quantitative. They have undermined our trust in subjective impressions and conceptual hunches such as those which were originally the source of the scientific revolution of the Renaissance. These advances have also undermined the subjective experiences from which value systems are developed.

A major part of the destruction by objectivization can be countered by the philosophy of psychophysical parallelism. This philosophy defends the subjective side of life, the reality of aesthetic values, and at least the possibility of a reasoned and solid system of moral values. It makes plausible that there be a Deity, in part a personification of our values, though it does not allow that that Deity have the traditional Christian attribute of omnipotence. But in the end that philosophy is not strong enough to defend against the strongest challenge of scientific materialism. This is the growing credibility of determinism as applied to the human brain. This belief has a potential to destroy the idea of personal responsibility, taken for granted in any system of moral values, and indeed to destroy the very concept of persons as such.

Determinism is such a powerful language for framing explanations that it has to be taken seriously (though there may be room for qualifying the reach of determinism, see below, chapter 14). Nevertheless, in practice no one can live their lives using only the insights they gain from the pure-blooded creed of neural determinism, without compromising to more commonplace ideas. There is indeed a great tension between the concept of determinism as used by scientists and the demands of everyday human existence. To a logician, and to Jacques Monod, the tension between these two world views may be quite intolerable.

However, when the chips are down, almost all of us prefer life to truth, and will compromise on matters of truth to make life possible. This is appropriate if only to accommodate to the fact that truth is relative (see chapter 5), an inaccessible ideal to which we can only approximate. As for the determinist creed, we may believe in it with our minds, but our hearts, which determine our actions, are compromised, at the practical level, to adopt more-or-less conventional moral stances. I believe this compromise is necessary at the metaphysical level, as well as at the practical level. I also believe that the nature of this compromise need not be an unprincipled retreat from intellectual rigour. It need not sacrifice the notion that the constructs from which our view of reality is to be built should be consistent and coherent, and in accord with empirical experience.

The word 'myth' has been used several times in the last pages. In defining the blatant lie in the modern world view Jacques Monod also uses the word, with some sympathy for the concept the word denotes. I believe that to reassert the reality and validity of those concepts which are essential to the life most of us cherish, we need to go to a deeper level, one which has not always been rational, but which in the modern world can be rational. This is the world of myth. How are we to understand this word?

Some questions arise which are insistent and provocative and will not go away. Yet they defy all attempts to provide an answer. Sometimes these questions have seemed unanswerable at one period of history, but at a later period the answer came to be provided from within science.

When my three-year old daughter asks me, 'Daddy, who made the moon?' she is asking a question which might have been asked by an adult thousands of years ago, and which might then have been answered by a traditional story or myth. Today we have from science some sort of answer about the origin of the moon and other heavenly bodies.

The first two of the basic religious questions ('Where did we come from?' and 'Where are we going to?') are, in general, of this type. In classical times they may have been unanswerable except by reference to myths, but nowadays science usually provides some sort of answer.

For instance, embryologists tell us of the processes involved in the origin of each individual, and pathologists assure us that our physical disintegration after death is complete. Evolutionary biologists tell us that the human species has developed by gradual change from quite different life forms. The actual mechanism of this change is generally believed to have been entirely natural selection, which has led to the slow emergence of humankind all the way from inanimate matter. A critique of this view is presented later in Part III. Regardless of the truth of the Darwinian view of the evolutionary process, there can be no doubt that the human form of life on this planet is of quite recent origin on the geological time scale; and that quite different life forms existed in the remote past from what we see about us nowadays. Thus, even though we may debate the mechanism of evolutionary change, the factual description of that change gives another sort of answer to the question 'Where did we come from?'

Cosmologists and astrophysicists provide us with a third type of answer to this question, in terms of what we know of the factual history and likely future of the universe. Ever more detailed and consistent descriptions are now being provided about the first moments of the existence of the universe, and its probable future demise. These cannot be tested empirically of course, being historical theories; but the extraordinary physical processes occurring in the extreme conditions which existed at the time of the Big Bang can to some extent be mimicked in modern particle accelerators. The data derived in this way are combined with the full rigour of modern mathematical analysis and computer simulation, and so give another sort of test of these conjectures about the origin of the universe.

It must be admitted that science sometimes even now has to recognize unanswered and unanswerable questions about the origin and fate of the universe and its inhabitants. One particularly striking example of this is found in physics and cosmology. The existence of the universe as we know it seems to depend on some extremely unlikely coincidences. Some of these are coincidences in what appear to have been the initial conditions of the universe. Had they been even very slightly different, the evolution of the observable universe could not have proceeded in such a way as to produce the set of galaxies which are observable, let alone the remarkably stable environment of the planet earth which has permitted the development of complex life forms. Even more remarkable coincidences have been identified in some of the basic constants of the physical universe. There are a variety of such constant values, such as the universal constant for gravitational attraction, or the ratio of the mass of the proton to that of the electron. There is no clear explanation of why these constant values take the quantities that they actually do. Nevertheless, it appears to be quite critical what these values are. With those basic physical constants taking exactly their observed values, the universe as a whole exists in a finely-poised balance. If those constants deviated by very very tiny amounts, that delicate balance would be disturbed, and the development of a relatively stable universe in which life-bearing planets could exist would not have happened. This is described in Paul Davies' book.[1] The question is, what interpretation should be given to these curious coincidences?

Some thinkers would invoke what is called the anthropic principle, which says that there is nothing at all remarkable about these findings. It is only in those universes in which all the conditions are right, that sentient observers can come to exist to contemplate the coincidence. There may exist in some undetectable insentient other places and times a vast number of other universes, where the coincidental conditions are not right for the emergence of conscious life. There is no suprise, but simple logical necessity that we exist in the former type of universe rather than the many versions of the latter.

Other thinkers would point to these striking coincidences as evidence for design in the universe. They suggest that the existence of the universe can only have come about by careful planning (perhaps by an intelligent creator), of the initial conditions for the universe and the physical constants governing the interaction of its components. In this respect, cosmologists are using an argument very similar to that of pre-Darwinian biologists, who argued from the evidence of design in living things to infer the existence of a Grand Designer.

However, between these two positions there is no rational basis for the choice. As Paul Davies, not himself a Christian, writes:

A conclusion can only be subjective. In the end it boils down to a question of belief. Is it easier to believe in a cosmic designer than the multiplicity of universes necessary for the anthropic principle to work? It is hard to see how either hypothesis could ever be tested in the strict scientific sense.[2]

Polkinghorne[3] also comments on this issue. He regards the view that there are many worlds, only those with appropriate physical constants and initial conditions supporting conscious life, as 'not . . . a scientific proposal at all . . . rather it is a metaphysical guess'. He also regards the alternative view, that there be a designer, 'not to be a knockdown argument'. Thus 'theism provides a persuasive (but not logically coercive) argument'.[4]

In other words, even for the questions about origin and end of the universe, scientific answers leave profound gaps that can only be filled on the basis of prior assumptions or beliefs about existence or non-existence of design and purpose in the universe.

For these questions it may be rather esoteric and academic which version we choose. The origin and fate of the universe is not of immediate practical significance to the majority of sentient beings, at least on earth. Admittedly Paul Davies writes, concerning the ultimate demise of the world (perhaps 10^{100} years hence): 'It is a scenario that many scientists find profoundly depressing.'[5] However, most of us have more immediate matters to make us depressed, and would not take the plight of these depressed cosmologists very seriously.

But when we come to the third of the great religious questions 'What are we here for?' 'What should we live by?', the question has a much more immediate practical bite for us all. Here, far more than for questions about our beginning and end, our attempts to provide rational answers are greeted with an ominous silence. We have then a question which we feel we should have an answer for, to help us in day-to-day living; but it seems that none is available, even in principle. These questions have immediate practical bearing on our daily decisions. Most of us try to take those decisions seriously. Should we do so? Can we afford not to? It is to deal with such situations that myths are still always necessary.

Traditional myths are stories which purport to provide answers to unanswerable questions, which are unsettling unless we have something approaching an answer. Since the questions to which a myth refers cannot be given a definite answer, it is pointless to ask whether the stories which constitute traditional mythology are true or not. Often their validity comes from the currency of the images and symbols contained in the story, for those people who accept the myth, rather than on the factual truth of the story. Polkinghorne has quoted the phrase: 'a myth is living or dead, not true or false'.[6] Regardless of their truth, such stories still have their function, to help us live with the anxiety of unresolved (commonly religious) questions.

The Bible is full of stories which fulfill the purpose of myths. The creation story of the book of Genesis is obviously a myth designed or discovered in order to deal with perennial questions about where the universe and its inhabitants came from. It can be compared with similar myths in almost all cultures. Such myths focus on the first two of our religious questions.

The story of the Garden of Eden and the eating of the tree of knowledge of Good and Evil is a very powerful myth. It is concerned with the Pandora's box which was opened at some stage early in human history, as human capacities for thought made possible the dilemmas of moral behaviour. Clearly this myth attempts to say something very basic about the third of our religious questions. The Maui legends in the Maori culture are powerful myths about the creativity of the human mind. The Christian story is an especially interesting one. It arose at a time and in a culture where some of the population at least were literate, and where history was recorded, rather than part of an oral tradition. In such a culture, factual history could be distinguished from myth, at least in principle. The Christian story claims to be factual history not myth; but, paradoxically, such a claim strengthens its power as a myth. Although this story is carefully constructed to fit the pre-existing myths of Old Testament culture, it is also blended with elements of the then contemporary Greek philosophy which clearly separated matter and spirit. It is a complex, powerful and subtle blend of symbols and images, making up a myth about the Deity coming to earth, redeeming us from our sinful nature, and conquering our greatest fear, of death. As such it is a myth about the question 'What should we live by?', and one which has been the inspiration for many cultures over the centuries.

As an example of the power of this myth I refer to a recent incident in New Zealand. In the early 1970s, at the Presbyterian theological college in Dunedin, an eminent academic was accused of heresy. The substance of this accusation is somewhat predictable, the denial of the historical truth of the biblical account of Christ's resurrection. One person who expressed an opinion on this subject was a staff member who had spent his life as a hospital chaplain, ministering to the mentally ill, the distressed and the dying. He asked how he could offer any hope to those to whom he ministered if the resurrection of Christ was not literally true. Much as I respected the person who expressed this view, I personally cannot believe in the literal truth of the resurrection. Nevertheless, I am left with a very similar unanswered question. How can one hope to rebuild the sense of 'personhood' in those whose lives have been devastated by mental illness, if, as was concluded in the previous chapter, persons do not actually exist, except as a delusion?

In Part II (sections 10.5 and 10.6) a concept of the Deity was developed, which was some way from the traditional Christian one, in that God was seen as the personification of Good, but having little (or perhaps even no) power. There is however a theme in some modern theological thinking which finds an important way in which this concept of God can be incorporated into some of the complex web of Christian mythology. The German philosophers Hegel and Nietzsche wrote of 'the death of God'. This idea came to have a quite different meaning in the writing of the twentieth-century German theologian Dietrich Bonhoeffer. Bonhoeffer was incarcerated by the Nazi regime and was executed in 1945. He saw, in the myth of Christ suffering and dying, a message for his times. It is only a God who is so powerless, and who suffers in such a human way, that can offer comfort and inspiration to modern humans who find themselves in equally powerless situations. God can help us most when he, like us, is powerless and suffers like us. Such a God is far more credible and helpful than one in whom is invested all the power and glory of the God of traditional Christian belief.

Myths such as these fulfil an important function, in that they may help us to live with anxieties and uncertainties. However, they can do this best only if they do not contradict any demonstrable facts. Paul Davies writes:

> No religion that bases its beliefs on demonstrably incorrect assumptions can expect to survive very long . . . To argue whether the date of the Creation was 4004 BC or 10,000 BC is irrelevent if scientific measurements reveal a 4½ billion-year-old Earth.[7]

Similarly it is pointless to spend time and energy on the search for parallels between the biblical creation story (which is a myth) and modern views of astrophysicists on the the Big Bang theory of creation. Likewise, a belief in a virgin birth may have been credible two thousand years ago, but becomes somewhat less credible when one knows something about reproductive physiology. The Christian myths, having lost their credibility with the advance of scientific knowledge, are thus now quite out of date in terms of the symbols they use.

I suggest that myths do not need to have the form of a story in order to fulfill the function of a myth. Basic (and rarely questioned) premises underlying the way we think may also have the function of myths. Just as with story myths it is impossible to get a definite answer as to whether these premises are true or not; and just as with these myths, these assumptions help us to live with the uncertainty of unresolved and unanswerable questions. In fact, just as with story myths, these assumptions can best fulfill their role in allaying our anxieties if we take them to be factually true (even though they are really statements of a quite different nature). This is rather similar to the traditional view of Christian mythology, that the Christian story is factually true, as a piece of history. Thus it is not surprising that some of the basic premises of the corpus of science are also given the status of being factually true; while they really do not merit that status, because they actually function as myths for the scientific age. We have already mentioned one of the questions for which any answer we adopt has the character of a myth. How do we view the extraordinary coincidences in initial conditions and physical constants in the universe which are necessary to produce a planet such as earth capable of evolving sentient beings such as ourselves? The answer we give to this question depends on prior assumptions, and those assumptions have the hallmarks of a myth.

However, scientific and conceptual premises of this sort are reached in a different fashion from traditional story myths. Their validity does not derive mainly from the power of the images and symbols they refer to. Instead their credibility arises from the fact that they do not contradict any demonstrable facts, and that there are no logical inconsistencies with the rest of the scientific corpus. Such a logically consistent structure may nevertheless be full of circular reasoning. Thus such very basic tenets of science are not likely to be objectively true, in the sense of being verifiable from facts external to this circular logical structure. This is what allows one to class these fundamental postulates as myths.

In Part I of this work, a variety of examples were given where the choice of a descriptive language had no *a priori* validation, but came to prove its merits much later. Such 'bootstrapping' occurred in early physics, for instance in the choice of quantitative descriptions, as superior to qualitative ones, or in the particular way in which Galileo chose to quantify time, or in the scientific emphasis on antecedent cause rather than the prescientific emphasis on final cause. None of these choices was self-evidently true before the choice was made; and they only became accepted as 'obviously true' when they had proved their worth over some centuries. There have been many examples of descriptive languages in biology, psychology and sociology which have not been properly grounded *a priori* in the wider corpus of science, but are adopted because of their usefulness within a particular subject. This same process of choosing fundamental premises on the grounds of their usefulness, rather than derivating them by reasoning from more fundamental premises, is also necessary within science but at a more basic, even metaphysical, level.

The really basic assumption, which makes the whole of the scientific enterprise possible, is the assumption of natural law. This assumption may be put in a stricter form, when it is even more mythical, by suggesting that there are *no exceptions* to the rule of natural law, in other words that the complete natural universe is strictly deterministic. These assumptions, and their mythical nature, are discussed in the next chapter.

14

Myths for the Modern Mind: Determinism as the Central Myth of the Secular Society

14.1 Determinism as an assumed answer to an unanswerable question

The most basic myth of modern scientific materialism is that of determinism, the belief that the world behaves consistently, according to the dictates of natural laws, in all regions of the universe and at all times, and without any exceptions. At the time of the ancient Greeks most philosophers did not clearly distinguish natural law from divine law. Moreover, in accounting for the regular succession of events in the world they did not distinguish necessity deriving from the details of antecedent events ('causal necessity' in modern terms) from the necessity deriving from a final purpose to which those events might be directed.

Some of the ancient Greeks, such as Democritus (an early proponent of the atomic theory), were however determinists who believed in the strict rule of natural law. This was clearly a belief for them, not an empirically tested postulate, since they rarely made empirical observations.

Isaac Newton appears to have seen a place for causation both by antecedent events and by the final (that is, divine) purpose to which events were directed. For instance, he writes: 'Lest the systems of the fixed stars should, by their gravity, fall on each other, he hath placed those systems at immense distances from one another.'[1]

In commenting on the fact that the larger planets (Saturn and Jupiter) are also the more distant from the sun, he writes that this 'surely arose not from their being placed at so great a distance from the sun, but rather were the cause why the Creator placed them at great distance.'[2]

In another letter he writes:

Where natural causes are at hand, God uses them as instruments in his works; but I do not think them alone sufficient for the creation, and therefore may be allowed to suppose that, amongst other things, God gave the earth its motion by such degrees and at such times as was most suitable to the creatures.[3]

Bertrand Russell discusses the subject of causal necessity versus final purpose as governing the events of the natural world. He writes:

I do not see how it could be known in advance which of these two questions science ought to ask, or whether it ought to ask both. But experience has shown that the mechanistic question leads to scientific knowledge, while the teleological one does not. The atomists asked the mechanistic question, and gave a mechanistic answer. Their successors, until the Renaissance, were more interested in the teleological question, and thus led science up a blind alley.[4]

Clearly in this historical shift in the way mankind thinks, there has been an *a posteriori* process of learning which modes of thought are apparently most profitable.

Since the start of modern science in the Italian Renaissance, the credibility of natural law, and the determinist belief in the strict adherence of all natural events to that law, has been growing steadily. Clearly it is fundamental to the whole scientific enterprise to believe that the universe behaves lawfully, at least some of the time, otherwise there would be no point in seeking out the principles of its consistency. But this is still an assumption or belief which guides scientists, just as much today as it was for Democritus. Strict determinism without any infringment of natural law is not necessary in a logical sense. It cannot be proved logically by any means that the universe behaves consistently without exception. For what premises could such a syllogism be based upon?

Nor is determinism a principle which science can ever prove empirically, from study of the universe. To show empirically that natural laws which fit a great deal of data apply with complete generality, that is with no exception whatsoever, can only be done when one has an infinity of information, which is not possible.

Let us consider the empirical status of determinism in more depth. We can ask two questions. Can we prove this idea? Can we disprove this idea? In both cases the answer must be no.

If we were hoping to prove the idea of the rule of natural law without any exception, we would need an infinity of information against which to test our conjecture. This is impossible. Suppose we had a smaller body of information, and hoped to test, as accurately as possible, our predictions of future events based on the current state of events, and our supposedly complete grasp of natural law. In some cases in the physical sciences, the correspondance between prediction from theory and empirical findings is indeed exceedingly precise. Penrose singles out the physical theories where this is possible as 'superb'.[5] Most of the theories in this category are from classical physics, and refer to very large-scale processes. One theory from modern physics which may be in the same class is quantum electrodynamics, which, for instance, can predict the magnetic moment of an electron to within one part in 10^{11}. However, most physical theories and theories in most other branches of science are nowhere in reach of such precision. Moreover, even under the unlikely condition of very complete and accurate information being available, there are limits to the accuracy of our inference, which would prevent us from ever making predictions with comparable accuracy. A body of mathematics – known as chaos theory – has been influential in recent years, which shows that, even with quite simple systems where every single interaction is assumed to be quite deterministic, prediction in the combined system is theoretically impossible, except in a statistical sense. Therefore, it is theoretically impossible to distiguish between experimental observations which are lawful in principle but unpredictable in practice, and those which escape completely the constraints of natural law.

The defender of the determinist case may seek support from commonplace events in the world of technology. He may point out that every time we turn a switch (or use any other piece of modern technological gadgetry) we are relying on the lawfulness of nature. He may say that in these cases the design of the technology has deliberately simplified the many extraneous influences which make it difficult to demonstrate determinism in naturalistic settings. Indeed he may have deliberately arranged to employ systems in which chaotic dynamics are avoided. When such simplification has been done, the lawfulness of nature becomes much more evident.

This argument is fair enough, but still does not rigorously exclude exceptions to natural law. Equipment does often fail unpredictably and without it being possible to find a detailed explanation of why and when it happened so. Moreover, most technology relies on mass events, involving large-scale force, mass, and energy (where Penrose's 'superb' theories may be applicable), rather than the microscopic events at the level of subatomic particles. Exceptions to natural law could easily be hidden in the population dynamics of many atoms, molecules or elementary particles, only a very few of which might defy natural laws as very rare events.

There is some evidence that such 'aberrant behaviour' actually occurs. Radioactive decay (and other 'quantum' events) are described as occurring by chance. The precise timing of such events cannot be described as necessary consequences of a natural law. The population of events of which a single such event is part may be statistically constrained. But the individual events *appear* to be random,[6] or events without an antecedent cause.

At the subatomic level there is also the well-known indeterminacy principle of Heisenberg, which suggests that the more accurately one attempts to measure one variable (such as the position of a particle) the less accurately one can measure another (e.g. its velocity). Although the mathematical rigour of such a principle can be applied only at this subatomic level, a similar principle, less formally stated, can easily be discerned at an everyday level, such as in human psychology. In attempting to understand the psychological events that have led a human being to behave in a certain way, a psychoanalyst may try questioning the person about those events. But the act of questioning changes the person's perception of the events. The act of obtaining information changes the person from whom the information is obtained, and thus there is a similar uncertainty principle.

So much for attempts to prove the determinist thesis. What about the possibility of disproving the idea that natural law reigns without any exception? When scientists claim evidence for lawfulness of behaviour of parts of the universe, they have almost always taken precautions to control and standardize all variables other than the ones being studied. But things are more complicated in the world outside the physicist's laboratory. To prove that such a naturalistic event, which appears to be an exception, really is a true breach of natural laws, one would need to exclude an infinity of possible interfering influences, some of which we now know about, others of which may be totally unknown at present. To disprove the idea of unblemished determinism, just a single well-documented exception to the idea of natural law would suffice to destroy the edifice of the complete lawfulness of the universe. But to obtain such a proven, *bona fide* example, one would need access to information about an infinity of possible events to exclude the logically possible occasional influences upon the event in question. Once again the completely rigorous disproof would require infinite knowledge.

What is more, some of the determinants of an event we might choose could be related to it in the indecipherably chaotic manner mentioned in the previous paragraph, while still actually being constrained by natural law. Thus many events which seem as if they are exceptions to natural law might still be determined by chaotic, though lawful, influences.

Thus, just as it would be impossible to prove the universe totally lawful, it is also impossible to prove definitively that any single apparent exception is really a *bona fide* exception to the usual natural laws.

Thus the belief in complete lawfulness of the universe can be neither proved nor disproved in a completely rigorous sense. Sure, there are plenty of events and phenomena in the world around us which seem to defy all the patterns of natural behaviour we are used to. It is arguable that these cases are more numerous and more typical than the cases where nature appears to behave lawfully. But there can be no proof either way. Logically speaking there is simply no way that the rule of natural law can be either proved or disproved to apply without exception.

In this context it is relevant to quote Newton again. Referring to his concept of gravity his celebrated dictum is 'Hypothesis non fingo.' This is usually translated as 'I do not offer an explanation.' On this theme he also writes:

> Hitherto I have not been able to discover the cause of those properties of gravity from phenomena, and I frame no hypotheses; for whatever is not deduced from the phenomena is to be called a hypothesis, and hypotheses whether metaphysical or physical, whether of occult qualities or mechanical, have no place in experimental philosophy.[7]

In other words, Newton confesses himself incapable of investing the regularities of nature which are summarized in his gravitational theory with the status of logical necessity. David Hume, the philosopher, would have agreed that the regularities of the world, however often observed, could never be thought of as logically necessary. Polkinghorne refers to the many instances where elegant mathematics is found to be a good description of the physical world, and quotes Wigner who writes of the 'unreasonable effectiveness of mathematics'.[8]

Let us survey from above (as it were) the cognitive capacity of our species with respect to the issue of determinism. Even from the standpoint of the materialist, it is hard to see how any living thing (such as myself, or the reader), a mere fragment of dust in the infinite cosmos, could come to represent within its nervous system such a universal generalization as the unblemished adherence of the natural world to the regularities of scientific law. This can be stated quite simply, because such a tiny fragment of matter as a human being (even if part of a social species which accumulates knowledge over the centuries) could never have interaction with enough of the exceptional phenomena of the universe to validly form such a universal generalization.

In other words *the belief in determinism without exception already has one important characteristic of a myth as defined above: It is an answer assumed to a question which, in principle, cannot be given an assured answer.*

Religious organizations are often criticized for their dogmatism on questions where there is no certain answer. In science it is equally important to be clear about the limits of what we can, in principle, know. It is important to be clear that the thesis of universal determinism is a belief, not a fact.

14.2 The psychological functions of the belief in determinism

The other important characteristic by which we recognize a myth is that it has a psychological function for the human mind. In other words, to show that the belief in determinism is of the nature of a myth we should ask: does the belief have a use, in allaying humankind's anxieties?

In this question, we are not dealing with the practical uses of determinism in relation to technology. These are the overwhelming majority of cases where, when it is put to the test, nature appears to behave consistently. As we have seen in the previous section it is impossible to assert that such lawfulness applies without any exception; but as far as technology goes, nature *is* sufficiently regular to suffice in practice.

But if we ask about the psychological uses of a belief in determinism (by which we identifiy that belief as a myth) we refer to the belief in determinism in principle. In this case we are dealing with a categorical statement that there be no exceptions to the rule of natural law whatsoever, whether or not those exceptions come to be observed by experimenters. Does such a belief help us (or some of us) to live, to reduce our anxiety in the face of otherwise unanswerable questions?

Determinism, if one believes it, provides the alternative of natural law to that of divine law which was dominant before the scientific Renaissance. Determinism as a belief has helped many people to throw off the shackles of other myths, especially the overbearing and (to many) incredible Christian mythology. Christian mythology was invented before the rebirth of science. It has several features which were fundamentally incompatible with the conclusions drawn about the world by that science. Some of these inconsistencies were not an essential part of the Christian message (e.g. that the world is the centre of the universe). Others were more important to the psychological function of the Christian myths as myths. Amongst these are the idea of God made flesh (a symbol, deriving from Greek thinking of the time, of a bridge between the world of ideas and the physical world); the resurrection of Christ (with much of the same symbolism, but also a symbolic triumph over mankind's greatest fear, of death); the redemption of sinful mankind (making reference to much older myths in the Judaic tradition).

These myths have their psychological functions, but have become incredible to an ever-increasing number of people since the Renaissance. The belief in determinism restored to such people a faith in their own senses. It was more credible than the belief in miracles, including the central myth of Christianity, the miracle of Christ's resurrection. The Christian myth of redemption was originally perhaps designed to remove a sense of guilt. But in later years, the doctrine of original sin and the doctrine of predestination could do nothing but burden people further with that same sense of guilt. In this fact lay part of the power of the churches, and still does. Determinism, the belief in natural law was, and is, a liberating influence from the domination of church power.

The liberating effect of a belief in natural law emerges strongly in the words of scientists themselves. We have already mentioned Laplace's quotation. Because of the demonstrations of natural law coming from Newtonian science, he could boldly assert, on the subject of God: 'I have no need of that hypothesis.' A century or more later Einstein asserted: 'God does not play dice with the Universe.' Even to such intellectual giants as these there appears to have been some comfort in the belief in natural law. For Einstein, a belief in natural law was so important that he (perhaps only half-seriously) personified that belief as the Deity; but it was a very different Deity from that which commanded belief before the birth of modern science. Christians who are also scientists may also assert the value of this aspect of the scientific creed.

Polkinghorne writes: 'Those who commit themselves to this trust in a rational cosmos, are asserting intelligibility to be the key to reality'.[9] Einstein also recognizes the unreasonbleness of a lawful universe. Polkinghorne[10] cites him as writing: 'as far as the propositions of mathematics relate to reality they are not certain, and as far as they are certain they do not relate to reality'. This view may be counterposed against the view of some Christian thinkers over the ages that their trust is validated by its *ir*rationality. For instance, Polkinghorne[11] cites Gardner, referring to 'religious faith' as 'unsupported by logic or science'.

The need for liberation from the shackles of religion is so strong that the package of materialism and determinism has strong appeal. But is it not possible to retrace our steps to a time before the Christian churches had such hegemony over people's minds? If we could do that we might rediscover the aspects of the human condition which led primitive man to invent the first religious myths. We might then find that the reasons for inventing such myths are largely unchanged. We could then search out positive reasons for adopting myths, rather than the negative one, namely the need for support in overthrowing organizations which have become so stale that they have forgotten the original reasons behind their own mythology. If we could do that we might find credible and useful myths, suitable for the modern era.

Determinism, supported by a basically materialistic philosophy, is the central myth underlying what I refer to as the secular society. It may be denied by the more sophisticated of scientists, especially physicists. But this myth now has a powerful hold on the popular mind, whose attitude to science is more naive. It is designated as a myth because it is an assumed answer to an unanswerable question, and because it has proved psychologically useful in overthrowing other outdated myths, from a previous age. Nevertheless, just as for the myths it has replaced, it is not 'objectively true'. This central myth of the scientific age has grown steadily in influence over the past five centuries. However, the process has accelerated in the past two hundred years, as a result of the development of other subsidiary scientific myths, derivatives of the central myth of determinism. These are described below. In contrast to Newtonian science these subsidiary myths are all beliefs about history. I hope to show that they have the same characteristics of other myths noted above, namely, they provide assumed answers to unanswerable questions; and they help mankind to live with the existential anxieties which would otherwise arise from the uncertainty of these unanswered questions. Just as with the central myth of determinism, the real function of these myths is to provide psychological support for those who would defy the authority and tradition of established religion. But in substance they are just as mythical as the myths of those religions (though undoubtedly nowadays more credible to most people).

Myths for the Modern Mind:
Subsidiary Myths of the Secular Society

15.1 'Classical science' versus the 'science of history'

The major triumphs of early post-Renaissance science – Newton's theories of gravitation and planetary motion – were the finest example of natural law revealed at that time; but these theories do not depend on a strict adherence to natural law without any exception, in the sense discussed above. There is no necessary conflict between Newtonian physics, where natural law seems to rule, and the microscopic events of quantum theory, where the rule of natural law is most dubitable. The latter, unpredictable events may be regular occurrences in a Newtonian universe, but because they are on so much tinier a scale, they need not influence the course of events at the Newtonian level.

Another characteristic of this 'classical' world view, which developed as Newton's ideas became assimilated into general culture of the times, emphasized that Newtonian natural law was a mechanism which, overall, tended to produce stability, or cyclical recurrences of events over the ages, rather than progressive change. As the Victorian hymn-writer E. H. Sears puts it:

> For lo! the days are hastening on,
>   By prophet-bards foretold,
> When, with the ever-circling years,
>   Comes round the age of gold.

The idea of progressive development was not typical of the thinking of the time. This can be said equally about astronomical events as about human societies. Both were viewed as relatively static, in the sense that people did not automatically believe in 'progress' as we do today. The same characteristic also applied to views on individual human identity.

Descartes' identification of critical self-awareness as a fundamental psychological reality had nothing of the developmental approach which modern-day psychologists would link with the concept of conscious awareness.

Nor was Newtonian science committed to the idea that natural law ruled without exception. The motive which led Newton himself to conceive his laws of motion (including planetary motion) and the theory of gravitation was not so much to create a scheme which realistically explained all known empirical facts in detail. Indeed, that scheme did not fit some of the empirical facts, and the reasons for some of the exceptions were left for later generations to unravel. Rather than this, Newton, like Galileo, had a faith, inseparable from his religious beliefs, that simple mathematical relationships were part of God's construction of the universe. Newton's own scientific ideas were an attempt to provide a mathematical description of the greatest elegance and beauty, rather than one which fitted all the empirical facts. To quote Newton himself: 'The most beautiful system of the sun, planets and comets could only proceed from the counsel and dominion of an intelligent and powerful Being.'[1]

Moreover Newton himself apparently believed in miracles, divine interventions, when those elegant mathematical prescriptions might be overruled. He considers the fact, additional to the law of gravitation, that the planets have a transverse velocity allowing them to move in circular orbits:

> The transverse impulse must be a just quantity; for if it be too big or too little, it will cause the earth to move in some other line . . . I do not know any power in nature which would cause this transverse motion without the divine arm.[2]

Newton also supposed the 'divine arm' to impress on the planets their diurnal rotation. Many of Newton's appeals to the 'divine arm' concern the initial conditions necessary to set the heavenly bodies in motion, which could have been part of the initial act of creation. But he also invokes the same divine intervention in the later history of the world.

> God made and governs the world invisibly . . . and by the same power by which he gave life at first to every species of animals, he is able to revive the dead, and has revived Jesus Christ our Redeemer . . .[3]

However, a body of religious thinking soon distorted Newton's own work, and saw in the Newtonian universe a mechanism like a clock which, once set going by divine edict, would then run on without any exception in the regular course of events. These were the Deists.[4] They presumably took, as a matter of faith, that natural law had no exceptions. However, as we have seen in the previous section, this belief can have neither logical nor empirical foundation. It therefore has some of the characteristics of a myth, and may be counted as a forerunner of the now-popular view that science implies unblemished determinism.

In the eighteenth century the belief in a static or cyclical universe started to be revised. Philosophers became more interested in progressive change; and after the radical change of the French revolution in 1789, the idea of steady or abrupt change, and progressive development, came to feature in a number of scientific or quasi-scientific theories. One of the earliest of these, for example, was the economic theory of Adam Smith, emphasizing for the first time the concept of economic growth.

In the mid-nineteenth century this type of theory started to flourish greatly, a radical change from the era before the French revolution. In the sociological area this was no doubt influenced greatly by that revolution. In the biological area it was also influenced by the developing science of geology, which showed, in the fossil record, that life forms quite different from what we know today had existed in past times. There were a number of quasi-scientific theories of social or biological change, such as the population theory of Malthus, or the evolutionary ideas which preceded Darwin's synthesis on biological evolution. The most celebrated historical theories of the time which claimed to be scientific were those associated with the names of Karl Marx and Charles Darwin, dealing respectively with human social history, and the history of life on earth. There have also been other historical accounts of human sociological development since then, largely drawing on the respectability of Darwinian theory.

Half a century after Darwin, Freud's ideas about psychological development of the human individual were presented, and had some relation to evolutionary theory. For instance Freud's hierarchical structure of the mind (including 'ego', 'superego' and 'id') seems rather similar to the hierarchy of functions postulated in the nervous system by neurologists such as Hughlings Jackson; and both systems arose naturally in an intellectual climate where evolution was supposed to occur by progressive building upon, and elaboration of, older structures and functions. Indeed, Freud's idea that the adult mind contains a repository of repressed memories of traumatic childhood experiences, and his designation of phases of development as 'oral', 'anal' etc., seem similar in style to the doctrine that the development of an individual recapitulates that of the evolution of the species.

All these theoretical constructions are part of the same *Zeitgeist*, the attempt to make scientific theories about historical or developmental processes. Of these three mentioned, Marxism and Freudianism have had many adherents, but neither has been generally accepted into the corpus of scientific knowledge and theory. Darwin's theory is the only one which has acquired the worldwide prestige of a truly scientific theory. This is perhaps because a specific, testable mechanism was proposed for the gradual change of life forms over the eons (in contrast to earlier formulations of biological evolution, which made less impact.) Just as Newton's theory of planetary motion relied on gravitational processes which could be demonstrated in the laboratory, so Darwin's theory of the origin of species relied on a process which could be demonstrated in the hear-and-now (or so it was claimed), that process of course being natural selection.

The change from Newtonian 'static' science to nineteenth-century 'historical science' apparently occurred without much conscious realization of the changed assumptions. But there were changes in underlying assumptions.

Central to this distinction between static science and scientific explanations of history is the distinction between 'nomothetic' and 'idiographic' descriptions. These are terms used by the psychologist Luria, who was interested in both, and knew the difference.[5] *Nomothetic science* involves the study of generalizable laws. *Idiographic science* involves interest in individual events for their own sake. The falling of an object under the influence of gravity is an example of the first. All cases of falling bodies are generalizable by virtue of the fact that all bodies are massive. The history of Richard Seddon (an early New Zealand Prime Minister) is apparently an example of the latter, unless one wants to make precise and strictly scientific generalizations about 'all New Zealand Prime Ministers'.

A serious question arises here. When do we allow generalizability and when not? In the case of Marxism, can the historical process be generalized from one society to another? In the case of Freudianism, can the ideas and complexes of individual psychiatric patients become generalized principles? Most seriously, referring to Darwin's ideas, can the origin of a species be generalizable from one instance of it to another?

In the physical sciences, the natural laws derive from (and are intended to describe) classes of event which are identifiable by reference to a *single explicit measurement*, which *can be made in actual practice*. Thus, the law of gravitational attraction, the laws of conservation of momentum, angular momentum, mass and energy, and the inverse square law in its various applications, can be tested as they apply to whole classes of events, defined by explicit measurements along the single appropriate physical dimension. For instance the law of gravitational attraction applies to objects by virtue of their mass.

In the case of the theories of Marx, Freud and Darwin this is not so. The events which are classed together to make generalizations (about social change, about human psychic development, or about the origin of species) are all complex events, not explicitly defineable, nor explictly observable. We have all seen massive objects falling under the influence of gravity, and the conservation of angular momentum is displayed every time we see someone riding a bicycle. But it is a far more elusive business to be certain that one has witnessed, for instance, the origin of a new species. At first sight, every instance of social change, every instance of individual psychic history, or every case of speciation has so many special circumstances surrounding it that it has to be regarded as a unique set of happenings, the individual elements of the set being unanalysed. One's immediate reaction to such events of history is thus to class them as 'idiographic' in Luria's terms, rather than 'nomothetic'.

15.2 Darwinism: the prime example of a 'science of history'

Let us look in more detail at the most important of these three cases, the process by which new biological species emerge.

Darwinian theory postulates two processes in interaction. *Random variation* (or 'quasi random' variation) is an observable fact, and is attributed to genetic mutation in neo-Darwinism. (There may be other contributory 'random' events, such as the chance isolation of a few individuals with particular characteristics in situations where they can reproduce prolifically, and so these individuals become 'founders' of a new and distinct variant.) *Natural selection* of the most advantageous characteristics produced by such variation and mutation is then held to be solely responsible for evolutionary change.

Firstly, consider mutations: *Single* mutations, in the modern view are unique, unpredictable events. As Jacques Monod puts it:

> A mutation is in itself a microscopic event, a quantum event, to which the principle of uncertainty consequently applies. An event which is hence and by its very nature *essentially* unpredictable.[6]

In other words, it could be suggested that a single mutation is part of idiographic science, an instance about which it is hard to generalize, rather than of nomothetic science.

Over the course of large spans of time, however, many mutations may occur, in the genome of a particular species. The process of mutation can be expressed quantitatively along a single measure, the mutation rate. This can be measured in practice by assessing the degree of congruence of DNA between different species; and this measure can then (in principle) be related to the time elapsed since those species are supposed to have diverged. Using such a measure it could be argued that genetic divergence and speciation are regularly repeated events (i.e. speciation occurs when genetic divergence exceeds a certain threshold), and so could be dealt with as lawful examples of nomothetic science.

To decide between these two views we need to examine the concept of randomness.

What does the word random mean? In statistical tables one may find a series of random numbers. In practice such a sequence of numbers may defy all attempts to see regularity in the sequence. In fact, however, such random number tables are generated in a quite regular and lawful manner. In modern times they would be generated by a computational algorithm, which usually needs to be 'seeded' by introduction of any chosen integer. Therefore, if one has the precise algorithm which was used to generate a particular random number table, and also knows the seed used to start the computation going, the sequence of 'random' numbers become easily predictable, and by no means random.

More generally, when one sees a sequence of events without apparent order or lawfulness, there is no way that one can exclude the possibility that the events are lawful, according to an as-yet-undiscovered principle. Therefore, one cannot prove a series of events to be random, in any absolute sense.

Likewise with 'chance' events like mutations. Logically speaking, one cannot prove that they are random. Monod's book focusses from its outset on the dichotomy of whether nature is 'objective' or 'projective' (i.e. directed to a final purpose). The idea that biological evolution depends on 'random' mutations is an application of the philosophy (or myth) that nature is not projective in Monod's sense, that it does not reveal any overall design intended to achieve a final purpose. However, since one can never prove a sequence of events to be truly random in an absolute sense, one cannot exclude the possibility that Nature *is* actually projective. One cannot rule out the possibility that the time and place of the occurrence of particular mutations are governed by some grander ultimate purpose or design.

This conclusion applies just as much to the specific combinations of mutations (which are summarized as mutation rates or degrees of genetic congruence between related species) as it does to each and every single mutation taken individually. Since mutations are the raw material from which evolution develops, one cannot therefore prove that evolution is determined by 'pure chance, absolutely free but blind' (Monod's words and his claim). The assumption that this *is* so, which is nearly universally made by modern evolutionary biologists, thus appears to have one of the characteristics of a myth, as defined above: It is an assumed answer to a question which is in principle unanswerable.

The alternative could be that, as part of a purposive development of the universe, the apparently random mutations in the genes, apparently controlled only by the statistics of causal or quantum processes, are in fact exceptions where natural law gives way to constraints of a totally different kind, indeed of a metaphysically different kind. These departures from regularity might be referred to as 'little miracles'.

Such events would, by their very nature, all be very tiny individual events. Also by their very nature they would all be incapable of being classified and 'tamed' as the repeatable individual events which science studies in the laboratory as nomothetic science. For both reasons, they could never be detected. But nor could their existence be disproved. The possibility of their existence would be essentially a matter of belief; and the option one chooses to believe would have one of the qualities of a myth.

This may not seem very satisfactory, but we will see shortly that the argument for the origin of species by natural selection suffers somewhat similar weaknesses. This need not be a cause for surprise if both beliefs are of the nature of myths.

However, once we realize that many events are not nomothetic but idiographic, we have somehow to come to terms with the latter. There seem to be three ways that idiographic events could be interpreted:

once one admits that there are individual events which cannot be tamed by science as instances of repeated patterns, one can simply say about them 'I do not know what to make of them.' But if one wants to systematize them, they could as likely be examples of a projective, purposive (though inscrutible) universe, as of one governed by 'pure chance, absolutely free but blind'. Neither of these choices is the sort which science in its strict nomothetic sense can make. Idiographic science has no bases to decide objectively between these alternatives. Any decision that is made is based on premises other than scientific ones, that is on the myths we freely choose.

Now consider the other process said to underlie evolutionary change, the process of natural selection. Natural selection can be demonstrated on the small scale, in laboratory experiments. Moreover, it can sometimes be inferred to a high degree of likelihood in naturalistic observations of evolution on the small historical time scale. The obvious and much quoted example is industrial melanism in a species of moth. Before the industrial revolution in Britain caused soot-blackening of trees and other substrates on which these species of moth might rest, they had a light colouring of body and wings. When the environment became blacker, these moths changed to a darker colouring, presumably because only those that had the darker colouring would be well camouflaged from predators (birds), and so survive to pass on their characteristics to their offspring. It should be noted, however, that this change is not the origin of a new species, but the relatively superficial change to a different form of a pre-existing species. It might be suggested that it is no more than conjecture to think that natural selection alone, working on the repertoire of mutations, can give rise to the vast range of living things that exists and have existed in the world.

A central phenomenon which needs to be analysed is speciation, the origin of new species. On the subject of speciation one might expect to find clear answers in Darwin's *magnum opus*. However, despite the title of this book – *On the Origin of Species* – it contains no detail about how new species actually arise. For the purposes of the following argument a 'species' may be defined as a group of animals which can breed with each other (and produce fertile offspring), but not with other groups of animals. In other words, a species shows 'reproductive isolation' from other species. The usual assumption, made by all evolutionary theorists up to about 1940, and by many modern evolutionary theorists, is that reproductive isolation (which defines a species) occurs simply as a result of geographic separation of different populations of the same species over periods of evolutionary history. This view of speciation is called allopatric speciation. Such geographic isolation may have been achieved by seas, oceans, major mountain ranges and so on. During the period of geographic isolation, the separated populations undergo genetic divergence, either by random drift resulting from the particular set of random mutations which occur in each population, or as a result of more directed change, the consequence of genetic selection to adapt to the different environments each population has to face. It is envisaged that, when such genetic divergence has proceeded to a certain degree, reproductive isolation (speciation) also inevitably occurs. One of the nicest examples comes from Darwin himself. He noted that windswept offshore islands (which would be well isolated geographically) commonly contained flightless species of insect. He suggested that this specialization arose because flying species would easily be swept into the sea, and thus would fail to produce offspring.

Alternatives to geographical isolation as a basis for speciation have also been suggested, but never fully substantiated. These are called sympatric speciation.

With regard to allopatric speciation Coyne writes:

> Surprisingly there is almost no empirical evidence for the most crucial aspect of allopatric speciation, the origin of reproductive isolation as a byproduct of [genetic] drift or selection.[7]

Both for allopatric and sympatric speciation, theoretical genetic models suggest that reproductive isolation and major adaptive change occurs much more quickly in small populations than in large ones. Thus, for the really dramatic and interesting evolutionary changes, most of which have to be detected from the fossil record, the chances of finding evidence of the crucial missing links become very small. Hence the decisive evidence for the claim that natural selection and mutation are the twin processes, by themselves sufficient for evolution to have occurred, is squeezed into a hypothetical realm which is mainly unobservable in fine detail, even in the here-and-now, and completely unobservable for historical examples.

Evidence for the existence of God has been sought in the 'gaps' which science has not yet been able to reach (the 'God of the Gaps', according to Coulson[8]). The hypothetical process of the origin of species by natural selection likewise appears to be confined to the gaps where observation is impossible. God may move in mysterious ways; but so, according to models of the evolutionary process, does Darwinian evolution.

Both for allopatric and sympatric speciation, what evidence there is, is of course collected from a few individual species, an infinitesimal fraction of all existing species, or of all the instances when speciation has occurred over the eons. If those very few examples are to be taken as paradigms for evolution of life as a whole, it is obvious that the assumption is being made that speciation is a nomothetic event, one where generalization is possible from a few instances to the general case. If this assumption is correct, the piecemeal approach to validating evolutionary theory would be valid. But it is an assumption, and it might not be correct. In fact, this assumption might be the single most important question about evolutionary theory. There seems to be an element of circularity in the reasoning here. Highly selected examples of speciation are chosen in order to throw light on speciation as a generality. Yet that step depends on the assumption that generalizations can be made about speciation. This begs the question on which Darwinian evolutionary theory rests.

Attempts have been made to render evolutionary theory plausible by working out the probability of evolution having happened the way it did. But this seems a strange pursuit. Quite apart from the technicalities of such an argument, which are considerable, several more general points can be made:

1. All premises for such an argument are based on observations made in the present tiny fraction of time in which humans have studied science. One cannot rule out exceptions at other times. In other words, the assumption is again made that evolution is a nomothetic process rather than a series of ungeneralizable idiographic ones.

2. Jacques Monod writes: 'Life appeared on earth: what – before the event – were the chances that this would occur'? Monod considers the 'possibility that the decisive event occurred only once'. He continues:

> This idea is distasteful to most scientists. Science can neither say nor do anything about a unique occurrence. It can only consider events which form a class, whose *a priori* probability, however faint, is definite.[9]

Monod assumes rather than proves that the possibility of life appearing on earth is a nomothetic event, one about which generalizations and probability calculations are possible. Nevertheless, if we are to take the logic of the Darwinian theory of evolution seriously, as reinterpreted after the discovery of the molecular basis of inheritance, we must envisage that the slight shuffling of genetic structure at the molecular level in a single individual case could result in that 'decisive event' – the origin of a new species – as an idiographic event. Monod appears to be limiting his interpretation of evolution to the modes of thought which science can comfortably handle. It is undoubtedly true that science can say or do nothing about a unique occurrence. But that is not a reason for denying the possibility of unique occurrences. It *is* a reason for being somewhat modest about what science can in principle achieve, and for recognizing the need for other ways of thinking.

3. To discuss evolution in statistical terms is rather like asking the question. 'What is the probability that a universe should exist in which "I" could emerge to contemplate the universe's existence?' As with discussion of cosmology, it seems reasonable to invoke here an anthropic principle that, given that we *do* exist contemplating our origin, the universe necessarily must have a certain form and history. The development, over the eons, of life forms with certain broad characteristics, then apears to be logically necessary, not a matter of chance. Statistical arguments are therefore not relevent.

This sort of question is crucial to our view of Darwin's theory of evolution, and the belief by modern Darwinians that all life forms, all species, have originated from the inorganic primaeval soup by the principle of natural selection.

In defence of the Darwinian version of evolution it is often asked 'What rational alternative could there now be to some version of Darwin's theory of the natural selection?' The implication is that no alternative has ever been suggested and found consistent with the rest of empirical data.

This sort of defence of Darwinism has occurred regularly in discussions I have had with my pro-Darwinian colleagues. But let me quote a more authoritative source. In a recent article in *Science*[10] Lenski and Mittler discuss some evidence purporting to show 'directed mutations'. Experimental evidence has been produced that in some bacteria the mutation frequency is greater for 'favourable' mutations than for 'neutral' or 'unfavourable' ones. The actual scientific issue is not directly relevant here. What is relevant is that the authors, commenting on this evidence, use, as an argument against the conclusion of 'directed mutations' that no mechanism can be suggested for such direction. In other words they use the assumption of determinacy, such as found in other biological systems, to defend the traditional Darwinian position. Yet this assumption is not a scientific one, it is a metaphysical one. Surely the evidence for directed mutations should be judged on its own merits, without recourse to unproved and unprovable metaphysical assumptions. This is not to argue against metaphysical thinking; but let us please be explicit about it.

Several other comments can be made against the 'there is no alternative' defence of Darwinism. First, this is perhaps not an adequate reason for accepting the theory. There are many aspects of the functioning of living things, which are undoubtedly simpler than the process of evolution, where we readily accept that we have no answer. In other instances we would expect to positively verify our favourite hypothesis of a biological mechanism by all means available, rather than accept it, by default, as it were, simply because no alternative can be suggested.

Musgrave,[11] in analysing the historical change of scientific ideas, has suggested that it is relatively rare for refutation of individual postulates to be a crucial determinant of major shifts of ideas. Instead, whole systems of ideas, with many auxiliary hypotheses buttressing a central core of ideas, are subject to experimental tests. When experimental results fail to confirm the system of ideas as a whole, it is usual to defend the central core of ideas, by showing how special circumstances mean that one or other of the auxiliary hypotheses no longer apply. Thus, to some extent, Musgrave suggests, the ideas which form a central core for a particular area of science are vigorously protected from attack, as though they are deemed 'irrefutable by fiat'. This is tantamount to admitting the point emphasized here, that some of the central ideas of science in general, and of specific areas of science, have something about them similar to myths. When a major shift of the central core does occur, it is generally possible only when there is a good alternative to this central core. For instance, in astronomy, by the end of last century some observations of celestial movements were known which were clear anomalies to Newtonian physics based on the central core of Newton's laws of motion. But Newtonian physics was not radically changed until there was a clear alternative set of central assumptions available, as advocated by Einstein.

In the case of evolutionary theory, the central core is the assumption that natural selection from amongst the naturally occurring variants of a species is responsible for all evolutionary change. As Musgrave states: 'Natural selection is the only plausible mechanism for evolutionary change' . . . 'It is the only game in town' . . . 'Natural selection has no serious scientific competitor.' This is true. There is no serious *scientific* competitor to this central core, however poor is the actual *validation* of it.

However, the central core of a scientific theory like Darwinism, that which is guarded most jealously, and which is most mythological in character, has implications not only for science, but also for the way we view ourselves, and therefore for the way we live our lives. These central beliefs therefore are one of the influences which determine how we answer that difficult religious question: 'What do we live by?' Thus, I suggest that although the central, quasi mythological core of evolutionary theory has little competition from within science itself, it is exposed to competition from alternative mythologies outside science.

The argument that 'there is no alternative' thus begs a crucial question. There may be no alternative to Darwin's theory within the metaphysical framework within which science is nowadays generally cast. But, for a hypothesis which attempts to give a comprehensive account of a historical process, it is exactly that metaphysical framework which is at issue. To assume that random mutation and natural selection are the sole arbiters of evolutionary destiny is to prejudge the issue. The assumption appears to amount to taking the deliberate decision *a priori* to exclude the possibility that nature is 'projective', that there is some direction or purpose to those apparently random events.

The alternative view of Darwinian natural selection, advocated here, need hardly influence the empirical study of evolution at all; nor need it be influenced by future research on the subject. Indeed, if either of these could happen the arguments I have used would be much weakened. Nevertheless, the alternative interpretation of the evidence I have suggested could have a major effect on the implications we draw from Darwinism about our place in the universe (as we shall see in section 15.4).

Let us be quite clear where the fallacy lies in evolutionary theory. The fallacy is not the notion of evolutionary change *per se*. The empirical evidence from the fossil record and from comparative anatomy leaves no doubt that life forms existed a long time ago which were very different from those around today. Darwinism was set up as an alternative to the prevalent idea of the time, that there was a special independent creation of each species. Darwinism, as a theory of evolution, was far more coherent than that idea, and far more in accord with facts of the fossil record, and the clear relationships in comparative anatomy between different species. However, all that was necessary to overcome those beliefs (which were attempted reconciliations of the biblical account with new scientific facts) was to argue for evolution, in the strict sense of historical *description*. Evolution by natural selection, as an *explanation* of historical change, is superfluous to that aim, and its basis in empirical fact was, and still is, far less satisfactory.

It is interesting here to contrast Newton's approach to Darwin's. Newton, having pointed out mathematical regularities describing the motion of the planets and other heavenly bodies which fitted the properties of an entity he called 'gravity', was content to say 'hypothesis non fingo'. He did not try to explain gravity. 'For the cause of gravity is what I do not pretend to know,' he writes to Richard Bentley in 1692. Darwin on the other hand, living at a time when bold 'explanations' (so-called), applying throughout history, were fashionable, achieved success exactly because he went beyond description and tried to explain the process of evolution in terms of a few simple premises.

Nor is the fallacy that the mechanism proposed – natural selection – can bring about *some* changes in the manner proposed by Darwin. However, all examples of biological change proven to be produced by natural selection are necessarily on a quite short time scale, and involve relatively minor changes. Admittedly there are a few examples where, by scrupulous and energetic laboratory or field work, the origin of a new species (with reproductive isolation) has been shown to occur under pressure from natural selection. However, these examples generally come from species with rapid reproduction rates (such as the fruit fly *Drosophila*). It cannot realistically be expected that similar work in the future will produce a substantially more complete proof of the role of natural selection in evolution, since the process of speciation is likely to consist of very rare combinations of events set against the backdrop of evolutionary history, only a minute fraction of which can ever be observed even in the here-and-now. Thus the fallacy comes in extending the mechanism of natural selection from the small scale to the geological time scale; that is, in assuming that mutation and natural selection are the sole determinants of evolutionary change throughout all history.

This fallacy is one which applies especially in historical theories – the arbitrary assumption that the circumstances which determine one example of change, itself beset by many special circumstances, apply universally, throughout historical time, when all the other examples may have their own equally special (but different) circumstances. Thus the real fallacy of evolutionary theory is to regard a series of idiographic events as generalizable, nomothetic science. Generally speaking, this fallacy is like concluding that the universe is lawful without exception, despite the fact that one cannot observe the infinite cases in which that lawfulness might be tested. Newtonian science did not make that assumption; and it was only when a debased form of Newtonian science came to have influence that fallacious historical theories could pose as science. In science generally, the formulation of the laws from which nomothetic science is built usually depends on laboratory experiments in which all imaginable extraneous variables are controlled. This is very different from the so-called generalizations made from the study of selected, but uncontrolled events within history.

Again one must try to be more specific about the nature of the fallacy. It does not apply to all historical scientific work. It does not apply, for instance, to geological arguments about how the shape of mountains and valleys arose. Nor does it apply to the cosmologists reasoning about the origin of the universe in the Big Bang. In both these cases we are dealing with mass events, where quantum events are swamped in population dynamics. The distinctive feature of evolutionary theory, which makes it so vulnerable to the confusion between idiographic and nomothetic science, is that biological evolution involves reproduction and transmission of information.

Information, unlike mass and energy, has a 'seed-like' quality, where a signal of microscopic dimensions can have an effect quite out of proportion to the mass or energy involved, provided it is expressed in the right way and at the right time.

An example will serve to illustrate this point about historical theories that involve information transmission. Supposing we were to meet someone who claimed to be the rightful heir to the French throne. At first we would be not a little sceptical of his claim; but suppose he was convincing enough for us at least to start serious investigation of it. To prove his royal lineage we would have to establish his family tree step-by-step back to one or other of the pre-revolutionary French monarchs. If just a single one of the links in this chain were proved false, his claim as a whole would also become quite implausible.

Similarly with the claim of evolutionary biology. The claim that all living things are descended by gradual change from inanimate matter, with only mutation and natural selection as the mediating processes, could be substantiated only if every single link in the chain of evolution could be shown to have occurred by these processes. Just a single instance, whether or not proven in practice, where evolution was driven by some other means, would suffice to undermine the edifice of Darwinism. More elegantly put, one can quote Alexander Pope:

> From Nature's chain, whatever link you strike
> Tenth or ten-thousandth, breaks the chain alike.[12]

Of course there are very few single instances where there is respectable proof that the twin processes of mutation and natural selection have given rise to a new species, this being but the smallest component of evolutionary change which Darwinian theory claims to explain.

Biologists, with good reason, are unhappy with arguments where there are long chains of reasoning, which are not supported at every step of the way by empirical data. They know very well how complex living things are, and need continually the reassurance of empirical data for every apparently secure logical step. This is the character of biology in every branch with the exception of evolutionary theory. But in arguments about macro-evolution, such obsession with empirical checking is curiously not thought to be mandatory. Indeed, such checks are not made at all, except in a most fragmentary way. Admittedly it would be quite impossible to carry out the necessary checks, if only for the reason that most of the changes one wishes to analyse occurred millions of years ago. Nevertheless, the differences in standards of proof between evolutionary biology and all other areas of biology seems astounding, though rarely noticed.

It is difficult to avoid the conclusion that for evolutionary theory the assumption has been made *a priori* that nothing but chance mutation and natural selection can possibly account for the actual known sequence of evolutionary change. The actual empirical evidence for this, even in individual cases of speciation and adaptive change is, to say the least, scanty. As for the wider claim of evolutionary theorists, that these two processes explain the whole process of change from inanimate matter to higher life forms such as man, the intellectual edifice seems far too long on logic and almost devoid of actual evidence.

One is forced to the conclusion that modern evolutionary theory serves as a myth for the post-religious age.

I am not the only one to reach the conclusion that Darwinism is in a category separate from normal science. Karl Popper[13] has questioned whether there can be any laws of history or of evolution, and has described the Darwinian theory as a metaphysical research programme, rather than a scientific theory in a strict sense. It should be noted however that his arguments against historical science were not restricted to realms of history dependent on information transmission (as was made clear in previous paragraphs). Another writer who (sometimes) recognizes the non-scientific role of evolutionary theory is Don Cupitt. He describes Darwin's book as 'the Genesis, and his theory the unifying creation-myth, for the new culture . . . Darwin had supplied the new age with its most important single myth.'[4] In this quotation Cupitt shows an attitude to evolution quite close to that advocated here. Yet at other times he seems to be persuaded of the scientific authenticity of this Darwinian theory.

15.3 Critique of Freud and Marx as theories of history

In section 15.1 two other figures of major influence on the modern mind were mentioned, as well as Darwin. These were Sigmund Freud and Karl Marx. The three names were grouped together as proponents of 'historical scientific theories'. Darwin is the one who has clearly been most deeply incorporated into the catechism of modern scientific thinking. Nevertheless, a few comments are appropriate to show that rather similar (though less subtle) flaws are made by Freud and Marx, whose 'theories' are also historical ones involving information transmission.

Karl Marx is the originator of a system of thinking which claims to understand human social development as a regular scientific process. His view of history is derived in part from that of Hegel, but also, as noted by Russell, owed a lot to the historical mythology common in Judaeo-Christian culture. For instance, Russell draws the parallels between the Judaeo-Christian ideas of the Second Coming and the Millenium and the Marxist ideas of the Revolution and the Communist Commonwealth, respectively. Marx, unlike Hegel, was a materialist, of sorts, and an atheist.

As explained in the previous section, in the theory of Darwinian evolution there has been considerable effort to validate a historical theory by consideration of actual historical evidence (though, as argued, such an attempt in principle cannot rigorously validate any historical theory). In the case of Marxism, the attempt to validate a historical theory by detailed historical research on human social development has been fragmentary in the extreme or non-existent. Russell writes:

Like other historical theories, it required, if it was to be made plausible, some distortion of facts and considerable ignorance. Hegel, like Marx . . . possessed both qualifications.[15]

If the importance of Marxism is taken to rest on its claim to be scientific, it is difficult to understand how it could have become so influential. However, it seems more likely that it was adopted because the form of its pronouncements had, as Russell noted, some similarity to the forms of religious thinking which preceded it. When they failed, a similar form of thinking, but with a materialist/atheist content rather than a theist content, could easily take over. Marxism clearly has one of the hallmarks of a myth, an assumed answer to imponderable questions about the destiny of human society.

Much of the thinking of Freud is also well known: his postulation of the unconscious mind, his ideas that neurotic illness arises from repression of trauma experienced in early life, his idea of sexuality in infants, his interpretation of dreams and other otherwise meaningless aspects of our everyday experience in terms of unconscious and repressed events, and especially in terms of repressed sexuality. He invented the technique of psychoanalysis for revealing the history in each individual from which adult behaviour, especially neurotic behaviour, arose.

A feature of psychoanalysis is the way it seeks to provide a specific interpretation for every single notable act or utterance of a patient. If this is supposed to be a scientific discipline, it seems to be making the same assumption, just as for Darwinism, that individual idiographic events, collected without the control of a laboratory experiment, can be used to arrive at very broad generalizations. Indeed Freud seems to make a virtue of this very habit, however questionably we may regard it. For instance, in his *Introductory Lectures on Psychoanalysis* Freud writes:

> Our technique with dreams is thus a very simple one . . . We shall . . . ask the dreamer how he arrived at the dream, and once more his first remark is to be looked on as an explanation.[16]

Take note of the special significance Freud placed on the subject's first remark. It is from innumerable instances of interpretation of such unguarded individual utterances that Freud built up such wide generalizations as the Oedipus complex. There is no attempt to classify these utterences into groups, each member being rigorously similar in some way to the others, so that they can be treated together; and there is no attempt to control all the extraneous other factors surrounding each utterance, and bearing on interpretation, when reaching his broad generalizations. In style, Freud's approach to understanding individual patients and their problems seems more akin to that of a literary critic trying to understand the symbolism within a work of literature. The idea that the symbolic nature of the behaviour and utterance of patients arises because of a disturbance in the brain mechanisms underlying symbolism is not explored. Instead, there is a complex attempt to give precise interpretation of the content, rather than the form of all the symbolic utterances. However the rich symbolism of those utterances *could* be related to abnormalities of brain mechanisms, because symbolism is a form of association, and association is a crucial principle of brain function, recognized by psychologists and neuroscientists alike.

Freud's style of reasoning appeals to scientists much less than does the evolutionary theory of Darwin. But there is a similarity in the use of uncontrolled idiographic fragments to build broad generalizations (about evolutionary or personal history). Few of the constructs advocated by Freud receive much independent validation from other areas of enquiry (e.g. from the neurosciences). Yet they concern provocative questions about individual idiosyncratic behaviour, which otherwise are unaswerable. In these respects Freudianism has one of the hallmarks of a myth.

15.4 Functions of modern historical myths for the 'post-religious age'

In this chapter the theories of Darwin, Marx and Freud have been identified as 'myths for the modern mind'. In chapter 14, part of the definition of a myth was 'an assumed answer to a question which in principle has no answer'. The discussion above has argued that this is so for Darwin's theory of evolution, as well as for the less reputable theories of Marx and Freud. Indeed, if history is regarded as a stream of idiographic events, without the control achieved in the laboratory of extraneous variables, any attempt to explain historical processes must be in terms of myth.

In addition, however, for a belief to be designated as a myth it had to have the practical characteristic that it helped mankind (or a section of it) to live more comfortably, that is to live more peacefully in the knowledge of those unanswered questions. In what sense do the 'theories' of Darwin, Marx and Freud have such practical usefulness? Each of them arose within Christian or Judaeo-Christian culture. I believe the real function of each of these has been to provide a belief structure for those who no longer find the Christian myths credible. This is of course a rather negative reason for adopting each of these belief systems.

How do each of the three deal with the great religious questions? The substance of all three of these belief systems says a lot about the first two religious questions, about the origin and fate of the universe and its inhabitants ('Where do we come from? Where are we going to?'). Since they are historical belief systems that is their prime purpose. They give some sort of answer to questions of origin and destiny of life on earth, or human society, and of the individual psyche. But what do these belief systems say about the third religious question: 'What are we here for? What do we live by?' This is how we recognize the psychological function of these belief systems for human beings in their existential troubles.

For Marxism the answer seems to have been that the individual fulfils the goals set by the state in achieving the ideal state. The state is presumed to be able to predict the future course of society, and therefore is an infallible authority which the individual must respect without the shadow of a question. Karl Popper, on the other hand, rejects the notion that any person or organization can predict future social history.[17] The psychological function of Marxism seems clear and fairly simple minded: to replace the metaphysical goal, sanctioned by the Christian religion, of striving for reward in the hereafter (offered by Christian religion) with the materialist goal of striving for the kingdom of heaven on earth. Unfortunately, in the absence of a belief in the afterlife, few would be alive and conscious, able to witness that ideal future society.

Sigmund Freud wrote as a doctor, one concerned with therapy, rather than as a philosopher or metaphysician. He was however explicitly strongly against the influence of religion in the society in which he lived and worked. For Freud the Christian religion specifically (and the surrounding Christian culture more generally) was the chief means of repression (or implicit coercion). He developed a strong antipathy to the hypocrisy of the over-civilized society in which he lived and worked. In the words of Philip Rieff:

Freud found the essential lie upon which culture is built in its zealous but faltering repressions. His way of mitigating them was, first, through rational knowledge, and second, a prudent compromise with the instinctual depths out of which rational knowledge emerges.

Rieff suggests that 'to avoid inefficient moral commitments, Freud offers us a better and securer standard . . . his "ethic of honesty"'.[18] This was certainly part of Freud's technique for therapy, in which a patient had to promise absolute honesty. In a wider sense, the enduring influence of Freud is that people are now more honest about their inner motives, and are more accepting of their natural needs.

However, honesty appears not to be a fundamental value which can be accepted without compromise. As Rieff writes:

> There is a risk in the ethic of honesty of which Freud is aware . . .
> Some of those who now take flight into illness would find the inner conflict exposed by candour insupportable . . . Honesty is not an ethic for weaklings . . . Neither will it necessarily render our nature more beneficient. Psychoanalysis prudently refrains from urging men to become what they really are . . . The new ethic fears the honest criminal lurking behind the pious neurotic.[19]

Thus in various ways Freud feels a need for compromise with the ethic of honesty. This implies that he must have had a more fundamental value system than just 'honesty'. However, this does not figure prominently in Freud's writings, nor is its philosophical or metaphysical basis made clear. Nevertheless it is clear that in his attempts to unravel the psychohistory of each individual, Freud was often explicitly trying to free his patients from the implicit coercion exerted by religious organizations.

These paragraphs explain some of the psychological usefulnesses which have given the 'theories' of Marx and Freud their share of adherents. The weakness in the reasoning behind them, dealt with in section 15.3, may explain why they have nevertheless not stood the test of time. But what about Darwinism, the most successful of the three?

A great deal of scientific advance leads to technological progress, that is, it has practical consequences for the way we lead our lives. It is difficult, however, to point to technological developments which derive from the Darwinian evolutionary theory. True, Darwinism has had a colossal impact on modern society. But this impact is not at the technological level, but at the level of what modern men and women in industrialized societies believe, especially what they believe about themselves. The impact of Darwinism is on account of the creed it implies, on its hold on people's minds, and the self-image it promulgates, rather than on account of its practical uses as technology.

Darwin himself was not motivated by any iconoclastic desire to undermine contemporary religious belief. As a young man, at the time of the *Voyage of the Beagle*, he had conventional Christian beliefs. In his autobiography (1876) he writes:

> Although I did not think much about the existence of a personal God until a considerably later period of my life, I will here give the vague conclusions to which I have been driven. The old argument from design in Nature as given by Paley, which formerly seemed to me so conclusive, fails now that the law of natural selection has been discovered . . . At the present day the most usual argument for the existence of an intelligent God is drawn from a deep inward conviction and feelings which are experienced by most persons . . . In my Journal I wrote that whilst standing in the midst of the grandeur of the Brazilian forest 'it is not possible to give an adequate idea of the higher feelings of wonder, admiration, and devotion, which fill and elevate the mind'. I well remember my conviction that there is more in man than the mere breath of his body. But now the grandest scenes would not cause any such convictions and feelings to rise to my mind. It may be truly said that I am like a man who has become colour-blind, and the universal belief by men, of the existence of redness, makes my present loss of perception of not the least value as evidence. This argument would be a valid one if all men of all races had the same inward conviction of the existence of one God; but we know that this is very far from being the case. Therefore I cannot see that such inward convictions and feelings are of any weight as evidence of what really exists.[20]

But in contrast to such scepticism, Darwin also writes in the same work of

> the extreme difficulty or rather impossibility of conceiving this immense and wonderful universe including man with his capacity of looking far backwards and far into futurity, as the result of blind chance or necessity. When thus reflecting I feel compelled to look for a First Cause having an intelligent mind in some degree analogous to that of man; and I deserve to be called a Theist. This conclusion was

strong in my mind about the time, as far as I remember, when I wrote the Origin of Species.[21]

Pulling these two themes together, Darwin confesses that 'the mystery of the beginning of all things is insoluble by us; and I for one must be content to remain an agnostic'.

Darwin himself was thus not the source of the bitter strife between science and Christian religion which was ushered in by the publication of his *On the Origin of Species*. The reader will note that Darwin refers to the 'law of natural selection' as an established fact. The critique offered above suggests that it is far less than an empirically established law, to be applied to all evolutionary history. Apart from that there seems little to disagree with in Darwin's agnosticism; merely to note that mankind may still need myths to allay his existential anxieties.

However, very soon another quite different mythology grew around Darwinism, and the needs that this fulfilled should be clearly spelt out. As on earlier occasions, a bold initiative of an eminent scientist became debased when conveyed to the popular mind.

As with the determinist myth, Darwinism has helped to liberate many people from the shackles of other quite outdated myths, promulgated by the established religions. Combined with the naive belief in the unviolated rule of natural law, Darwinism has provided a world view which seems more or less complete, apparently leaving but few natural phenomena without explanation, at least as far as living things go. To adherents of this world view it can be asserted even more strongly than by Laplace that there is no need of a hypothesis (such as the theistic myth) of anything which stands outside that mechanistic, valueless universe.

Such may be the psychological function which made the Darwinian theory of evolution attractive to many people when it first appeared 130 years ago. But what have been the actual consequences of the increasing adoption of that theory as an aspect of popular belief and culture? Darwinism has been held up as a justification for ruthless competition in economics; as justification for racist doctrines in large parts of the world for substantial parts of the last century; as justification of sociobiological explanations of a variety of human behaviours. At a more personal level it might persuade a women who is unable to bear children to regard herself as one of evolution's failures. And with all of these, there is the implicit denial of the importance of personal subjective experiences of pleasure and suffering, which are counted as mere epiphemonena on the vast landscape of evolutionary change. This is despite the fact that these experiences can be counted as the only *a priori* source on which we can base our daily value judgments.

What is the value content of this popularized view of evolutionary theory? Some proponents of evolutionism would claim that evolutionary theory is not valueless. The concept of biological 'fitness' – interpreted simply as reproductive success – could be considered as the overriding value which derives from Darwinism. But if that value comes to be supreme, our heirs are destined to live on a planet overcrowded to the point where adherence to any of the older values of civilization cannot be possible. Is that what evolutionists want? This sort of argument has already been discussed, under the heading of the 'naturalistic fallacy' – the appeal to so-called biological fact to support concepts of value, which are really quite independent from matters of fact. If reproductive fitness were defined as the sole criterion of value, one may simply ask 'why?' Does existence and proliferation of life have a supreme value independent of the quality of that life? Is there not a value scale more enduring than existence of life, however squalid, in the here and now?

We may sum up by noting that all three of the proponents of historical 'scientific theories' have served to promulgate ideas which help mankind to allay the anxieties of the post-religious age. As a generalization one might even suggest that the idea of progress, which developed about the time of the French Revolution, is another important part of contemporary mythology, seen more in the ideas developing from Darwinism and Marxism, than in the work of Freud. The consequences of mankind's adoption of this myth can be criticized, like those resulting from Darwinism and Marxism. Progress for some people has often been bought at the expense of great suffering for others. Admittedly there are still many ways in which the lot of humankind can be vastly improved. But, in the view of the environmental crisis (which is closely related to the idea of economic growth as 'progress') closing in on us, it might be more suitable to the 'New Age' to readopt the myth of a static view of history, such as prevailed before the French Revolution and the Industrial Revolution.

15.5 A metaphysical alternative to determinism, to the assumptions of Darwinism, and to other modern myths

In section 15.2 the 'orthodox' belief of modern evolutionary thinking was discussed, that evolutionary change occurred as a result of selection from countless mutations, themselves absolutely random, and blind to any final purpose. The conclusion was reached that this belief is quite unprovable (as is the idea of 'absolute' randomness), but was an answer asssumed about a question where, in principle, no firm objective answer can be found. In other words this belief is a myth.

As an alternative (or 'heterodox') view, there is the possibility that apparently random mutations in the genes are actually aberrant events, perhaps at the quantum level. These aberrant events, though apparently random, may be exceptions where natural law and the logic of statistics give way to constraints of a totally different kind, indeed of a metaphysically different kind. This possibility need not contradict any known empirical fact.

Such aberrant events may be part of the universe as a whole, occurring in situations other than genetic mutations. This opens the further possibility that the universe as a whole is projective, that is, it has a tendency, however slight, to move towards a final goal. This possibility likewise need not contradict any known empirical fact. Such departures from regularity might be part of a purposive, projective universe. If so they might be referred to as 'little miracles'.

Assuming that such events were quantum events, they would be very tiny events, which would never be detected unless very special equipment was used, and then to detect only a very minute fraction of such quantum events. Thus, such little miracles would not manifest themselves in the obvious, overpowering manner of the classical miracles of the Old and New Testaments. The influence of such miracles would be much smaller than is admitted by this usual concept of miracles, or as believed by Newton, for whom the Deity was all-powerful, as well as omniscient and benevolent. Moreover, by their very nature, these miracles would be individual (idiographic) events, incapable of being classified and 'tamed' as the repeatable events which nomothetic science is capable of studying. Therefore, not only would their detection be extremely difficult, but, even if it were accomplished, it would never be possible to work out how they fulfilled any final purpose. Thus, their existence and the purpose they might subserve could never be proved. But neither could these possibilities be disproved. The supposition that such quantum events serve a purpose would then, like the assumption of absolute randomness to mutation, have the quality of a myth. The possibility of the existence of such purpose-fulfilling aberrations would be essentially a matter of belief, as would be the possibility of absolute randomness to mutation.

If ever the macroscopic consequences of such events could be tracked down to their microscopic origins, they would be very tiny insignificant events. This view of miracles thus seems to be consistent with an idea of a God who, though the personification of good, actually has only a very little power. 'Quantum theology' is not a theology for developing ideas about the omnipotence, the power and the glory of the Deity. It is a theology in which God moves very discretely and rarely, and is usually overpowered by causal necessity.

Although such little miracles could in principle occur in any part of the natural world, the possibility of aberrant events could be especially significant in the biological world where information transmission is so important. In chains of cause and effect relying on complex patterns of information processing the occasional aberrant behaviour of a few molecules would be impossible to detect, but could sometimes precipitate major transitions of state. Because of the great complexity of biological systems, there are a great many possible histories which could unfold, differing by only relatively minor changes of initial conditions. In other words, there is a very complex set of 'bifurcations' possible in the 'state-space' in biological systems. The apparently 'uncaused' microscopic events of quantum physics could thus, in practice, be directly related to macroscopic events, in the same way as the survival of Schrödinger's cat depends on quantum events, in the well known 'thought experiment'.

Such a microscopic event might determine the modification of a single base-pair in the genetic code. Jacques Monod has already been quoted (section 15.2) to the effect that 'A mutation is in itself a miscroscopic event, a quantum event, to which the principle of uncertainty consequently applies. An event which is hence and by its very nature *essentially* unpredictable.' Yet such a modification of a single base pair might start the cascade of events which leads to the origin of a new species.

If a quantum event determined a microscopic event in a human brain, it could likewise account for the otherwise unpredicted adoption of a new decision on how to act, by that person. The decision itself might have a serious moral dimension, if the person concerned was, at the time, on the horns of a difficult ethical dilemma.

Although it would in principle be impossible to decipher the workings of such processes, there is no reason categorically to rule them out, nor to conclude that there could be no projective or purposive significance to their occasional occurrence. As with the supposition of absolute randomness, free but blind, there can be no proof, and whichever possibility one has in mind is a matter of belief, not of proof.

Polkinghorne regards the existence of evil in the world as the most difficult area for reconciliation of science and religion. He distinguishes between physical evil (such as the occurrence of natural disasters) and moral evil (perpetrated by humans), the latter being the more difficult to assimilate into his scientific/religious perspective. With regard to the latter, he suggests, half-seriously, that 'original sin was the only experimentally verifiable Christian dogma'.[22] Many other people also find the existence of evil the most perplexing aspect of their religious world view, and it persuades some to abandon that view.

In section 10.5 I suggested a view of the Deity as a guarantor of values, but far from all-powerful. In fact the actual power of this God was limited to the occasional imperceptible little miracles discussed in the previous paragraphs. When tragedy strikes, its emotional impact is always difficult to assimilate, especially if it is a result of a human perpetrator. Nevertheless, from a logical point of view, the image of God as having goodness but little real power may be helpful. Natural disasters reflect the workings of the mostly- deterministic universe. We can also regard the workings of the human mind/brain as 'mostly deterministic'. The mechanisms of the human mind/brain of course include purposeful planning and execution of actions, but this does not conflict with a 'mostly-deterministic' view of humans. Purposeful actions fulfilling a particular motive can readily be programmed in a computer and, in a very different, but still essentially mechanistic way, are likely to exist within psychophysically-defined human nature. In fact, those regretable human actions which we would most readily identify as 'evil' probably reflect a pathology of one of the most potent of human motives, the impetus to control one's environment. Thus one need not regard 'evil' deeds of one's fellow human beings as an indication of the existence in the universe of evil (in the metaphysical sense), but rather of the fact that God has only a little power over causal necessity and the misfortunes that it haphazardly produces.

Aberrant events, whether in evolution or human psychobiology, which escape from causal necessity but which may fulfil a projective goal, if they occur, can be regarded as only one sort of miracle. In a previous section the possibility of life forms evolving where human mentality could exist was considered in statistical terms. But this was regarded as a profitless excercise. The coincidences necessary for our existence could be regarded as either logically necessary but un-miraculous (invoking the anthropic principle), or as *prima facie* miracles. The same can be said for the coincidences in the physical universe, which make likely the existence of life-bearing planets.

But, if we recognize the subjectivitity of our own being at face value, we are confronted with another far more obvious type of miracle. Our very existence as conscious entities contemplating our own existence is utterly miraculous. The arguments from the philosophy of mind were discussed in Part II of this work. Let it suffice to remind ourselves that the philosophy of psychophysical parallelism (also referred to as epistemological dualism) allowed us to undertake unconstrained scientific examination of the natural world, without undermining any fundamental sense of human values. Central to that philosophy was the separation of subjectivity from the objective world, as parallel but independent forms of reality. The existence of subjectivity *per se* can in no way be derived from what we know about the matter of the brain. If we accept this at face value, it is quite miraculous; and the only reason why many of us do not recognize it as such is that it is such a commonplace, everyday miracle.

Likewise, we may ask about the meaningfulness of life; but in the end this is not a question for intellectual answer. It is not an issue which has to be explained or justified in terms of something else. It is a first premise for most people most of the time, which is more or less synonymous with a childlike acceptance of our own subjectivity at face value.

Many people of scientific orientation would deny that they have an inner conviction about the meaningfulness of life. They might deny this by referring to the supposedly objective valueless universe around them which has no regard for whether they exist or not or whether they experience pleasure and fullfilment or pain and suffering. They do not recognize the mythical quality of this belief. But though they deny with their minds the projective, purposive nature of the universe around them, most of them would resolutely affirm with their manifest behaviour their commitment to projective, purposive behaviour. Can they not jump from their own instinctive search for purpose in their own lives, to the myth that the universe also is projective? The question seems appropriate, especially when there is not (and cannot be) any conclusive proof either for or against that conjecture.

15.6 Can we ever deliberately adopt a myth?

The answer to the above question can be given emphatically in four monosyllables. We have no choice! When our backs are against the wall, and the void also opens up in front of us, we have to take the risk, and actively construct a framework of ideas in which the world is intelligible, and the constructs useful and meaningful as a basis for our lives. Pilkinghorne writes:

> Rational enquiry is not characterized by an unwillingness to take intellectual risks, so that we cling alone to that which is deductively certain, but it is bold enough to venture on the construction of a metaphysical scheme, whose justification will lie in its attainment of comprehensive explanatory power.[23]

Some academics (scientists and others) may object to such deliberate myth-construction, and adopt a stance of studied objectivity. But to take such a God-like 'objective' view of human strivings and values is striking a pose beyond that which humans validly can achieve. In surveying global history these advocates are denying the vast suffering (and ecstasy) of life and the evolutionary process, and thus these attitudes implicitly deny the reality of those values by which we rate that suffering and ecstasy. But hardly any of us, least of all these proponents, really maintain such objectivity when faced with an infinitesimal fraction of that suffering or ecstasy in their daily lives. We cannot escape from the subjective view of the world, try as we might. Only those who are not involved in wrestling with the question 'What are we here for?' can adopt such a philosophy. Their aloof, detached viewpoint is really placing them on the side lines of all-important decisions; or else they make firm value decisions blindly, without realizing that that also has implications for fundamental absolute values and their possible metaphysical basis.

To those who insist that human values are all relative, I suggest that they contemplate some of the modern giants whose lives have been single-mindedly devoted to matters of value. Take for instance political prisoners such as Andrei Sakharov or Nelson Mandela or, in another realm, Mother Teresa. Each of these has had his or her life on the line for many decades over matters of personal value. That is the hardest currency there is for values. Relative their values may be, and indeed human constructions rather than 'objective facts'; but undoubtedly more robust, in both emotional and logical terms, than that of the bystanders who flaunt their freedom from social determinants of values.

Earlier in Part III, several common beliefs were designated as 'myths for the modern mind'. These included the belief in unblemished, clockwork determinism; the belief that the universe continues on its determinist course, blind to any final purpose; and the beliefs derived from these such as Darwinism, Freudianism and Marxism. But all those myths serve their real function as antitheses to pre-existing Christian myths. (They may not have been constructed with that purpose explicitly in mind; but they nevertheless serve that function, and derive their enduring popularity from that function.) They are not recognized as myths, because that would undermine their function as alternatives to religious belief.

If we do recognize these beliefs for what they are, myths for the post-religious age rather than proven scientific facts, we may feel less compulsion to adopt them as our own beliefs. But whether we accept these particular myths or not, we do still need myths, of one variety or another, to live with those great religious questions, especially the third and most difficult one, 'What should we live by?' Paul Tillich writes: 'One can replace one myth by another, but one cannot remove the myth from man's spiritual life.'[24] P.228

It may seem strange to plead for our conscious adoption of beliefs, which we also recognize as myths. After all, the tenor of some of the preceding paragraphs is that myths can perform their psychological function most effectively when we forget that they are myths and regard them as proven facts. Such was the status of the Christian myths. Such, it has been argued, is the status of those supposedly proven scientific facts, which have been redefined in this work as myths for the post-religious age. How can we accept a belief, when we also know it to be a myth?

I think the circumstance in which this can be legitimately done, without sacrifice of either intellectual integrity or rigour in thinking, is when the question addressed by the myth is both of vital importance to our existence, and also in principle unanswerable. In these circumstances we may make a free choice to adopt the belief which makes social and personal life possible, provided it does not involve any logical contradiction, nor contradict any empirical facts. Since the question resolved by such adoption of belief is not answerable in any objective sense, we are not likely to be compromised or constrained by either logical or empirical considerations. After all, if such deliberate adoption of a myth were subject to either of these constraints, the question could thereby be answerable.

The strategy is one readily adopted in practical matters but more problematical perhaps in philosophical and metaphysical ones. It is simply this. 'If it works, use it.' Of course, if there are empirical reasons against the myth/belief we adopt, it will not work, and so we should not use it. It is exactly when the void of unanswered and unaswerable metaphysical and existential questions opens up before our feet that we are forced to such decisions about which myths we adopt. Those who would prefer to remain in a state of deliberate agnosticism on such questions may well be those who have never faced that void, or who do not recognize it when it confronts them.

The most general example of such a decision is the question cited near the beginning of this work, from Jacques Monod's *Chance and Necessity*. Monod asserts that nature is objective rather than projective (i.e. directed to a final purpose). Remember also that Bertrand Russell suggested that it was impossible for the pioneers of science to know in advance which of these two possibilities was most likely to apply to the natural world; and that it is only with accumulation of scientific knowledge that the generalization could be hazarded that natural law, blind to any final purpose, was the more useful pattern for science to seek. But, within the limits set by quantum physics, there is still the freedom to choose the myth that the world is projective, though the movement towards the final goal is achieved by tiny, undetectable miracles, rather than by dramatic large-scale exceptions to natural law.

Thus, whatever the usual derogatory connotations of the word 'myth', I am not against myths. All I ask is that those myths be credible (that is, logically coherent, and not in disagreement with empirical fact); that we openly recognize our need for myths; that we recognize which are the mythical elements in our belief structures; and that we are honest about the psychological functions they perform for us. In this quest for honesty, there is some similarity with the 'ethic of honesty' recognized above in the writings of Sigmund Freud. However questionable Freud's work was as science, the ethic of honesty about our fundamental and subjective needs has much to commend it. The honest acknowledgment of the mythical elements in our belief structures, and the needs fulfilled by those myths (at once intellectual and emotional), can be seen as part of a similar ethic of honesty.

Much has been written in recent years by liberal Christian

* GOD HAS TIME ON HIS SIDE

2018

theologians about 'demythologizing' their religion. Cupitt traces this process back to the latter part of last century.

> People at that time were highly conscious of having come a long way and of standing at the end of a rich and complex process of historical development.
>
> However, from the 1880s a different conviction was taking shape, most conspicuously in the thought of Nietzsche. The new science-based industrial culture was emerging, and it was becoming clear that it represented a violent break with all previous tradition. The chief new feature . . . was that human thinking and human valuations were much more radically autonomous than ever before, being no longer grounded in any authoritative, coherent and secure vision of the cosmic order. In science-based culture nothing is sacred because everything is dubitable, truth is fragmentary, disconnected and socially neutral . . . There is a total absence of what ordinary folk variously describe as 'absolutes', 'certainties', 'Truth' with a capital 'T', or 'Meaning' with a capital 'M'.[25]

However, while the contemporary scientific view denigrates many of the previously accepted social and religious beliefs as myths, I want to argue that we should not be disdainful about the fact that some of the most cherished beliefs of our society are unprovable, and therefore 'myths'. We should accept with humility our need for them, in the face of the insoluble but yet provocative religious riddles. We should recognize our personal myths for what they are. We should not pretend that our personal myths are historical facts (as is characteristic of Judaeo-Christian religions). Nor should we pretend that they are proven scientific facts or theories (as is characteristic of scientific materialism). What they are is answers to those riddles which we assume when there is absolutely no definite evidence for a particular answer to the riddle. And we assume these myths because, faced with the abyss of uncertainty, that assumption makes life possible.

On this matter, Polkinghorne tries to have the best of both worlds, to 'have his metaphysical cake as well as eat it', so to speak. Despite his assertion that one needs actively to construct a metaphysical framework he fails to acknowledge this 'bootstrapping' approach to certain truths. He believes

that the New Testament can be used as an evidential basis for supporting the claims of the Christian faith about its Founder, Jesus Christ . . . The life, death and resurrection of Jesus is not just a tale, however evocative, but a wonderful fusion of the power of myth and the power of actuality.[26]

Possibly, this fusion of myth and actuality, of truth as human construction and as what corresponds to reality, is an essential part of main streams in Christian thought. After all, the incarnation of God is 'the word made flesh'. To many this is a great attraction of Christianity. However, Polkinghorne is not dogmatic about this approach, and realizes that many aspects of his synthesis are not logically coercive.

For myself, I cannot structure my metaphysical beliefs in this way. I think there is a sharp divide between what is myth, a human construction, and what is publicly demonstrable actuality. The two parts of my definition of a myth have already been given; that it is an assumed 'answer' to a question which is in principle unanswerable; and that it helps relieve the existential anxiety which those provocative questions would otherwise leave us with. A question cannot be both answerable and unanswerable at the same time; and if we adopt a belief *a posteriori*, just because, in the lack of any real evidence, it proves useful in allaying our existential anxiety, that belief may be undermined if it can be tested from public facts. The historical conflicts between the church and science have come about in exactly this way. Polkinghorne seems ready to accept that the book of Genesis can be taken as poetry and myth, but not as fact; but the events of the New Testament, to him, are simultaneously fact and myth. If the life, death and resurrection of Christ are actualities, one would expect, after two thousand years, that a consensus would have been reached on the subject. In scientific matters, such agreement *is* reached: The principles of nuclear physics which permit the construction of nuclear weapons are agreed in the USA, in Russia, in India and in China.

Don Cupitt writes that 'religion is not "natural" or "innate" but is a human construction'.[27] This idea, which is central to his book, is later expressed in the following way:

When we understand that religion is simply human we have not abolished it but have begun to grasp its true import. Human beings fufill themselves by projecting and enacting their desires symbolically.[28]

He then goes on to discuss the work of Ludwig Feuerbach who, in the second half of the last century, put forward a similar view but was widely misunderstood, as undermining religious beief. The suggestion that we should ackowledge the component of myth in our own beliefs, without then discarding those beliefs, is along the same line as Cupitt's and Feuerbach's.

For instance Cupitt in his book *Only Human* occasionally writes explicitly about human values. He says that when he attends a family wedding ceremony, or prays for the sick, there is no implication of 'occult causality', but rather a 'value affirming and life-structuring symbolic action'. 'The affirmation of our values is a far greater and more important thing than the application of techniques.'[29] However, Cupitt apparently wants to do this without metaphysics. But does he not realize that, with the growing credibility of neural determinism, those values are under threat, not only at a superficial level, but also at the metaphysical level? I have no doubt Cupitt's value system accepts the existence and value of each human person. But our previous discussion of neural determinism suggested that the very idea of a *person* (whose marriage we might celebrate, or whose sickness we might care about) has no scientific basis, and this because of the metaphysical position espoused by modern science rather than because of more superficial successes of science.

Earlier on in his book Cupitt appears to run away from the threat he recognizes in neural determinism. He writes

While it is possible . . . to learn to look at animals and plants and see them as simply natural products of chance and time, variation and selection, it is more difficult consistently to think of one's own thinking as mere natural process and as a product of evolution. There are horrors ahead here with which few of us have yet grappled.[30]

The suppositions about the nature of reality coming from modern science, especially biological science, and the metaphysical package that goes with it, appear to leave no room for Cupitt's or anyone else's values. If Cupitt wants to affirm or defend those values it is a hopeless task unless it is done at the metaphysical level.

Therefore, in contrast to Cupitt, I suggest that metaphysical suppositions about the nature of reality are still crucial parts of the myths which we need to construct and believe.

Cupitt writes:

Above all, religion itself is no longer an external apparatus of domination but an inner spirit of liberty.

So, at least, said the New Testament. But Christianity needs a vesture, and the Christianity we got was Christian Platonism, the faith corrupted by being allied with dogmatic metaphysics, and embodied in an authoritarian institution.[31]

In this book, the aim has been to show that we should not scorn those old metaphysical questions, but that we should approach them, willingly and without dogmatism, and without the authority coming from a religious institution. Metaphysical questions may be unanswerable, but we cannot avoid metaphysical assumptions as part of our mythology. But let those assumptions, and their mythical nature, and the needs which they fulfill for us, be explicitly acknowledged.

The drift of the preceding section is that the question of whether the natural world is or is not directed to a final purpose is actually not answerable, even in principle. The remarkable coincidences in cosmology of the initial starting conditions, and of the values of fundamental physical constants, could be interpreted, arbitrarily, in either way. In biological evolution, the mutations on which that evolution appears to depend could likewise be interpreted arbitrarily either as truly random and purposeless events, or as ones coordinated in some totally inscrutable way to achieve a final goal. There is no way to answer such questions. The belief we adopt depends entirely on which myth we find more credible or in other ways appealing. But make no mistake: *whichever* of the two beliefs we adopt *is* a myth, an assumed answer to an unanswerable question, which helps to make personal and social existence possible.

Perhaps, then, the most important myth I want to reconstruct is that the universe has some projective aspects to it.

At this stage reference should also be made to the thermodynamic law, the Law of Increasing Entropy. This is said to be the most fundamental of physical laws. It is a historical law, stating that randomness and disorder will always increase, that there is a progressive degradation over the course of history in the order and information content of the universe. This law is a statement similar to the Darwinian claim that natural selection is the sole explanation of evolution. Both of them are theories that are supposed to apply to the whole of history. If the Law of Increasing Entropy really *is* a true description of the empirical behaviour of the universe, it is the ultimate contradiction of the thesis that the universe has the slightest projective element to it.

In origin the Law of Increasing Entropy had an empirical basis, that for 'heat engines', studied in the laboratory, efficiency was always less than perfect. This empirical fact could also be predicted by statistical deductions about the kinetics of gases which stated that there would always be an increase in disorder. This principle has then been applied to the cosmic scale. But it is not clear to me that there is any actual empirical evidence that it does apply on the cosmic scale. Indeed, how could there be? If entropy is disorder, it is in the realm of information rather than the dimensions of mass and energy. To make a statement about disorder in the universe as a whole requires us to have infinite information about that universe. Observations of distant galaxies seen from a vast distance would give us no inkling of the degree of order or disorder on the small scale, which could completely change the entropy balance.

Thus we have a situation closely parallel to that which applied to evolution of life forms. A principle of change over time can be derived from very small-scale observations and then, by a massive extrapolation based on logic but not empirical demonstration, it is said to apply universally. But the only way to provide an empirical test of its universal application requires infinite knowledge.

Thus it appears that the Law of Increasing Entropy applied at cosmic level is not really an empirical law, but a mathematical one, a logical necessity *provided one makes particular assumptions*. The key assumption is one we have already considered, that of unblemished determinism, that the laws of nature apply in all parts of the universe, and at all times, and without any exception. Given such an assumption, the logic of statistics can prove that there will be a progressive increase in the disorder of the universe. To put it another way, irrefutable logic will prove that it will always be vastly more likely that we can shuffle a pack of cards to a state of disorder than that we could 'unshuffle' them back to their original state of order.

However, if the assumption of unblemished determinism should fail, the Law of Increasing Entropy could also fail. Thus, although the logical deduction we would make is that it would be virtually impossible by the usual procedures for shuffling a pack of cards to 'unshuffle' them back to their pristine original order, nevertheless that is a possible empirical outcome. If that were to occur, we might attribute it to a rare event whose statistical likelihood was astronomically remote. But equally, we could attribute it to an interference in normal natural laws, perhaps, in effect, to the intervention of an intelligent and powerful Being, Newton's 'divine arm', or, to continue our present metaphor, to the intervention of a 'Celestial Cardsharp'.

We have already seen that the assumption of unblemished determinism cannot itself be evaluated within science. It is not accessible to test empirically. On the contrary, this assumption is the central faith for science, especially for the physicist. Thus, the same point made about Darwin's theory of evolution can be made about the Law of Increasing Entropy. They are both too long on logic, and too short on actual empirical evidence. In this light, both are myths.

It may be suggested that it is a bolder myth to suppose that the Law of Increasing Entropy gives way to the Final Purposes of the Celestial Cardsharp, and one that requires greater interference with natural law, than anything suggested so far. But if we bear in mind the astonishingly unlikely coincidences in the apparent initial starting conditions and values for physical constants, which are thought to have been necessary for the cosmological development of the universe as we consciously are aware of it, it may not seem so bizarre to question the empirical status of this law.

16

What are the Necessary Myths?

[handwritten: TWO CRITERIA P. 208 ① VITALY Needed ② UNANSWERED   P. 216-219 C.F. INDISPENSIBLE MYTHS INDE   Necessary myths]

Let us sum up, by listing the structure of mythology that is necessary to answer the third (and most difficult) of the great religious questions. From what has been written so far, it is obvious what most of them should be, and the surprise is that some of them are anyway universal items of implicit belief.

1. *Nature is projective.* The modern faith of the secular culture, in a deterministic universe, blind to any final purpose, was not a feature of the original scientific Renaissance, in the times of Galileo and Newton. It emerged a century after Newton, and grew more popular, as one of the later manifestations of nineteenth-century historical science. The pioneers of science did adhere to the myth I reconstruct here that the universe may be directed to a final cause. Ironically, as the accelerating development of industrial and technological society became an actuality, the metaphysical belief that nature as a whole is projective has gradually declined. However, logically this is not a contradiction. The inscrutible goals towards which nature is directed in a metaphysical sense may have nothing at all to do with the apparent goals of contemporary 'progress' of human societies.

As I have suggested above, the movement towards this final purpose may be achieved by 'little miracles'. These may be involved, quite imperceptibly, in the origin of species, in some personal decisions, and in social history. On a much grander scale, but still imperceptibly, they may reverse the trend apparent with the logic of determinacy towards increase in entropy. Although these suppositions cannot be proved, there is also no empirical fact which conflicts with them. The real conflict is the conflict of myths, the myths of determinism and Darwinian evolution on which modern scientific culture is based, compared with alternative myths where persons, values and a purpose to the universe can be conceived. The latter myths help us to give an answer to the third (most difficult) of the three great religious questions 'What are we here for? What do we live by?'

2. *The reality of subjectivity.* This is the source of many of the insights from which science developed at the time of the Renaissance, especially in physics, but this has been largely forgotten in an age dazzled by the highly practical, but more superficial triumphs in the less fundamental branches of science. Accepting the reality of subjectivity has many other implications. For instance it implies that the subjective view of time (as an 'ever-rolling stream') must also be accepted, despite its lack of congruity with the physicists' view of time. The reality of subjectivity is also the only real *a priori* foundation upon which human value systems can be based. Thus, along with an acknowledgment of the reality of subjectivity as such, it is necessary to ackowledge the reality of pleasure and fulfillment, or of pain and suffering. To postulate any of these realities is not logically necessary, nor of course are they objectively true. If we are to acknowledge these realities, it can only be by fiat, as *a priori* constructions of myths, making it possible for us to think in useful ways about the puzzling condition in which humanity is placed.

3. *The reality of persons.* This is of course a quite fundamental part of the belief systems of any and every culture. In practice, anyone who really rejected this belief would be labelled as psychopathic, or its equivalent. However, there is no basis in neuroscience for postulation of that metaphysical entity mysteriously integrating the activities of many millions of separate neurones. Anyone who sincerely adopts the scientific materialist package, especially its modern developments as cell assembly theory, should not believe in the reality of persons. Cell assemblies can in theory exhibit all the functions of persons and, according to the scientific materialist package, have a stronger claim to reality. Therefore, if we are to acknowledge the reality of persons it has to be by fiat, an addition to cell assembly theory which is unnecessary in strictly scientific terms. Once again we construct a myth to allow us to survive. If we are prepared to acknowledge this myth, it allows us also to postulate the reality of personal decisions. Admittedly, human behaviour may generally be subject to the constraints of a deterministic nervous system. But, in the projective universe given by our primary myth, that usual deterministic behaviour may be overriden at times, when the person as such may, in some special way, be exerting their identity.

4. *A God who combines goodness with severely limited power.* This part of the mythology is derived from all the above three myths. God is seen as the universal integral of all subjectivity. Since all human values are derived from this subjectivity, God is also the universal repository and

limit of subjectivity

guarantor of our values, and thus can be regarded as all-loving. God is also the initial creator of the universe, and then sustains the universe either by guaranteeing the consistent operation of natural laws, or the consistent operation of parallelism between the mental entities and their corresponding physical events. In addition God may have a very limited power to override the constraints of natural law, as demonstrable in the 'here and now', in the 'little miracles'. Since those exceptional events would never be recognizable they could never be analysed in the physicist's laboratory. Since subjectivity is the most important defining feature of a person (the third of our myths) and God is a universal subjectivity, it would also follow that God, if comprehensible at all to us, has some of the attributes of a person, the personification of all human schemes of value, and of human powerlessness.

5. *The existence in principle of absolute truth and of absolute values, however inaccessible these might both be in practice.* These two are expressed as 'in principle', since it is quite impossible to get accurate access to what these absolutes might be in actual practice. Nevertheless, with a belief in such absolutes, we are impelled to take the moral side of human life seriously. However, since these absolutes are also inaccessible in practice, we cannot be too certain or dogmatic about any of our provisional moral insights.

Some of the above beliefs are almost universally accepted by people today. Others are the subject of wide disbelief in 'Western' style countries. Nevertheless, there are strong logical relations between the above items of belief. These may be so strong that we have to accept or reject that set of myths as a whole. If it was possible to be more honest and integrated in our belief systems, we might realize the inconsistency in holding to some of the beliefs from the above list, and rejecting others in the names of 'scientific materialism'.

We thus have the scientific myth of absolute determinism, and the other major developments of that myth, especially Darwin's theory; and we have alternative myths, of the existence of persons, of values, of a subjective world as counterpart to the objective one, and of a purpose to the universe, albeit usually overwhelmed by the necessity of natural law. The latter myths are compatible with a considerable degree of lawfulness in the natural world, and therefore do not flagrantly conflict with scientific observation. They are, however, I believe, fundamentally incompatible with the myth of absolute determinism free from exceptions. That myth cannot be proved or disproved in any rigorous sense, though obviously natural law applies a great deal of the time. Both mythologies can thus be reconciled with empirical 'fact', such as it is. The scientific materialist mythology can perhaps be regarded as the intellectually more parsimonious of the two. On the other hand, the mythology which constructs the concepts of persons and values helps the possibility of a humane social existence. There are no *a priori* reasons to choose one rather than the other of these two; and there are no constraints other than their respective usefulness (as demonstrated *a posteriori*) to help us decide between these mythologies and the world views which follow from them. It is an entirely free choice, and, in the end, a metaphysical choice.

Notes

1. Introduction

1. G. H. Raner and L. S. Lerner, letter to *Nature*, 358, July 1992, p. 102.
2. J. Z. Young, *Doubt and Certainty in Science: A Biologist's Reflections on the Brain* (1950 Reith Lectures), OUP 1950.

2. Definition of Scientific Materialism

1. See, for instance, M. Bunge, *The Mind-Body Problem. A Psychobiological Approach*, Pergamon Press 1980.
2. Don Cupitt, *Only Human*, SCM Press 1985, p. 140.
3. Jacques Monod, *Chance and Necessity. An Essay on the Natural Philosophy of Modern Biology*, Collins 1972, p. 30.
4. 'Projective' is a different meaning from 'subjective'; but the two are related, because if the universe is projective in nature it implies the existence of a cosmic mind, purposefully developing its projects.

3. Materialism and Definitions of Mind

1. See R. Penrose, *The Emperor's New Mind: Concerning Computers, Minds and the Laws of Physics*, OUP 1989.
2. P. S. Churchland, *Neurophilosophy: Towards a Unified Science of the Mind/Brain*, MIT Press, Cambridge, Mass. 1988, p. 351.
3. G. M. Edelman, *The Mindful Brain*, MIT Press, Cambridge, Mass. 1978.
4. M. Polanyi, *Personal Knowledge*, Routledge and Kegan Paul 1958.
5. S. M. Kosslyn, J. Brunn, K. R. Cave and P. W. Wallach, 'Individual Differences in Mental Imagery Ability: A Computational Analysis' in *Cognition*, 18, December 1984, pp. 195-243; A. Paivio, *Mental Representation: A Dual Coding Approach*, OUP 1986.

4. The Scientific Obsession with Exclusive Objectivity

1. See J. Piaget and B. Inhelder, *The Psychology of the Child*, Routledge and Kegan Paul 1973.
2. See N. Feather, *Mass, Length and Time*, Penguin 1959.
3. In Galileo's inclined plane experiments quite accurate timing was

necessary. However, according to Stillman Drake (*Galileo: Pioneer Scientist*, University of Toronto Press 1990), the method he used was not accurate absolute timing but relative timing of the rate of descent of two different objects. Apparently he devised a method of ascertaining, with considerable accuracy, the equality of timing between two rolling bodies by listening to the 'beats' made in two strings, struck by the two objects.

4. P. C. W. Davies, *God and the New Physics*, J. M. Dent 1983.
5. B. James, 'Psychiatry, Science and the Seduction of Emma Bovary' in *Australian and New Zealand Journal of Psychiatry*, 14, June 1980, pp. 101-107.
6. H.-J. Gundersen, 'The New Stereological Tools: Disector, Fractionator, Nucleator and Point Sampled Intercepts and their Use in Pathological Research and Diagnosis' in APMIS, 96, October 1988, pp. 857-81.
7. Weber and Fechner as cited in R. Granit, *Receptors and Sensory Perception*, Yale University Press 1955, ch. 1.
8. Ibid.
9. E. L. Thorndike, *Animal Intelligence*, Macmillan, New York 1911.
10. J. B. Watson, *Psychology from the Standpoint of a Behaviorist*, J. B. Lipincott and Co., Philadelphia 1929, pp. 1, 2.
11. These debates have had their counterpart in earlier science. The Renaissance astronomer Johannes Kepler concentrated on establishing simple numerical relationships between astronomical measurements without looking for any deeper logic in the pattern of those observations. Science in its more typical form appeared with Newton, for whom the quantitative details of astronomical relationships took on quite new meaning when he defined the properties of gravity. Gravity could not be directly observed, but only inferred. It is therefore similar to some of the internal strategies of psychological information processing – such as 'reinforcement – which have been given greater credence after the hard line behaviourists lost their sway.
12. Watson, p. 15, italics his.
13. Ibid. p. 360
14. C. Hull, *A Behavior System*, Yale University Press 1952, pp. 244–45.
15. B. F. Skinner, *The Behavior of Organisms: an Experimental Analysis*, Appleton Century Crofts 1938, p. 440
16. Ibid., p. 441.
17. Ibid., p. 7.
18. B. F. Skinner, *Reflections on Behaviorism and Society*, Prentice Hall, Englewood Cliffs, NJ 1978, pp. 111, 110.
19. Ibid.
20. See J. Marsh, (ed.), *Experimental and Theoretical Studies of Consciousness*, CIBA Foundation Symposium No. 174, Wiley and Sons 1993.
21. Eg. R. W. Sperry, 'Mind-Brain Interaction: Mentalism, Yes; Dualism, No' in *Neuroscience*, 5(2), 1980, pp. 195–206.

22. See e.g. G. Ryle, *The Concept of Mind*, Barnes and Noble, New York 1949 and M. Bunge, *The Mind-Body Problem*.

23. L. J. Cronbach and M. E. Meehl, 'Construct Validity in Psychological Tests' in *Psychological Bulletin*, 52, 1955, pp. 281-302.

24. K. R. Popper, *Conjectures and Refutations: The Growth of Scientific Knowledge*, Routledge and Kegan Paul 1974.

25. K. Jaspers, 'The Phenomenological Approach in Psychopathology' (translated from a paper given in 1912) in *British Journal of Psychiatry*, 114, 1972, pp. 1313–23.

26. H.-J. Haase, 'Clinical Observations on the Actions of Neuroleptics' in H.-J. Haase and P. A. Janssen (eds), *The Actions of Neuroleptic Drugs. A Psychiatric, Neurological and Pharmacological Investigation*, Amsterdam 1965, pp.1-98.

27. A. R. Luria, *The Making of Mind: A Personal Account of Soviet Psychology*, Harvard University Press 1979, p. 177.

28. J. Monod, *Chance and Necessity*, p. 146.

29. R. Penrose, *The Emperor's New Mind*, p. 413.

30. Ibid., p. 424.

31. The revised version of the DSM – III remedied this absurdity by creating a category of 'provisional schizophrenia'.

5. *Exclusive Objectivity in Matters of Value*

1. It may be unfair to attribute this practice entirely to the passion for objectivization of value judgments – it probably results from the very difficult problem of assessing very large numbers of students in a manner that is 'fair and seen to be fair'.

2. A. Smith, 'Qualms about QALYs' in *The Lancet*, 16 May 1987, pp. 1134–36.

3. M. Polanyi, *Personal Knowledge*.

4. G. E. Moore, *Principia Ethica*, CUP 1903.

5. But note that the anti-sex attitude of Christianity is not actually very strong in the New Testament itself, and does not exist in the Old Testament. Reference to Mary as a 'virgin' only occurs twice in the New Testament, and one of these references is quoting Isaiah, whose original Hebrew version really means 'young woman' not 'virgin'. Apart from this, there is Paul's advice that it is better to remain celibate. The real origin of the anti-sex attitude of Christianity is the Greek influence at the time the Gospels were written, which probably influenced Paul, reinforced by St Augustine three centuries later.

6. K. R. Popper, *Conjectures and Refutations*.

7. J. MacMurray, *Reason and Emotion*, Faber 1935, p. 187.

8. Popper, op. cit., p. 226.

9. Bertrand Russell, *A History of Western Philosophy*, Allen and Unwin 1961, p. 56.

6. *Destruction by Objectivization*

1. Don Cupitt, *Only Human*, pp. 189–90.
2. John Polkinghorne, *Reason and Reality: The Relationship between Science and Theology*, SPCK 1991, p. 59.

7. *Origin of Scientific Materialism*

1. K. Jaspers, 'The Phenomenological Approach in Psychopathology'.
2. P. C. W. Davies, *God and the New Physics*, p. 8.
3. Ibid., p. 3.
4. E. Schrödinger, *Mind and Matter*, CUP 1959, pp. 101–102.
5. Aldous Huxley, *Ends and Means*, Chatto 1940, p. 56.
6. Some years ago I had this experience, in meeting a person who survived the vast massacre which led to the foundation of the state of Bangla Desh.

8. *Subjective Reality*

1. See M. Bunge, *The Mind-Body Problem*.
2. P. S. Churchland, *Neurophilosophy*, p. 356.
3. Ibid., p. 324.
4. Ibid., p. 326.
5. R. Miller, 'Striatal Dopamine in Reward and Attention: A System for Understanding the Symptomatology of Acute Schizophrenia and Mania' in *International Reviews of Neurobiology*, 35, 1993, pp. 161–278.
6. A. L. Blumenthal, *The Process of Cognition*, Prentice Hall, Englewood Cliffs, NJ 1977.
7. H. Woodrow in S. S. Stevens (ed.), *A Handbook of Experimental Psychology*, John Wiley and Sons, New York 1951, pp. 1223–36.
8. P. J. Snow, B. M. Lumb and F. Cervero, 'The Representation of Prolonged and Intense Noxious Somatic and Visceral Stimuli in the Ventral Orbital Cortex of the Cat' in *Pain*, 48, January 1992, pp. 89–99.

9. *Psychophysical Parallelism*

1. Bertrand Russell, *A History of Western Philosophy*, p. 620.
2. Don Cupitt, Introduction to *Only Human*.
3. R. Miller, *Meaning and Purpose in the Intact Brain*, OUP 1981.
4. J. C. Eccles in K. R. Popper and J. C. Eccles, *The Self and its Brain: An Argument for Interactionism*, Springer Verlag, Berlin 1977.
5. J. Polkinghorne, *Reason and Reality*.
6. Ibid., p. 25.
7. P. C. W. Davies, *God and the New Physics*, p. 82.

8. G. Ryle, *The Concept of Mind*.
9. J. Searle, *Minds, Brains and Science* (Reith Lectures for 1984), BBC 1984, p. 14.
10. P. C. W. Davies, op.cit., p. 92.
11. Ibid., p. 94.
12. Ibid., p. 96.
13. A. R. Luria, *The Making of Mind*, ch.4.
14. Ibid., p. 80.
15. Don Cupitt, *Only Human*, p. 187.
16. J. C. Eccles, *The Self and its Brain*, p. 314.
17. Ibid., p. 366.
18. D. van Lancker, 'Personal Relevance and the Human Right Hemisphere' in *Brain and Cognition*, 17, September 1991, pp. 64–92.
19. P. C. W. Davies, op. cit., p. 90.
20. Ibid.
21. Ibid., p. 141.
22. R. Penrose, *The Emperor's New Mind*.

10. *'Epistemological' Dualism*

1. J. Monod, *Chance and Necessity*, p. 148.
2. P. S. Churchland, *Neurophilosophy*, p. 321.
3. J. S. Mill, *A System of Logic* (1843), 7th edn Longmans 1898, p. 376.
4. B. F. Skinner, *Reflections on Behaviorism and Society*, p. 101.
5. J. Marsh (ed.), *Experimental and Theoretical Studies of Consciousness*.
6. J. Searle, *Minds, Brains and Science*, p. 18.
7. Thomas Traherne (1637–1674), 'Dreams'.
8. R. W. Sperry, 'Mind-Brain Interaction'.
9. J. Polkinghorne, *Reason and Reality*, p. 79.
10. P. C. W. Davies, *God and the New Physics*, p. 191.
11. Ibid.
12. B. Russell, *A History of Western Philosophy*, pp. 446–47, 556–69.
13. M. Dunbar, *Catherine: The story of a young girl who died of anorexia*, Penguin 1986.

11. *Organized Religion and its Relation to Metaphysics*

1. J. Polkinghorne, *Reason and Reality*, p. 19.
2. Ibid., p. 28.
3. P. C. W. Davies, *God and the New Physics*.
4. A. M. Renton and D. L. Miller, letter in *The Lancet*, 341, January 1992, p. 310.

12. *Weakness of Psychophysical Parallelism*

1. P. C. W. Davies, *God and the New Physics*, p. 142.
2. See M. Straker and J. Tamerin, 'Aggression and Childhood Asthma: A Study in a Natural Setting' in *Journal of Psychosomatic Research*, 18, April 1974, pp. 131–35.
3. Samuel Beckett, *Waiting for Godot*, Faber 1956.
4. M. Sperling, 'Asthma in Children: An Evaluation of Concepts and Therapies' in *Journal of the American Academy of Child Psychiatry*, 7, 1968, pp. 44–58.
5. Advocates of psychoanalytic reasoning may object here and say that the blame of parents for causing their offspring's illness is not an attribution of *moral* guilt. Against this I cite Bruno Bettelheim (*The Empty Fortress: Infantile Autism and the Birth of the Self*, The Free Press, New York 1967, pp. 64–68) who, within the context of a psychoanalytic account of autism in infants, refers to the parents of such infants as no better than concentration camp guards.
6. R. Miller, letter in *Journal of Psychosomatic Research*, 32(1), 1988, p. 118.
7. According to Bertand Russell (*A History of Western Philosophy*, p. 358), the reason why St Augustine rejected sexuality is that it is 'beyond the will'. Certainly the physiology of sex gives some support to that, since the sexual organs are controlled by either the autonomic nervous system or the endocrine system, rather than the so-called 'voluntary' nervous system.
8. B. Libet, 'Time of Conscious Intention to Act in Relation to Onset of Cerebral Activity' in *Brain*, 106, September 1983, pp. 623–42.
9. Don Cupitt, *Only Human*, p. 187.
10. Ibid., p. 188.
11. Cited by Davies, op.cit., p. 25.
12. Cupitt, op.cit., p. 34.
13. J. Monod, *Chance and Necessity*, p. 110.
14. Cupitt, op.cit., p. 171.
15. C. D. Frith, 'The Positive and Negative Symptoms of Schizophrenia Reflect Impairments in the Perception and Initiation of Action' in *Psychological Medicine*, 17, August 1987, pp. 631–48.
16. Monod, op.cit., p. 158.
17. Ibid., p. 166.

13. *The Creation and Uses of Myths*

1. P. C. W. Davies, *God and the New Physics*, ch. 13.
2. Ibid., p. 189.
3. J. Polkinghorne, *Reason and Reality*, p. 79.
4. Ibid., p. 80.
5. Davies, op.cit., p. 204.

6. Polkinghorne, op.cit., p. 33.
7. Davies, op.cit., p. 33.

14. Myths for the Modern Mind: Determinism as the Central Myth

1. H. S. Thayer, *Newton's Philosophy of Nature*, Hafner, New York 1953, p. 42 (excerpt from Newton's *Principia*, Bk III).
2. Ibid., p. 49 (letter from Newton to Dr Richard Bentley, 1692).
3. Ibid., p. 64 (letter from Newton to Thomas Burnet, *c.*1681).
4. Bertrand Russell, *A History of Western Philosophy*, pp. 84–85.
5. R. Penrose, *The Emperor's New Mind*, p. 152.
6. In fact, as explained in section 14.2, it is impossible to prove that a set of events is truly random, rather than being constrained by an as-yet unknown principle. It is thus possible that the radioactive decay of a single atom is fully lawful, but at a level so small that it has defied empirical analysis so far. But, since there is uncertainty on this matter, it remains impossible to prove the thesis of determinism.
7. Thayer, op.cit., p. 45 (excerpt from Newton's *Principia*, Bk III).
8. J. Polkinghorne, *Reason and Reality*, p 76
9. Ibid., p. 6.
10. Ibid., p. 12.
11. Ibid., p. 50.

15. Myths for the Modern Mind: Subsidiary Myths

1. H. S. Thayer, *Newton's Philosophy of Nature*, p. 42 (excerpt from Newton's *Principia*, Bk III).
2. Ibid., p. 52 (letter from Newton to Dr Richard Bentley).
3. Ibid., p. 66.
4. See P. Byrne, *Natural Religion and the Nature of Religion: The Legacy of Deism*, Routledge 1989.
5. A. R. Luria, *The Making of Mind*, p. 23.
6. J. Monod, *Chance and Necessity*, p. 112.
7. J. A. Coyne, 'Genetics and Speciation' in *Nature*, 355, January 1992, pp. 511–15.
8. C. A. Coulson, *Science and Christian Belief*, OUP 1955, p. 20.
9. Monod, op.cit., p. 136.
10. R. E. Lenski and J. E. Mittler, 'The Directed Mutation Controversy and Neo-Darwinism in *Science*, 259, 1993, pp. 188–194.
11. A. E. Musgrave, 'Is Evolutionary Theory Scientific?', unpublished lecture, Otago University 1984.
12. Alexander Pope (1688–1744), from 'An Essay on Man' (1732–34), 11.245f.

13. K. R. Popper, *The Poverty of Historicism*, Routledge and Kegan Paul 1957.
14. Don Cupitt, *Only Human*, pp. 37f.
15. Bertrand Russell, *A History of Western Philosophy*, p. 705.
16. S. Freud (1846–1939), *Introductory Lectures on Psychoanalysis*, Penguin 1973, p. 134.
17. Popper, op. cit.
18. P. Rieff, *Freud: the Mind of the Moralist*, Methuen 1960, pp. 315, 316.
19. Ibid., p. 322.
20. Charles Darwin, *Autobiography* ed. N. Barlow, Collins 1958, pp. 87, 90, 91.
21. Ibid., pp. 92f.
22. J. Polkinghorne, *Reason and Reality*, p. 99.
23. Ibid., p. 11.
24. Paul Tillich, *Dynamics of Faith*, Allen and Unwin 1957, p. 50.
25. Cupitt, op.cit., pp. 141f.
26. Polkinghorne, op.cit., p. 63.
27. Cupitt, op.cit., p. 116.
28. Ibid., p. 130.
29. Ibid., pp. 123f.
30. Ibid., p. 34.
31. Ibid., p. 206.

p. 208

16. What are the necessary myths (1-5)

Index